In *Around the World in Seventy Years* you'll discover the joy of being used of God—long after you may have thought He couldn't use you anymore. Sir James Matthew Barrie, author of *Peter Pan*, wrote, "The life of every man is a diary in which he means to write one story, and writes another." Betty's dream-story was about her desire to be a faithful Christian, devoted wife, and a dedicated mother, living out her faith in service to God. But divorce brought her hopes and dreams crashing down, and she seriously doubted whether God could still use her. If you've ever wrestled with that question, you need to read how Betty Smith discovered how God could and would use her in ways she had never thought possible, and you will be inspired by an adventure that will keep you up into the wee hours of the morning—hanging on to every word—like I did!

—Reverend Dr. Jim Howell
Senior Minister
Grace United Methodist Church
Atlanta, Georgia

Betty Smith is one of the most godly, sold-out-to-God women that I know! I have had the privilege of knowing and ministering along with her for almost thirty years. She is very powerful in helping others in prayer. I strongly recommend her story.

—DAVID A. PHELPS JR.
President, Looking Unto Jesus Ministries Inc.
Perry, Georgia

What a joy for me to travel around the world through this book with my friend Betty who is continually about the Father's business. This book touches the very heart of folks who have never ventured into the realm of missions. It inspires, encourages, and empowers those who will answer our Lord's call for us to be and build disciples of Christ among all nations, tribes, and peoples.

It is not necessary for me to try to describe her physical person to you because the moment she opens her mouth to pray, the Oracles of God pour forth. She truly makes a friend, is a friend, and brings those friends to Christ.

—JANE GUNTER
Director, Family Life Ministries
East Point, Georgia

Betty Smith has written from the heart, sharing with the reader her personal moments, teaching moments, and soul experiences as she journeyed on the path God led her. One who loves the Lord begins to journey with Betty as her partner, experiencing the surprises, difficulties, joys, and successes in dealing with many diverse cultures. This book reveals the heart of one who is committed to her God and His work for her, but it does more than that; it draws the reader to a deeper commitment as they journey with her. This book is a treasure revealing God's work.

—**GILLIAN GROWNEY**
Volunteer Assistant Chaplain, Christian City
Union City, Georgia

Reading *Around the World in Seventy Years* was so exciting! I couldn't wait to reach the next chapter. It made me want to run, jump on a plane, and go on missions immediately. The information was so compelling, it satisfied the innate desire for learning the real purpose of life. The courage, sacrifice, and integrity of the author made this book great.

—**DAVID R. MOORE**
Attorney at Law

AROUND
THE WORLD
{IN SEVENTY YEARS}

BETTY T. SMITH

CREATION
HOUSE
A STRANG COMPANY

AROUND THE WORLD IN SEVENTY YEARS
by Betty T. Smith
Published by Creation House
A Strang Company
600 Rinehart Road
Lake Mary, Florida 32746
www.creationhouse.com

General facts about Israel and its history are from *Look Upon Zion—A Guide to Israel*, 2nd ed. by Ezra Eini (edited by Reed Holmes). Privately printed in Israel.

Cover design by Amanda Potter

Library of Congress Control Number: 2007938624
International Standard Book Number-13:
978-1-59979-282-8

First Edition

08 09 10 11 — 9 8 7 6 5 4 3 2 1
Printed in the United States of America

To my precious jewels:
You light up my life and make me proud to be called
Mom, Mother-in-Love, and Grandma Betty.
My heart overflows with love for you!

ACKNOWLEDGMENTS

My deepest gratitude is extended to the following special people who made this book a reality: First, Allen Quain and Ginny Maxwell at Creation House, who guided me through this overwhelming maze of publishing; David Moore, my very first editor; Kathryn and Richard Bennett, whose computer skills brought me into the twenty-first century.

Second, my fellow missionary partners, who "represented" Jesus each step of the way. Special thanks to the leader of each mission: Walter Boyd, Rick Bonfim, Derryck McLuhan, Adis Rasmussen, David Rushton, Terri Ablett, Alan Winter, Tricia Cunningham, Charles Kennedy, Steve Foster, and Rich Terry.

Third, all the "senders," who launched me financially and covered me in prayer. The congregations of Atlanta City Church, Mt. Olive Baptist, and East Point Presbyterian outdid themselves. It would take another book to list each contributor, but Brother Grogan and Mickey Reeves, I just had to call you by name!

Fourth, these dearest of encouragers: My Reunion Sisters, Joann Winkles, Ruth Wingo, Jill Growney, Polly Jackson, Lyla McCurdy, and Lenora McCrea; my very own sister, Pat Freeman; my prayer partner, Wanda Mardis;

"Pastor Tilly" Welborn, who had the vision of the golden pen; and "Pastor Jim" Howell, who emphatically insisted this book be published.

Fifth, my church family at Powder Springs First United Methodist Church, who accepted me so lovingly as one of their own from the get-go!

Thanks again. I appreciate each and every one of you!

ONTENTS

PREFACE

When our Wales mission team departed from London for the flight home, I was providentially seated by Dan, a professor of World War II history at a university in London. He did not come from a Christian family and said he was not religious. "Great," I replied. "Neither am I! However, I am into a 'relationship' with the Lord." He was graciously attentive as I shared my testimony, along with choice details about the Wales mission. We agreed that we must have a passion in our life. He was passionate about lighting minds and seeing lives changed. So was I!

He was writing a book about World War II memories so they would not be lost, and challenged me to write about my mission trips. I confessed that he was not the first one to tell me this; actually, he was the fourth. We made a commitment to each other: he would finish his book, and I would write mine. I have kept my word; hence, this book you hold in your hands.

INTRODUCTION

My goal in life since I was a young girl was to be a good wife and mother, to grow old with the husband of my youth, and be surrounded by loving children and many grandchildren. In a movie I had seen, a man told his sweetheart that what he wanted when they were old was to keep their teeth in the same glass. I didn't want to go quite that far, but I did agree with the sentiment. I was well on my way to accomplishing my goal until a certain Sunday afternoon in June 1978, when my husband of twenty-six years announced to me that he was leaving home to be alone and think about what he was going to do. This was unbelievable; it couldn't be happening! Yet as he spoke, I sensed that I was on the Rock. The winds and waves were crashing in on me, but I was not going under. I begged my husband not to leave, but to no avail. He "thought" another eighteen months, but on February 1, 1980, the divorce he sought was granted. So much for my goal!

The following years were most difficult because I was so sure that at any moment he would be coming home, so I was straddling the fence between the past and the present. I believed with all my heart I could "confess it and possess it," and all it would take was faith and perseverance on my part to have my marriage restored. My Lord patiently showed me that He has given each of us a free will, and that included my husband. He had the right to make what I was sure was a very wrong decision.

I was asked this question by my Lord: "Do you think that I can take all this muck and mire and make it a firm foundation upon which you can grow?" That was a no-brainer; of course He could, and that is just what He did! Not overnight, but in the fullness of His time.

After my husband left, each day I would look in the bathroom mirror and say, "Lord, help me make it through this day." Then after many, many days I was at last able to say, "Lord, I don't want to just make it through this day. I want to make a difference in my world," and that was the pivotal point. My life made a turn—away from me and toward His world. It was *His* goal I sought, not my own.

I had led a very sheltered life and did not leave the state of Georgia until my honeymoon in 1952, when we went to Florida. After my husband graduated from college, we went to Kansas for his tour of duty with the U.S. Army. After the birth of our second son, we went back to Florida because of my husband's job, and there our final child, a beautiful daughter, was born in 1965. Shortly thereafter, we moved back home to Georgia. The only other times I left Georgia were on lay witness mission trips through the United Methodist Church to Alabama, Virginia, and South Carolina. You could say that I was not well traveled, but in 1985, the Lord opened an exciting, adventurous door for me. That story, dear reader, is what I want to share with you.

CHAPTER 1
PERU

FEB 1985

My friend Linda is very fluent in Spanish and was scheduled to serve as a translator on a mission trip to Chincha Alta, Peru, sponsored by the North Georgia Conference of United Methodist Men. She had night vision problems, so I volunteered to drive her to the first team meeting. The leader, Walt, who also coordinated many of the regional lay witness mission trips on which I had served, asked if I would consider going on this foreign mission because one team member had withdrawn. I protested, saying that I had no money (which was true) and no passport. The team sat me in a chair and prayed that, if the Lord had chosen me, it would all develop according to His will. Within one week, I had my passport and the money. Even today, I cannot trace the sources of the funds; just different people handed me cash and checks. The Lord's will was the Lord's bill, and He paid it.

The majority of the team rendezvoused in the Atlanta, Georgia, area and drove to Newberry, the home of Walt's mother, for a scrumptious meal. This was an important part of the mission because this dear saint ministered to us with her kind hospitality, and we, in turn, showered our love on her. As a mother, I know what it means to have your children come home and give you a hug. Walt said he hugged his mother three times!

The transmission support on one of the vans broke when we ran over a curb, but the Lord gave us a preview of His loving care by immediately providing a welder, who completed the repairs in about thirty minutes for only $18.50. You couldn't beat that with a stick! We continued on to Miami, Florida, where three more team members from Augusta joined us: George, Vivian, and Tom. Mike and Diane, old mission friends who were living in Miami at that time, met us there and graciously parked our two vans at their home to save us money.

We flew from Miami to Kingston, Jamaica, for a short layover, and then on to Lima, Peru. It was a bit hectic at the airport, with the team scattered because of the crowd. Thankfully, a gentleman came to our aid, and we went through customs with no inspection at all! Here was God's hand again on our behalf. We were met by Florenzio, Carlos, and Geraldo (all brothers) and Julian, who had been working with Carlos in the Amazon area. They took us into Lima to exchange money, eat, and buy some food to take with us. The team was dispersed, doing various errands, so some gave out tracts while they were waiting for everyone to come together. Paul (we called him "Tall Paul") paid some little boys to shine his shoes, and this gathered a little crowd, opening the door for other members of the team to come and share. Linda and Walt were answering questions posed by a lady named Livia, who said she was a Christian, and Sixto, who wanted Jesus to come into his heart. Linda prayed with him and encouraged Livia to continue ministering to him, since we had to leave.

We drove south in the bus for about three hours to Pueblo Nuevo, just outside Chincha Alta. I could not believe myself, there on a bus in Peru. I was a missionary! We drove along the coastline with the sea on one side and mountains on the other, many of which were decorated with mysterious carvings. One had the scene of a giant bird, and it was called Hummingbird Hill. The people in the area where we worked spoke Spanish. They are a beautiful people, with olive skin, dark hair, and dark brown eyes. They are also a loving people, eager to embrace, laugh, and share with you.

In addition to the Augusta men, our team of fifteen included Walt and Charlotte, Haygood and Bertha, Joel, Bubba, "Tall Paul," Grace, and Linda. Ken and Del were to join us later in the week, making a total of ten men and five women. We stayed in the Pueblo Nuevo Methodist Church compound area, which consisted of the church sanctuary, where we worshipped and held services; a kitchen and eating area; classrooms on the first floor; and various other rooms on the second floor. Some of the ladies and I shared one of those upper rooms and slept on straw mattresses, which were quite comfortable.

The first night we were there, the people had a feast for us: whole chickens (feet and all), vegetables, juice, and a beautifully decorated cake! The chickens were a sacrifice for them, because it meant they were giving up their source of eggs. Some of the team had been on the first mission, so they were excited to see old friends, plus it was important for the local people to see them return because it showed a depth of commitment to the project. We were the second team, and a third team would come later to complete the project. The children sang for us, waving Peruvian and American flags. The women were presented with flower bouquets, and the men with carnations. It was a grand occasion, and I immediately loved these special children of God. Still, at the end of the evening, it was so good to get to bed!

Charlotte and Walt were staying in a room on the first floor, but Charlotte quickly abandoned Walt because of the *cucarachas* (cockroaches) and came to stay with her girl-friends on the second floor, where we were blessedly bug-free. The men were not as blessed.

One of the primary purposes of the mission was to construct an office building next to the church, which involved forming, mixing and pouring concrete columns. Also, the men made four doors, sixty-four lap desks for the children, and repaired some broken equipment. Many of the local men were of great assistance, especially Macedonia, and laboring together was an effective way to witness for Jesus.

On our first full day (Sunday), some of the men went into the city jail with three of the local leaders who led Bible studies on Mondays and Wednesdays, as well as church services on Sundays. Our guys shared in both the women's and the men's cells. All the women were believers, so the team prayed with them for favor with the judges and salvation for their families. Pedro, one of the locals, opened the service for the men, Bubba and Florenzio shared, and Walt gave the invitation, at which time twelve prayed to receive Christ. Bibles were given to those in the study groups.

Later in the week, some of the men returned to the jail. They ministered briefly to the women, with Bubba speaking, and then they went into the men's section for Bible study. Tom presented one of the men with a pair of pliers to help him in his work, and the man testified that this gift was an answer to his prayers. The prisoners are not fed by the city, but must earn their food by working. They gave our men crafts they had made, which was a sacrifice, as they could have sold them in exchange for food. Walt gave a word of encouragement, and nineteen-year old Pancon, who was a real terror and hated by everyone at the jail, came forward to surrender his life to Christ. This made an impact on the other prisoners, and six more came forward, for a total of seven salvations that day.

Linda, George, and I were sent to a Sunday school for children held in a local home with adobe walls and dirt floors. The study group was called "October 13" because that was the day it started. George taught a lesson about seed, and the children illustrated their responses with crayons and paper we had brought. It was astonishing to see how the children valued the crayons and paper. They would take only one crayon at a time, being very gentle so it would not break, and then they would return it, asking for *otra* (another) crayon. They only expected one piece of paper, because paper was so difficult to obtain.

Two other visitation teams were sent out into the neighborhood that morning, with members of the teams sharing their testimonies. Each team had four salvations, for a total of eight! The church was encouraged to go out and do likewise!

Other members went with the pastor and some children from the church to the local radio station for teaching, sharing, and singing. It was a festival day, and the children were allowed to pour water on adults, so our guys got drenched!

The team had brought non-perishable groceries from America (canned meats, crackers, peanut butter, etc)., and we put it all together. We were trying to make our meager groceries last by coming up to the girls' room to eat our lunch alone, but our Peruvian friends wanted to be with us, so they came up, too. We had one big smorgasbord of American canned goodies. The Lord was faithful to multiply our "loaves and fish" every day, and it was so much fun!

Another thing that struck me was how God had put this team together. For instance, this was Grace's first mission trip, and, in fact, her first time to ride on an airplane! She had a gift of organization and kept us running like a well-oiled machine. I thanked the Lord for choosing her "for such a time as this."

Later that afternoon we held Sunday school classes at the church, and then the classes came together for more singing and teaching. I am convinced that the angels must sing in Spanish because the language is so beautiful! Even though we had been going for over three hours, the altar was full. How sad that we don't see that at home! Most Americans are too antsy to sit through services that last that long.

That evening we split into two teams. One went to the Union Church for singing, testimonies, and a message by Vivian. Approximately sixteen people came forward for prayer at the altar call. The other team went to a Methodist Church in Chincha. The pastor spoke and Walt shared, but there was no response to the altar call. A big rally by the Communist Party was going on in the square concerning the upcoming elections, and this was quite a distraction.

That night in bed, I thought about our God and His comments at Creation—it had been a very good first day!

The following morning (Monday), we got into our schedule. While the men were doing construction work— with the encouragement of lots of the local kids—the women were sent out with the pastor and his wife to a local village, San Isidro, to hold morning classes for that week. In the States, we call it vacation Bible school. We all piled into the pastor's truck, taking along with us some boards, papers, coloring books, crayons, and candy. These children were precious; we wanted to take them all home with us. The first day they were all cleaned up, fresh as little daisies. But each day they wore the same clothes, so by the end of the week, the little daisies were drooping, though still adorable!

We met in a house that had two rooms, with dirt floors and straw mats for walls. One room was quite large (probably the living/bedroom), the second room was apparently the kitchen, because there were the remains of a "campfire." We made benches out of our boards, which we laid over some rocks, and quickly filled them with approximately fifty-four children that first day. Our numbers steadily grew as the week progressed. Many of the children had infected sores, most likely caused by the unsanitary water conditions and poor nutrition.

At our first session, an adult couple from the neighborhood came to join us. They were named Adam and Eve, and I promise this is the truth! Stranger than that, the pastor led Adam and Eve to Jesus, and they were gloriously converted. The whole trip would have been worth it, had it only been for these two, but as the mission unfolded, many more were added to the kingdom, including three more adults.

On our last day at San Isidro, we decided to bring oranges as a special goodbye treat. Some of the mothers came for the celebration, and they brought a fruit drink they had made. They only had a few glasses, and the team was invited to drink first, so standing on God's promise that nothing would by any means harm us (Mark 16:18), I chug-a-lugged mine down, thanking them profusely, because this was done out of their love for us and at great cost to them financially.

We estimated that we had approximately ninety in attendance, so having enough oranges for everyone was going to be a problem. It would be awful to leave someone out! Linda stood at the doorway and gave out oranges as the people left, so we could be sure each person got just one; meanwhile, Bertha and I stood over by a wall, praying for multiplication. As the last person walked out the door, Linda held up one orange, and the rest of the team broke into laughter and praise. Just as our second floor lunches were multiplied like the loaves and fish, our Lord had done it again! Then we walked outside, and one of the local men came running up; he had been blessed to get work for the morning and asked if there were an orange for him. "Of course," Linda replied, handing him that last orange. But the greatest miracle was that fourteen children that day had invited Jesus to come into their hearts! The angels were rejoicing with us.

In the afternoons that week, we returned to the "October 13" Bible study for teaching and sharing by different members of the team. The adults stayed in one room, while Linda and I went into a separate room with the children and teenagers. One particular day, I was speaking and Linda was translating, but at one point, after I had said a clause or two, there was only silence. I looked over at Linda, and she was staring out the open door, mesmerized by a big rooster strutting around in the yard. She realized what had happened and turned sheepishly to look at me. I started laughing, and said, "Well, if you want them to go to hell, that's up to you!" Some of the teenagers knew enough English to understand what I said, and we all exploded into laughter.

We had different assignments each evening, going to local churches to share our testimonies, pray, and minister to those who came forward. It was a very tense time because of the elections; the communists were trying to get into power. At one church in Chincha, there were iron bars running perpendicular across the front, like stores in the U.S. sometimes have for protection from vandalism and theft. While we were sharing, someone ran a stick across the bars, making a clank-clank-clank noise and causing everyone inside to jump. We decided to move into the city plaza because that was where the people were. We sang, shared testimonies, gave out tracts, and prayed with nine people to receive Christ. Members of the Communist Party were on a flatbed truck nearby with loud speakers, making it difficult to speak above the noise, but still God's Word went forth! In fact, we returned to the plaza a second night after a brief service at the church where Linda and I testified, and this time six more made professions of faith!

Each day there were gunshots and reports of killings. It was not unusual to see people coming down the street carrying coffins on their way to another burial ceremony. At one church service, a woman was trying to tell me about her husband. My Spanish was very limited, and she kept using the word *muerte* over and over, getting louder each time because I could not understand what she was trying to communicate to me. (Why is it that we think by increasing the volume we can bring understanding?) I thought her husband had died of illness or natural causes, but she was saying he was murdered. I never got the details, but I did understand her pain and tried to express my sorrow as I prayed for her. While she could not understand my English, she did comprehend my love and concern for her as my sister in Christ.

On our last day after the party at San Isidro, we went to the beach for a baptism service. Over forty went with us and six were baptized. That evening, the church gave us a farewell party, and we again combined our resources. It was really a bittersweet time, knowing that home was waiting, yet not wanting to leave our new friends. Over two hundred people came, including the mayor and other politicians. We were so happy that Ken and Del had safely arrived. Certificates were given to all the members of the team, and there was a special presentation to Ken on behalf of the North Georgia United Methodist Men. The service closed with a symbolic dedication of the church building, which was to be finished on the next trip.

A friend of mine had given me eighty dollars to give out during the mission trip, asking that I hold it until the Holy Spirit revealed to me the recipient He had chosen. I had been watchful, but so far had no leading. That last night, as

I was talking with the pastor of the local church there, I knew he was the one. As I gave him the money and explained the details, he was overcome with emotion. They had six children, and because the church members were so poor, his income was meager. From that exchange, we established a relationship that continues to the time of this writing. Another friend of mine and I helped pay for meals for two of his sons when they later attended seminary. One of those sons, Efrain, attended Duke University in North Carolina on an exchange student program, and he is following the footsteps of his father as a pastor in Peru.

The team had to leave very early the next morning, and many of the congregation stayed there all night, some even sleeping on the concrete floors so they could be there when we left. I shall never in my life forget piling into the backseat of that bus, looking out the rear window and seeing them wave goodbye with tears in their eyes as they sang to us. I thought my heart would burst with a mixture of love and joy, sadness and pain. Even today, I can recall that scene vividly, and it still brings a lump to my throat.

We then traveled north to Arequipa to look over some possible future church planting sites. This part of Peru is in stark contrast to Chincha. Here it is mountainous, lush and green, while Chincha is flat, sandy, and barren. We toured a convent of the Dominican Order that had been built in 1579 and an elaborate Jesuit Church. I was impressed with the ornate carvings and statues, especially in light of the beggars who were sitting at the front door. More contrast here—rich versus poor. Carlos and Julian, our Peruvian brothers, joined us, and we were riveted by Julian's testimony during our devotion time. It was a joy to be with these "mighty men of valor" in a relaxed setting. However, it did make it harder to say goodbye, as there was more time for them to burrow into your heart.

For me, the mission was over when we left Chincha, and I just wanted to go home so I could have a good cry. I actually felt guilty that I was in such a beautiful place, eating high on the hog while our friends in Chincha were struggling. We did witness and pass out tracts at every opportunity, and Walt especially zeroed in on our guide, a lovely young lady named Betty, giving her a Bible with study guides.

We were blessed at the airport in Lima to get all our baggage checked through, and Del, our cameraman, was able to retrieve his ticket and passport, which officials had held in exchange for allowing his equipment to come into the country when he first arrived. We had a ten-hour wait, so there was time for a final dinner at a unique restaurant named La Rosa Nautica, which jutted out over the ocean. There were real roses to decorate the tables, and the music and the food were excellent. Of course, in Peru, because of the money exchange rate, everything was cheap. There was more business conducted up to the last minute at the airport, as Ken met with Florenzio and went over plans to finish the church at Pueblo Nuevo. Geraldo, Carlos, and Julian also stayed with us until the end. If we could bottle their zeal and love for the Lord and give just a sip to our church members in the U.S., we would have a mighty revival!

We retraced our steps to return home, flying to Jamaica and then into Miami, where we picked up our vans and shared our exploits with Mike and Diane. We said a fond farewell to our Augusta crew and settled in for the long drive to Atlanta. It was fun to share our stories, and while we were all exhausted, it was a good tiredness.

The official number of salvations was sixty-five, but that was just a fraction of the lives that were touched. Not everyone needed to be saved; many already knew Jesus. Others simply needed to be encouraged in their faith, to know that there is a family of God who cares enough to come to them no matter the distance and the cost.

But I also had been changed—I had been bitten by the missions bug! My life was not over; in fact, I was entering into a new phase, and indeed, the best was yet to come.

CHAPTER 2
MONTERREY, MEXICO

FEB 1986

At last it was time for bed. Poor Hagood and Tom shared a room next to the ladies' shower. Lord, bless them for that!

The next morning (Saturday), we were up bright—nearly so, at least—and early. First there was breakfast at the hotel, then the housekeeping duties, including exchanging money (at the time of our trip, the rate was 465 pesos to the dollar) and getting all the supplies ready to disburse.

Mark's team left early for their assignment to Apodaca. The other two teams went to Guadalupe, but on arrival at the church, we found that the meeting had been moved to Delfín's home. He had been a Christian for three weeks and was on fire for the Lord. The little house was packed out. Linda gave her testimony in Spanish, and there were a lot of tears. Because of the crowd, the meeting was moved to the backyard. Two other team members shared, and Pastor James of their church spoke. A lady named Letícia was saved, and shared that she had felt the Lord drawing her to that meeting.

A woman asked me to pray for her because she was experiencing respiratory difficulties and feeling bad in general. She came to me later in the evening, and said she felt fine—no more problems. I was so grateful that the Lord healed this dear lady and that He could use me. I just needed to be faithful and available while He did the work.

It was at this meeting that one of the brothers told Linda that Jesus smelled like a melon. Linda was puzzled and asked him to explain. He replied, "Jesus is Jesus, no matter the language or the nationality. You see the same Jesus in people. It's just love." Just as sure as a ripe melon has a good smell, so do His true disciples exude the aroma of His love.

Then it was back to our dorm for team reports. We were elated to hear Mark's report of twenty-three salvations and one infilling of the Holy Spirit. At this time, we were given the schedule for the rest of the week and some ground rules. There were some definite no's, such as no strawberries, no smoking, and nothing from vendors. We were cautioned to eat only a small amount of fruit and to speak slowly, using short sentences with simple words. Another important thing for us to remember was to accept the refreshments offered. Refusing such an offer is very offensive, as to most it is a great sacrifice and they want to be of service. It was also explained that we should say that we are from the United States or North America, not just *America*, as our Mexican brothers and sisters consider themselves to be Americans also.

The next day was Sunday, and our team was assigned to Apodaca for Sunday school and morning worship. The church was a concrete block structure about the size of a single car garage, located on a small lot with a fence around it. The bathroom was in a neighboring house, but the neighbor had grown weary of the intrusions, so the team had to rough it. Missionaries particularly need endurance in the bladder department!

Gabino and Graciela were our interpreters—such a genteel couple. Gabino said it was very important that we come on mission trips because the communists were offering so much, but Christ is the only answer. He advised that we be honest and tell the people if we were nervous. By sharing our testimony, he said, we could show the people they are welcome to share theirs.

The pastor's name was Juan Francisco, and he stole our hearts away. He was a seminary student at Juan Wesley, scheduled to finish that July. He knew he was called by the Lord, but felt inadequate and unloved. He preached a terrific sermon from Nehemiah about how we are to build with a brick in one hand and a sword in the other. That sermon is still vivid in my mind.

Several of us gave our testimonies. Bubba spoke and one of the local men shared. A lovely young girl played a beat-up guitar. Later in the week, Penny led a campaign to get her a new one. Other ladies on the team worked with the children, who especially loved the instant Polaroid photographs.

After lunch with Gabino and Graciela, we returned to Apodaca for more visitations. Bubba, Linda, and I went door to door throughout the neighborhood, which was predominantly Catholic. At one home, three ladies were assured of their salvation as we shared the EE presentation. Meanwhile, back at the plaza, the rest of our team bought ice cream for approximately thirty-five children and handed out coloring sheets.

Our entire team had coffee and cake at the home of Augustín and Angelina, and then we returned to the church for the evening service. Linda was to interpret, but one of the local young ladies named Pearl took over. This was very important because Pearl was supposed to help us visit that afternoon but had hidden from us because she was afraid. Now the fear was gone!

Penny, Paul, and Kim testified as a family, and then Linda shared. Bubba gave a short message and then an altar call. Eight came forward for salvation, sixteen for the baptism of the Holy Spirit, and two for deliverance. This church had not originally wanted us to come because they were poor and had nothing to offer rich North Americans. Praise the Lord that they repented of this false assumption!

We all came together that evening for sharing. Walt's team had gone to Guadalupe for Sunday school and morning worship. Charlotte and Bertha taught the children, several of the team testified, and Walt spoke on the topic of the Holy Spirit. The team split to have lunch in different homes, and in one home, four generations were represented. Instead of a visitation, the church had prepared a party in honor of the team and to celebrate a birthday. Then everyone went to the plaza, where people were playing bingo, a band was playing, and vendors were trading. When the band took a break, the team got up and sang and Pastor James spoke, inviting the people to the evening service while the team gave out tracts. At the subsequent service, several of the team shared, and the pastor spoke. At the end of the day, a total of nine had prayed for salvation, four for the baptism of the Holy Spirit, and one for healing.

Mark's team had been to Nogalar, where approximately three years previously he had been pastor. Several members of the team shared and Mark preached. At the altar call, two came forward for salvation and two for the infilling of the Holy Spirit.

The consensus was that it had been a very fruitful day!

The next day (Monday), the entire group descended on Wanda and Randy, our local missionaries, for breakfast. We had grits, heart-shaped biscuits, and sweet fellowship. Then there was time for shopping in Monterrey and lunch at VIP's, a very nice local restaurant. (Some suffering for Jesus, right?) It was good to encourage Wanda and Randy and to receive their wise counsel. It was also very important for us to get into the marketplace and build bridges of friendship.

Our team went to Guadalupe for more afternoon door-to-door witnessing. The object was to contact as many people as possible by handing out tracts and coloring sheets and inviting them to a house meeting that night.

Linda and Earl were in the poorest section of the neighborhood, where there were box springs for doors and thatch walls and roofs. Their first visit was to a lady who was very sad because she needed money and could not sell her *murachas*. Linda asked her what murachas were, and the lady led her to another part of the house where there were chickens. Linda pointed to them, but the lady shook her head and continued to lead Linda into another section of the house where there were pigs. "Murachas," said the lady, pointing to the pigs. So Linda and Earl had to question what the Lord was trying to show them in the middle of a pig pen. The bottom line was that because they cared, the lady and her husband came to the house meeting that night. They learned the truth of the saying, "I don't care how much you know, until I know how much you care."

The second stop for Linda and Earl was the most exciting. A man was sitting in a chair in his yard, and they walked up to invite him to the meeting. He said he was an *evangel* (an evangelist) and was glad to see them spreading the Word. For years he had worked in water up to his knees, and this had left him crippled and unable to walk. They asked if they could pray for him, and he agreed, falling down on his knees in the rocks and the dirt. Linda and Earl likewise fell to their knees. They prayed and were starting to leave as the man got back in his chair. Then Linda hastily put down her Bible and purse, grabbed the man's knees, and started praying in the Spirit. She felt power going through her hands, and the man jumped up yelling, "I'm healed!" All three of them were dancing in the street, praising the Lord!

The evening meeting was held in the backyard of a local home. Several of us shared and Bubba spoke. A young man named James came forward, wanting to get right with the Lord. He became a valuable asset the remainder of the week, translating in the door-to-door witnessing and in the services. Our translator that night was Rose, a beautiful, petite woman and a real fireball for Christ. She was very excitable, and Paul's driving was a real test of her faith. At the conclusion of the service, nine prayed for the infilling of the Holy Spirit and one prayed for healing.

At the team meeting later that evening, Walt's team to Apodaca had an interesting story. Tom and Wanda, as his interpreter, went into a small courtyard where Tom gave the EE presentation to the father of the household. Meanwhile, two other gentlemen approached and Tom continued, witnessing to all three. Then he noticed that Wanda had left and Pearl was translating. All three men wanted Jesus to come into their hearts. As they were kneeling, Pearl asked if she could pray also, since she was not sure of her salvation, so all four prayed. At the evening service, Pearl told the congregation that the two men who had walked up were her father and grandfather. Three generations of her family were saved at one time! She shared how before she had felt so unimportant, and now she was important. As the service ended, two more came forward for salvation and two for the fullness of the Holy Spirit.

Walt admonished us that being unable to speak the language was no excuse for not sharing or praying with people at the altar. The Holy Spirit is not hindered by our lack of language skills.

Mark's team had been to Jerusalem, one of the larger churches, for visitation, and they had a packed-out service that evening. There were twenty-one salvations, eighteen of these being children. One of the adults who prayed for salvation was the mother of one of the children who had prayed also, which made it extra special. Twelve came forward for the baptism of the Holy Spirit, and there were many prayers for healings.

The following day (Tuesday), some of the team met with Florenzio and Maria, missionaries, at the El Paso Hotel. They were in the process of gathering materials from the Old and New Testaments to use in Columbia, Peru, and Mexico for discipleship. The plan was to disciple small groups and then send them out to repeat the process.

Florenzio's vision was a "floating" seminary, using the multiplication formula. He reported that in the past when people were reached for Christ, they were not discipled, so cults were able to come in and take them. The new way was much more effective. After all, Jesus told us to go and make disciples!

Later that morning we had a chapel service at the Juan Wesley Seminary. It began with songs of praise and worship in Spanish and in English with piano and drums. Even the offering was special, with the congregation walking down the aisles to put their money in the plates. I thought to myself, "The Lord must be loving this!" Then, to my amazement, I was asked to give my testimony. I told them how awestruck I was to be in this place at this time. A few years before I felt my life was virtually over, and now my Lord was using me as a missionary! There was a release of so much love in the chapel that it seemed to flow like a river, with everyone crying and hugging each other.

A young student shared about being pastor of a church far away. He had lost much sleep traveling back and forth and was very discouraged. After being there five months, the church experienced revival, and seventy-five people were saved. Now he was praising God!

Pastor Mark preached from Ephesians. The illustrations he used in that message have remained in my memory to this day. He said that Christ hit the ball out of the park, so we can run slowly, touching every base. Also, he encouraged us to check our view: as you stand on top of Lookout Mountain, Tennessee, from where you can see seven states, don't lose your perspective by looking down at the backside of a passing buzzard. We must believe enough, he said!

After the service, the team split into two groups for lunch with the students, as they could not accommodate all of us at once. Each team member sat at a table with three students. We practiced our Spanish while they practiced their English, and we had more fun time to get acquainted and build relationships.

Our team met at four o'clock to pray for the other teams going out, especially for Hagood and Tom, who were to speak, and for the "pig lady" to sell her *murachas*. We returned to Guadalupe for door-to-door witnessing prior to the evening house meeting. James, the young man who had rededicated his life the night before, was there to help translate. The team split into pairs so we could cover more homes, giving out tracts and inviting people to the service.

Linda, Paul, and Penny shared at the service, while I worked with the children. It was such a joy for me to work with the little ones; their hearts were so soft! Four adults prayed for salvation and healing.

We ended the day with the usual team meeting. Mark's team had returned to Jerusalem for afternoon home visitation, during which time six people accepted Christ. At the evening service, five adults and fifteen children were saved.

Walt's team had been back in Apodaca for an afternoon prayer meeting/taco party. He presented the gospel to approximately twenty-five people; five were saved and four prayed for healing.

On the way to the church for the evening service, Pearl urged Tom to visit a special home. The lady there responded affirmatively to the two EE questions, so Tom prayed with her and left. She came to the service and testified how before Tom came to her home, she had asked the Lord to send someone to pray with her because she needed encouragement. Our God is in the details.

Members of the local church led three people to the Lord after the service (a good example of Florenzio's discipleship principle). As Tom was leaving, Lily, the interpreter, asked him to pray with a little nine-year-old girl who was crying because she wanted Jesus in her heart. Our Lord warned us not to hinder the little children from coming unto Him, and Tom was so glad to introduce this little one to Christ!

As we concluded our reports, members shared personal needs, and we prayed for each other. It was vital that we wrap ourselves in prayer! Our Lord was moving, and we wanted no obstructions.

The next day (Wednesday), we had our second morning chapel service at the seminary. Mark continued to preach from Ephesians. He urged us to know God and to see God's power in us—that same resurrection power that changed death to life. The altar was filled with those seeking a deeper commitment.

Our team was assigned to Jerusalem. Prior to the service, we met with Pastor Eddie and his local group for home witnessing. We merged our team into his and went to specific homes. At this point, Arturo, one of the pastor's members, staged a minor revolt, not wanting to go. He said it was "women's work." Pastor Eddie was embarrassed, and at last Arturo consented to go. When Arturo saw someone come to the Lord, suddenly he couldn't be quiet. There is no higher high on earth than introducing someone to Christ!

Our little team-within-a-team saw four professions of faith that afternoon. There was a Catholic lady in one home, and as I knelt at her feet she accepted Christ. In another home, there were three beautiful teenage girls who prayed for salvation. The total count on visitation was nine salvations.

On the way back to the church for the evening service, we passed teams of Jehovah's Witnesses covering the neighborhoods. We were told by one of the teenagers who had prayed earlier that this cult had been in her home, and she had been very confused by what they said. She was grateful that Christians had come to tell her the truth.

This was to be the last meeting at the Jerusalem church, and it was important that the rest of the children be reached with the gospel. Approximately eighty children attended, so we divided them into two groups: the saved and the unsaved, or the *sheep* and the *goats*, as they are called in Matthew 25:32. Diane, Earl, and I testified in the service, and then I slipped out to entertain the little saved sheep. Bubba gave the message, and at the altar call there were six professions of faith, two who prayed for the infilling of the Holy Spirit, and seven for healing. Penny and Linda worked with the unsaved children and led twenty-six little goats to the Lord!

After church, the team was invited to a local home for *sopapillas*. These are little fried cakes that are covered in butter and sprinkled with sugar. Yummy—not just the food, but the fellowship. A crucial ingredient in evangelism is to share with people in their homes and to let them serve you. Their hospitality removes any barrier between you, and they receive what you say not as "preaching" but as from a friend to a friend, sharing good news. Jesus was a prime example of being a good receiver so He could, in turn, give.

Then it was back to El Estudantíl for praise reports. Mark's team in Guadalupe had conducted door-to-door visitations and held a house meeting that evening. At the conclusion of the service, eighteen prayed for the infilling of the Holy Spirit. Janet shared the gospel with the children, and twelve received the Lord.

Walt's team went to Escabado and held a street service. Scripture was read under the streetlights, and two people accepted Christ. Charlotte and Bertha worked with the children, who were too numerous to count, and there were twelve professions of faith in that group. Another amazingly blessed day!

Thursday morning came quickly. We had our final chapel service with the seminary students. Mark preached again from Ephesians, this time about how we are all special. No matter our origin, Jesus has done a work in our lives and we are one. Then the team came to the front and the students prayed for us to take revival fire back home. President Baltazar gave a prophecy from Isaiah 35:7–8:

> *And the parched ground shall become a pool, and the thirsty land springs of water: in the habitation of dragons, where each lay, shall be grass with reeds and rushes. And an highway shall be there, and a way, and it shall be called The way of holiness; the unclean shall not pass over it; but it shall be for those: the wayfaring men, though fools, shall not err therein.*

My pastor preached from this text on my first Sunday home, and I told him how we had been given this same word in Mexico.

It was difficult to bid farewell to these new friends, but we had to leave for a luncheon appointment with the Guzmans in their home. It was a great time to relax, enjoy a delicious meal, and hear the current news from friends in Peru. Too soon, it was time to say good-bye and get back to work.

Our team was assigned to San Nicolas, a mission church of Jerusalem that held its services in a combination residence and grocery store. The team divided for witnessing in homes designated by Pastor Eddie, plus cold-knocking as time permitted. Pastor, the now red-hot Arturo, Penny, and I shared in a young couple's home. The husband, wife, and grandmother accepted Christ, and the couple came to the service that evening. The local men took good care of them, and pastor promised to follow up. It was encouraging to see them bring to church the New Testaments we had given them earlier.

At another home we had visited that afternoon, three ladies were saved and one of them also came to the service. Penny, Wanda, and I worked with the children during the service. One of these was a little boy with whom Randy had prayed for healing during their visitation. He was super-hyper all evening, so I suggested to Randy that next time he pray for healings for the children at the end of the service, not before!

Arturo presided at the service, which was held in the front yard of the home-store. All the living room furniture, plus extra chairs, were moved into the yard. Paul gave his testimony, and a local lady delivered a dynamite sermon. We wanted to ship her to the U.S. to be a missionary to us. Ten prayed for salvation, five for healing, and four for the baptism of the Holy Spirit. In the children's group, eleven came to Jesus.

The teams came together for late-night reports and sharing time. Mark's team was sent to Nogalar. This church was in its sixth week of EE training, and the locals joined with the team for visitation. Mark reported that a husband for whom they had prayed when Mark lived there had now accepted Christ, and his wife presented the gospel in the EE program that night. A total of four were saved in the home visitations.

Walt's team had returned to Guadalupe to pass out tracts and invite people to the evening services. In the U.S. we need at least a week's notice; in Mexico fifteen minutes is sufficient. Six prayed that night for the fullness of the Holy Spirit, six for healing, one for assurance of his salvation, and six children came into the kingdom. It was thrilling to see how the Lord was moving.

Friday came too soon, our last day of ministry. We had a noon luncheon at Santa's home, which was located a few blocks from the San Nicolas mission church. Santa's aunt gave her testimony, telling us a story about her son that involved a Ouija board and demon possession. This was very exciting, especially when Linda, our translator, squealed; she had misunderstood and thought Santa's aunt had been "burned" instead of "shoved," and we had to wait for her to translate it correctly into English for us. This made us all more determined to learn Spanish. The end of the story was that through the deliverance of the son, the entire family, including Santa's father, had been led to Jesus.

We had a delicious lunch of typically Mexican food, and then some of the team returned to the seminary to prepare for the farewell party (*despedido*) that evening. The rest of us stayed at Santa's home, as the witnessing that afternoon was to be in that area.

While waiting there, the aunt requested prayer for healing and to receive the baptism of the Holy Spirit. Members of the team laid hands on her and started praying. Linda felt the "electricity" again, and knew the lady was healed. As Linda prayed in the Spirit, Santa's mother interpreted, "Thank Me. Give Me your family, your problems. I will take care of you." After this, the sister of Santa's brother-in-law stopped by to visit. She was given the EE presentation and accepted Christ as her Savior.

Our team met up with Pastor Eddie and went to designated homes in the area for visitation. One lady with serious marital problems was counseled, and Pastor assured her of his continued support. When we concluded our assignments, there were seven professions of faith, two of these being children of a mother who had come to Jesus the previous night. The Lord was saving families!

We proceeded to the seminary to assist the others with the party. We wanted to start late, which would have been the usual since some of the team had not returned, but President Baltazar insisted we proceed on time. He gave a message entitled, "Remember Jesus—He Remembered You." This was an especially meaningful service. We were one in Christ, united by what Jesus had done for us by His love, by our love for Him, and for each other. We ended with communion—how appropriate!

Then it was party time, and almost everyone went downstairs for the festivities. However, Gabino, one of our translators, asked for prayer for the circulation in his legs, so Randy, Wanda, Diane, and I stayed in the chapel with him. As he knelt down at the altar, we laid hands on him and prayed, sensing the sweet presence of the Lord all around us. Gabino was such a gentle man. How we loved him, and how much more Jesus loved him!

When we went down to the party, we almost panicked. There were so many people! Peggy wanted to get more bread for sandwiches, but we agreed there would be enough food. Al said, "If you believe, why aren't you in line?" So we got in line, and, of course, there was more than enough. I remembered how Jesus had fed the five thousand, and there were twelve baskets left over. I also recalled how He had moved miraculously for us in Peru with the oranges. After stuffing ourselves, much as we had all week in our "suffering for Jesus," the program began.

President Baltazar played the accordion and led us in singing Spanish, English, French, and even Arabic melodies, the last of which he said came from the camel caravans. The students did skits, and Noel sang an American country-western song. Some of the guys did a routine as soldiers, and our own Mark made a terrific monster, scaring Peggy, and making us all laugh. There were some improvisational duets, and we "matched thumbs," a game where everyone must find someone whose thumb looks like his. We ended by joining hands, forming a huge prayer circle. Santa's mother gave Joshua 1:9 as a prophecy to all:

> *Have I not commanded thee? Be strong and of good courage; be not afraid, neither be thou dismayed: for the LORD thy God is with thee whithersoever thou goest.*

Then they sang to us the lovely Mexican farewell song to friends. It was very touching; no one wanted to loose hands and leave. We were bound together by cords of love. Very slowly, we said our goodbyes to those who had become especially close, exchanging addresses and promising to write.

Finally, the teams were all back at El Estudantíl for our last meeting there. It was time for bed, but it was so hard to unwind and let go. The Lord had been moving mightily, and had graciously allowed us to be a part of His awesome plan. I did not want to move from the extraordinary back to the ordinary.

Saturday morning came, and we left very early for the airport—so early we beat the sun. It got cold again! We had a little time to spend with Randy and Wanda while the vans were being returned (at more cost than we anticipated). It was not easy leave this inspiring couple who had become so dear to our hearts, and the tears flowed.

Tom didn't hang up his passion for EE, and on the plane from Monterrey to Houston, he led a young man named Benjamin to the Lord. I tried to witness to Charles, a businessman from New Jersey, but there was that old American resistance that kept him from making a commitment. However, he did take some tracts to read later, so seed was planted for another to harvest. There are no small things in God's kingdom.

We held our final team meeting in the chapel of the Houston airport. Various members spoke about the specific events of the week which were outstanding to them, and then we got down to some very personal deep sharing. The trip had not been just for us to minister to others, but indeed, for the Lord to minister to us. It was just as Mark had told us at the beginning of our mission, but he did not say I told you so. He simply led us as we offered prayers of thanksgiving and praise.

We continued on the last leg of our journey—Houston to Atlanta—which was uneventful; it was just a time for me of quiet reflection. This had been a good one! The kingdom had been increased by at least 210 new births, but by more than an increase in quantity. There had been an increase in quality as well, for this was not the same team that left Atlanta the previous week, and certainly there were some chosen ones in Monterrey who were not the same either.

The great commission is to go into all the world, and the promise is that signs and wonders will follow those who believe (Mark 16:15–18). Certainly the Lord had kept His Word. We had seen and been a part of signs and wonders, all to His glory and our amazement!

Still, there was that sense of being not quite finished.

CHAPTER 3
BRAZIL

JUNE 1987

The North Georgia United Methodist Men were partnering with Rick, an evangelist in the Methodist Church whose headquarters are in Athens, Georgia, and who also has a ministry in Brazil. Pastor Rick was building a combination worship center, clinic, and base for missionaries in Niteroi, near Rio de Janerio. We were the first team in, laying the foundation for the building and doing general construction during the day. We had Bible study every morning at eight o'clock, and worked until four o'clock in the afternoon. In the evenings, Pastor Rick would speak in certain local churches, and the team would minister to the people. This mission trip was a challenge, both physically and spiritually. To say that I was in way over my head would be a gross understatement!

The team of ten women and eight men drove in two vans from Atlanta, Georgia, to Miami, Florida, leaving on June 13—my fifty-third birthday! Prior to our departure in Miami, we briefly visited Roy and Barbara, who served with Wycliffe Bible Translators. From Miami we flew into Rio and then went by bus to the Niterói Palace Hotel. I was surprised at the very nice accommodations, and I was so pleased to have my buddy, Linda, as my roommate.

After breakfast in the mornings, we rode the local bus to the work site. Actually, the team was a sight! When we left, we were clean and neat, but when we returned in the evenings, we were caked with mud. It was obvious we had been working all day, and that gave us opportunities to share with our co-riders because they were hard workers as well. It was equal footing here. Even though we had very limited vocabularies in Portuguese, we were unlimited in our enthusiasm and good cheer.

An example of our limited language skills was with the Brazilian workers on the job site, which was located on the side of a gigantic dirt hill that seemed to go straight up. We had to move piles of gravel from one place to another, and it made no sense to us *gringos*. We would pick up a piece of gravel and take it over to another place and lay it down in mock fashion: "Is this what you mean?" And the answer would be *sim*, or "yes". Every day there was a new pile, so we made up a song:

> *Old Pastor Rick had a pile,*
> *E-I-E-I-O.*
> *Move a pile here, move a pile there—*
> *E-I-E-I-O!*

We also helped dig the footings, unload bricks, and carry buckets of concrete. The guys made a ramp of boards for me, and I would be up at the top with a load of dirt, run down the ramp, and dump it over when I got to the end. The team knew not to get in my way because once I started, I could not stop!

Pastor Rick decided that we should fast for three days, saying it would sharpen and energize us. I had fasted before in my Christian walk, but it didn't seem logical to me to go without food while doing such strenuous work. Still, he was the leader, and I was confident he knew his stuff. We did drink juice from freshly squeezed oranges, and it was delicious! One of our team members, Dusty, was a sixteen-year-old student, who got so hungry. One of the guys suggested he chew gum, which was a big mistake. His stomach kept thinking food was coming down, but it didn't (for three days). At a team meeting, Rick said we could eat a banana because it was mostly water. In the elevator returning to our room after the meeting, I whispered to Linda that I was going to our room to "drink a banana." We both exploded with laughter, and our teammates thought we had finally lost it!

The atmosphere in this part of Brazil was bizarre. At night you could see fires up on the mountains and hear the drums. On street corners, witches were dressed in beautiful white dresses, and had their wares set out on tables. Many people wore big pendants with the occult symbol of Magumba on them. Satan was on the prowl, and we ran into him headlong at many of the meetings.

At one particular meeting, Rick informed us that the building we would be meeting in was rented until 9:30 p.m., at which time the lights would be turned off, indicating that time was up and we were to promptly leave or be left in the dark. Rick preached and then gave an altar call. The people were directed to come to one area for salvation, to another for the infilling of the Holy Spirit, and to another for healing. My assignment was to help pray for those wanting the baptism of the Holy Spirit, and kneeling before me was a handsome young man in his late twenties or early thirties. He kept his eyes closed at first, and I was able to establish by questioning him that he had previously accepted Christ. He continuously hit himself on the chest, repeating over and over, "Knives in my heart!" When I touched his face, it appeared that he had a fever because he was so hot; however, his hands were icy cold. He opened his eyes, and they were not blood-shot, but solid red with jet-black pupils. I felt like I was looking into the eyes of the devil himself, so I immediately said, "I plead the blood of Jesus Christ over me and over you from the tops of our heads to the tips of our toes!" Maybe it was selfish to pray over me first, but how could I help him if I were incapacitated?

I continued to pray, but my prayers were hitting a wall, so I called for David, one of Rick's assistants. As he talked to the man, he told me there was a generational curse and we had to break the power of witchcraft to the tenth generation. Then David started coughing so uncontrollably that he could not pray, so it was up to me. I handed David a mint (every good missionary has mints in their pockets), then I anointed the young man with oil, and in the name of Jesus starting casting out this "demon of witchcraft" from each generation before him. I was pleading the blood, building hedges of spiritual protection around him, and praying every way, but still he was beating his chest, saying "knives in my heart." Then the lights started flickering off and on. "No, this cannot be," I thought. We were not finished yet—this man was not free! A young lady walked up behind the man, and I said, "Come with me; we'll go downstairs," and they obediently followed. When we got outside, David started to pray, but the man still had the feeling of knives so David called Rick over. Rick spoke to the man and then to the woman, and then he prayed over them. The man responded, "Peace in my heart, peace in my heart." I asked Rick to explain to me what he had done that was effective, and he said that you just do whatever works. This man and his wife had made an occult pact, and when they came to Christ, the pact had to be broken. It was not enough just for the man to renounce Magumba, but it required his wife also, as they were "one flesh." This really drove home to me the seriousness of marriage. We take so lightly that concept of being one flesh, but it is a reality and is far-reaching.

At another service, a lady came who had also been involved in witchcraft. She came at the invitation of her sister, so we were especially praying for her. At the altar call, she came to the front and proceeded to go berserk. She was foaming at the mouth, thrashing around, and breaking the holds of several strong men who were trying to calm her. They got her under the big cross that was hanging on the wall, and as they prayed, she got quiet. They were able to take her outside the sanctuary and minister privately to her. She came back later, a new creature in Christ, set completely free and at peace!

At this same service, I was praying for a young man who needed specific direction for his life. I was standing in front of him, and Linda was kneeling in front of him, beside me. All of a sudden, it seemed like a powerful lightning bolt struck my arm, which I had raised in the air, jumping from me into Linda and then into the man. It was a three-way charge, and we all felt it. The man was overjoyed at the presence of the Lord, and I was in shock, literally. This was really church!

The Lord moved again in a sweet, compassionate, and quiet way at a service that was very small. A young woman there was going through the heartache of her husband leaving her, and she wanted us to pray that he would come back home. I could feel her pain and was able to share my similar testimony with her, assuring her that Jesus would be her Husband (Isaiah 54:5). Life was not over for her; she was not alone because her Maker would walk with her through it all, and she would be victorious. We prayed that her husband would come back, but even if he did not, God's plans for her were good (Jeremiah 29:11). We told her that because of His promises, she would be happy again. I was living proof of that, and since our Lord is no respecter of persons, He would do it for her as well. I still have her card in my Bible and pray for her when I see it.

We had so much rain one day that the construction site became a sea of sticky mud, so Rick suggested that we take the next day off. Several of us took him at his word and went to a local shopping center. However, Rick changed his mind and sent word for us to get back on the job. It was good while it lasted, but we had come to work, so we obediently returned.

The Bible studies were especially meaningful each morning, as Rick is a powerful teacher and also a talented guitarist. He gave many on the team words from the Lord, and he told Walt that Charlotte, his wife, was like a soft, downy pillow where he could come home. Those words described Charlotte perfectly. How I wished for a personal word for me, but it never came during our mornings together. However, as we were leaving the airport at Rio to go home, David gave me an encouraging word—I was doing just fine! Perhaps that was just his opinion, but even so, it was appreciated.

I have such fond memories of Dusty, our sixteen-year-old who is now a preacher himself. In addition to his problem with fasting, he got into a struggle with a bidet toilet. We had a meeting in Walt and Charlotte's room, and he excused himself to go to the bathroom. He came out with water all over the front of his pants, not knowing how to work that contraption!

Another time, the team had gone to check on our departure, and while in the building, we divided by gender to use the bathroom facilities. The ladies had gone into one side of the restroom, but there was no stall left, so I went on the other side. When I came out, nobody on the team was there. I walked out to the front of the building, and both vans were gone. I decided to wait at the door until they realized I was missing, and in a short time they pulled up. Dusty darted out of the van, grabbed and hugged me, saying he'd never let me out of his sight again—and he didn't!

When we ministered at the churches in the city, we encountered a great number of young people. Dusty was so powerful, especially when ministering to them, but I did get a little alarmed. He would get so excited that he would start slapping them on their throats, wanting them to get their prayer language. He seemed to think he could shake the Holy Spirit into them, and the Holy Spirit was honoring his zeal.

We took a break from our work one afternoon and went by train up Corcovado Mountain to the monument of "Christ the Redeemer." It was an overwhelming sight—Christ standing with arms outstretched, looking over the coastline of Rio on the Atlantic Ocean. The statue itself is ninety-nine feet high, and the distance between His hands is ninety-two feet. It is constructed of reinforced concrete and coated with small triangles of soapstone, making it gleaming white in the sun. From there we could also see Sugarloaf Mountain, and down on the coast there was the famous resort of Copacabana. Christ was watching over it all, and He was watching over us!

The whole team greatly admired Enio, another of Rick's assistants. He drove us, guided us, labored with us, and just in general was a true brother. However, my dear Linda's feeling ran deeper, and the feeling was mutual. Her heart was torn between staying and returning home, but since she had two sons waiting for her, the decision was obvious. She had been married to a man who passionately loved her, but he died many years before. Perhaps Enio could have loved her with the same passion, but it was not to be. My heart ached at her pain when she had to say goodbye.

It was hard for all of us to leave, as the building had just begun and there was so much more ministry we could have done, were it not for the time constraints. Still, home was calling. We left Rio, retracing our path into Miami, and then by vans back to Atlanta, arriving on June 29, 1987, which would have been my thirty-fifth wedding anniversary.

On this mission, I saw the reality of the marriage covenant. When a man and woman join in holy matrimony, they truly are one in the Lord, and the breaking of that covenant has serious ramifications. This truth made me even sadder that my marriage had failed, but I understood more clearly why the enemy is so hell-bent on destroying marriages. The Bible says that one will chase a thousand, but two will chase ten thousand (Deuteronomy 32:30). Satan wants to split the home and rip away that power. Yet, while the devil is very real, he is no match for the power of our God!

CHAPTER 4
ZIMBABWE

JULY 1990

This particular trip needs a bit of prologue. On a certain Saturday afternoon in June 1987, my mother and I went to the movies to see *Out of Africa*. As I watched the movie, it seemed that I was actually there in Africa, walking on red dirt (like in my home state of Georgia), seeing thatched huts, and feeling the sunshine on my shoulders. The people were beautiful, and I instantly loved them. I prayed silently, "Lord, would You let me go to Africa?" The next day the team I went with to Brazil attended a commissioning service at Marietta First United Methodist Church. As I entered the sanctuary, Walt, our leader, approached me saying, "How would you like to go to Africa?" My immediate response was yes! He then explained that it would be a couple of years down the road because Nyika had to finish his studies at Emory University's Candler School of Theology. Nyika, the son of Chief Mutambara, was being sponsored the bishop and the North Georgia Conference of Methodist Men. Nyika graduated in 1987, and upon his return home to Zimbabwe, he became a teacher and village administrator at Mutambara Mission. Nyika set in motion the plans for a construction and evangelism team to come to the Mutambara Province. Approximately three years later the plans were finalized, and sixteen volunteers from seven different churches were set to go, including awestruck me!

We flew from Atlanta to London, where we had a short layover and did a little sightseeing. It was hard to believe that I, Betty June Terry Smith, was actually seeing Buckingham Palace! Little did I know then that I would be passing through London again on future mission trips. We flew from London to Harare, the capitol of Zimbabwe, and from there drove by bus for five hours to Mutambara.

The scenery along the way was magnificent. I saw poinsettias as big as trees and hedges of marigolds. Aloe trees were vivid shades of red and orange, and the mountains seemed to stumble across each other. For some reason, I had not expected mountains. We stopped for lunch at a teahouse, which we called "The Teahouse of the August Moon." It was like something out of the movies: a rather sprawling pink stucco house trimmed in white that had been transformed into a restaurant. The tables were set with beautiful white linen tablecloths, fine china plates, glasses and silverware, and decorated with vases filled with fresh flowers. The waiters wore brilliantly white uniforms, which made their skin look even darker than it was, and they were all extremely kind and courteous. Gorgeous roses were blooming in gardens all around the house. Also, the food was delicious, which was an added bonus because just the atmosphere fed your soul. I was overwhelmed!

It was dark when we arrived at Pastor Peter's house in Mutambara, where our new friends awaited us, singing to us in Shona as we stood in Pastor's front yard. After a fine meal and some sharing, the team was assigned to their host homes. The mission compound is separated by a river, and Ron and I were sent to the other side while the remaining fourteen stayed on the more populated side. This was the first time missionaries had been sent to the other side of the river. It turned out to be harder physically to be on that side, but it also turned out to be more rewarding, at least in my view. Ron lost about twenty pounds by the time we departed, and even quit smoking. I had tried to get in shape before I left, doing a lot of walking, and that was a lifesaver. We walked at least four miles every day, but it was a joy because on the walks we had personal contact with the people.

It was already dark when we got to the home of Dorcas, my hostess, who became like a sister to me. There was no electricity on that side of the river, so my little room had a candle and a small lamp with a burning wick to keep out the mosquitoes. They did have a small television set, which was powered by a car battery; it was black and white, and the shows were ancient. It was as if I had stepped back in time.

The next morning Dorcas took me on a little tour of her property. Her house was light green stucco, and there was a lemon tree on one side with lemons the size of softballs. She took me to the back yard to show me her African kitchen, which was a thatched hut. As we were walking away from the hut to see her chickens, I looked down and saw the red dirt puffing up from my feet. I felt the warm sun on my shoulders—all that I had experienced almost three years before at the movie. I knew I was where I was supposed to be, and I started to weep. This upset Dorcas, and she asked, "Why are you crying? You didn't come here to cry." "No," I replied, "I came here to love, and tell people about Jesus!"

Dorcas told me about her family. Her husband worked in Harare, and he either came home on the weekends or she went there. She had two grandchildren living with her, Little Dorcas and Kennedy, and she was providing for their education. Two other boys, Ngwarai and Farai, were "helpers." Farai was attending school at that time, and she planned to send Ngwarai next quarter. She had eight children, six were married and had their own homes. One son, Quinton, was going to a boarding school and wanted to be a preacher. Years later I heard he had died, but I never learned why. Her daughter Ebbar was still unmarried, but she was in love. I met her boyfriend, Baricosa.

Dorcas and sixteen other women had formed a group called the 17-Ladies Co-op. Naomi, Ron's hostess, was president of their group; Dorcas was vice-president. I told her that back home I was in a ladies circle with twelve women, and we were called "The Dorcas Circle." That was a cute little God-incidence and another confirmation for me.

On our first full day at Mutambara, the team met for a reality check. Tentative projects had been planned, but we had to determine whether or not they could be completed within our time frame. After touring the mission area, the men felt the half-mile of irrigation piping could be laid, and the swinging bridge—the only way across the river for three miles—could be repaired.

Later Dorcas asked if we would be able to put a roof on the building of their co-op so they would be able to care for children, teach mothers about parenting and nutrition, hold their business meetings, and do their various projects. The men graciously agreed to add this to their list, and not only did they put on a roof, but the team painted the building as well, to the delight of the ladies of the co-op. Incidentally, they also had a field where they grew tomatoes and peas. The profits from their produce were divided among the families, and they planned to buy sewing machines to make school uniforms. I was inspired by the great courage and strength of these women, especially Dorcas and Naomi. They were pioneer women, real trail-blazers!

Two of the ladies, Elinah and Phillipah, came to visit me on the second morning, Saturday. They came to the front yard, calling out, "Is the mother of the house here?"

Dorcas and I met them at the porch, and they were dancing and singing to me, "Alleluia, Jesus!" I danced and sang with them. They had brought me water from the irrigation ditch down the road so I could wash. My suitcase had been temporarily misplaced by the airline, so my wardrobe was seriously limited. They became dear sisters to me.

The drums started early in the afternoon, announcing the meeting of the Jeneneska Church, and the team had been invited to come. I didn't know what denomination this was, just that it was the Chieftain's church. The musicians were dressed in beautiful African garments of blue and white, and they were really "getting down," as we would say in America. The women were also dressed colorfully, and it was like a scene from the movies. I sat with one group of the ladies on a straw mat, and when they started to dance, I joined them. They were showing me the steps, being very patient with me, and they also showed me how to "hoot," African-style: you purse your lips and move your tongue up and down real fast, like our yodel. The chief spoke briefly, and then he called on Walt, our leader, to come forward. Walt gave his greetings and then called on Huey, next Reese, and then me to give our testimonies. When I shared that I was single, the chief's bodyguard came up beside me. He was a short little man, wearing a wine-colored polyester leisure suit with a white shirt and "fried-egg" tie, and he had no teeth in front. When I saw him, I jumped and said "Oh, my!" Everyone started laughing, and my ladies' group started their hoot, yodeling "Bett-Tee, Bett-Tee," over and over. For the rest of the time we were there, whenever I entered a meeting, I was greeted with "Bett-Tee" from my own cheering section. It was so precious, and I was so grateful because I loved them so much. Nyika said if I could stay another five years, I would become one of them. That would be an honor.

That evening I was lamenting to the Lord that I had not spoken very well, how I wished I had been more eloquent. Then He spoke to me in my heart:

> *These are my children. I have children all over the world—red, yellow, black, and white, some with eyes brown, some blue. Some eat sadsa and some hot dogs, but they are all my children. It saddens my heart when I see some of my children so poor, and then those who have so much (even called by My name) not helping, not sharing. But the day is coming when all my children shall be received; there will be no more need. I did not call you here to make flowery speeches. I brought you here to be My love. Was not that my call? Come, walk with Me, and be My Love.*

I remembered when my husband had left and the Lord had promised that He would walk with me through it all. He gave me the invitation, "Come, walk with Me, and be My love. The best is yet to be." What an affirmation!

On that first Sunday, we visited the Mutambara United Methodist Church, and Dorcas went with me, although she was a member of the African Independent Church. Some of us, including me, worked with the children, presenting lessons, singing and praising the Lord, and giving out balloons. At the main service, the team was introduced, and we had the preaching service. After lunch the ladies on the team met with the ladies of the church, sharing and exchanging testimonies. That evening the entire team attended a Bible study, with more teaching and sharing. It was a jam-packed, delightful day, made even better for me by the news that my suitcase had been found and would be delivered on Tuesday. Clean clothes and underwear are a blessing we take so much for granted!

On that first Monday, after the morning team meeting, the physical work began. The men split into two teams: one working on the swinging bridge and the other on the irrigation project. The bridge project moved rapidly. However, the water project was another story. The ground was like rock and there were not enough tools.

The ladies also split into two teams, one going into Mutare that day for shopping and later working at the 17-Ladies Co-op building, getting it ready for the men to roof and paint. The other team, composed of Glenda, Charlotte, and me, were assigned to the hospital to catalogue books for Clemonts, the German instructor for the nurses. This project lasted several days, so we were able to have tea with Clemonts on different occasions, and it made for some very interesting conversations. Clemonts was on a two-year assignment with the Peace Corps, and he seemed to be very informed on the politics of the area. At that time, Mozambique, only twelve miles away, was in a war with Zimbabwe. Soldiers from Mozambique would come into a village, force young boys to kill their parents, and then the boys, emotionally broken, would follow the soldiers and join them. There was a camp of Zimbabwan soldiers on the compound, and we had been specifically instructed not to associate or talk with them, as they were on duty. Their presence made the mission compound like an island, so we were not seeing the real situation. Clemonts urged us to talk to the people, as we would probably never have this opportunity again. He said he was a former Roman Catholic, and he agreed that denominations did not matter—what counts is what we think of Jesus Christ. We did not get deeper into this subject, as we had to return to work. Later I was pleased to meet Alexander, his roommate, a born-again, turned-on, radical Christian, and I was assured that God had His own plan for Clemonts. Alexander was sure to be a big part of it.

The ladies were able to visit the three schools on the compound. There was a primary and a high school on the more affluent side, and on the other side of the river (where Ron and I lived) there was another primary school. The team was appalled by the fact that a water ditch ran beside the school on the poorer side, and farther up the road cattle were walking across that same water that the children were drinking and playing in. We brought the matter to the attention of our men, and took up a collection for a well. After we left, the well was constructed, and not to be outdone, the government added more wells in the area.

We went to different classes in the schools, where we answered the children's questions about the United States. Some examples: Are there cars in the United States? Is the sky blue there? Does the sun shine in the United States? Most of them thought all American men carried machine guns, because the only movies and television shows they saw were about the FBI and Elliott Ness. In one class, the children sang "Polly, Put the Kettle On" to us, and another song equivalent to "If You're Happy and You Know It." They were delightful; you just wanted to bundle them all up and take them home. We had brought lots of goodies to give away, but in many classes there were so many children that sometimes we would not have enough of one item for everyone. In those instances, we left them with the teachers to dispense later. It was very important to be wise in our giving. It is easy to leave someone out when there are so many, and when only one or two receive, the others feel slighted or that they are inferior.

The principal of the high school invited the team to come in the evenings and conduct some classes. We divided into different subjects, and to my amazement, Darryl and I were assigned to teach on Sex Education. Of course, we had the biggest attendance. Talk about being out of your comfort zone! Still, we had fun, and I believe a little educating did take place. I learned that when God calls, He equips, and He has a great sense of humor!

The ladies on the team had a very special meeting with the 17-Ladies. We met at their building site, where they danced for us, and then we moved into the school classroom for our meeting. Our team was very impressed with the ingenuity and drive of these seventeen women. They had organized with a minimum of assistance. The Zimbabwe Association of Women's Clubs gave Naomi and Dorcas bookkeeping lessons, and they had a manual. A lady was fined if she did not attend a meeting. Their projects at that time were the garden (peas and tomatoes), school uniforms, panties, and socks. There were approximately 175 students who did not have uniforms, and their group was willing to make the uniforms if we could provide the fabric. We shared our testimonies, and they gave us peas from the garden. Then they sang us a song about learning and making progress. Their motto is Forward—Progress. If all the women in Zimbabwe were like these seventeen—watch out world!

In the midst of my awesome mission, I had a jolting experience. You can count on the enemy to try to strike fear into you. The moon shines brilliantly in the dark night skies, and I had many times gone to the outside toilet with no problem. One night when I stepped inside, I saw a huge rat the size of a dog sitting on the ledge. I ran outside shaking and crying, "I want to go home. Oh, Lord, please get me home!" I started praying fervently, and at last the peace came. I will say that for the rest of the mission, I never went to the outhouse at night, and even when I went during the day, I carried a broom and starting swinging it as I walked in. I was the ultimate picture of a brave missionary.

One afternoon at lunch, Dorcas and her daughter Ebbar and son Quentin, presented me with a beautiful crocheted tablecloth. What a blessing! I thanked them profusely through my tears as I raved over the handiwork. This was genuine gratitude from my heart, but I noticed also that it lifted them up and made them feel very good about themselves, as well they should have. We must be cautious not to make those to whom we minister feel that they are somehow lacking or inadequate. We are all God's family, in this together! One universe, under God.

The day after that, two of Dorcas' cousins, also members of the 17-Ladies Co-op, came to visit and presented me with more crocheted pieces as thanks for gifts of earrings and bookmarks. I tried to explain that I was not the source of the earrings and bookmarks, as I had brought gifts for the children, but they insisted that I keep the gifts because they could not thank everybody and I was there, which was an advantage to my being a "country cousin" of Dorcas. I was reaping where I had not sown.

At one special meeting with the local United Methodist Women, each lady there gave her testimony, and we united in prayer for unsaved husbands and children. That is a universal need and a source of pain for so many women. In that, we are so much alike.

Some of the team took a day off from our work to do some sightseeing. This is an important part of missions because people love their countries, and want to show off a bit. It builds good relations when you can "ooh" and "ahh" over those things and places that are a source of pride to them.

Our destination was Chimanimani, which means "squeezed in." It was appropriately named because in the midst of this huge chain of mountains, our spot, Bridal Veil Falls (not to be confused with the falls of the same name in Yosemite National Park), was neatly tucked into a valley. Along the way we saw donkeys, cows, and goats in the fields and on the road, guinea hens feeding on the grass, and women carrying huge bundles on their heads going to wash clothes in the river. The women on the team were in the car being driven by Dorothy, Nyika's wife, and the vehicle was in bad shape; the hand brake did not work at all. She was driving in the middle of the road, passing on curves with hairpin turns at a very fast speed. Glenda was next to me, and we would just smile at each other and pray. I whispered to her, "Do you feel like you could leap off a burning building—like Superman?" I was so aware of our divine protection.

We were way ahead of the men, who had decided to go to the animal sanctuary but had not told us. Dorothy drove us to the Mozambique border (this same Mozambique that was at war with Zimbabwe). The weather had turned foggy and misty—downright spooky. The gate was locked at the crossing, and a guard walked up. We explained that we just wanted to put our feet across the border so we could say we had been to Mozambique, but he would not allow that, saying we had to come back in the daytime. This was quite out of character for Dorothy, who is usually meek and mild-mannered, but it did give us ladies an adventure we would never forget. I do wish I could say I had been to Mozambique, but close is still good.

My relationship with Dorcas deepened, and one morning at breakfast she shared with me that her husband had another wife, which is legal in Zimbabwe. His father had told him to put away the other wife and not hurt Dorcas, which her husband had done. However, the father had died, and she feared that the other wife had returned. She was not certain of this, but people were talking. I shared with her how my husband had left me, so I could relate to her pain. She said that she continued to pray, go to church, and stay close to God, and I nodded in agreement. I could again see God's hand in putting me in Dorcas's home; there was a special bond between us as women who had been wounded in spirit, but refused to quit.

We went to Dorcas's church, The African Independent Church, the second Sunday we were there, and I was asked to do the children's sermonette. I had the children sit on mats and shared with them about giving so that it would be given back to them. I gave the first child a piece of candy, explaining to the children that as they received, they were to pass it on, and they would be given more. It started out well, but as they went down the line, some of the children started hoarding and not passing on. They really did not trust that they would get more. All the adults had a good laugh, but we could see ourselves in this scenario. At the end I made sure all the children had equal amounts of candy.

The team was introduced, and I was asked to go and sit with Dorcas. The chief had sent word that Ron and I were living with people on this side of the river, and that as he walked by, he saw a white woman gaining weight (meaning me)! After church there were refreshments, and the ladies of the church requested that our ladies stay and meet with them. We shared testimonies and I taught on the Proverbs 31 woman. Afterward, the whole church met in a huge circle in the front yard, and we sang a song about Africa. We joined by crooking our little fingers together and holding our hands in the air. This was such a moving experience for me, as I knew that not just little fingers were joined but our hearts as well.

One afternoon Dorcas and Aunt Margaret took me to the hospital to visit Grannie Miriam, an elderly lady who had suffered a stroke. I could never figure out the relationship between Dorcas and "Aunt" Margaret, because everyone was called "aunt" or "aunti." They seemed to be cousins or related in some way, but sometimes it simply appeared to be a term of endearment or devotion. I was asked to pray for this precious lady, and we left some money to help her with expenses. When I returned to visit her a few days later, she had been moved from ICU and the doctor said she would fully recover. God is so good, all the time!

It was a joy for me to walk the river road, because each time I would encounter divine appointments. There was the old man who lived in a shack close to the river, and finally one day he spoke to me. The students along the way always wanted to talk because they wanted to practice their English. They especially liked my accent, and they were very polite. Monkeys were in the trees, and other little monkeys (the children) would jump up and down and yell at me as I passed by.

One young man working on the co-op building was named Never, and he was having problems with his mother. He had chickens, and his mother wanted him to keep them inside so that no one else would want the house. The team had given him some wire and lumber so he could fence them in, but this was upsetting his mother. I stopped by to talk with her, explaining that it was good that the chickens were outside because it was not healthy to keep them in the house. She seemed to agree wholeheartedly with me, but I had to wonder what she really thought.

Dorcas told me about her son, named Memory, who joined the army and went off to war. He took his suit with him so if he died, he could be buried in it. She said she cried constantly and could not pray. Then one night she had a dream. Her son Memory told her that if she kept crying, he would not return. She joined a group of ladies at the Methodist Church who met every Wednesday, early in the morning, for two years, praying for several hours for the safe return of their children from the war. Every woman who prayed had her child return home. She related how one day they were told that a group had returned to a city close to Mutare, so she went there on the bus and saw Memory. She said that he was still a solder because it was what God had called him to be.

Our ladies met one afternoon with the Methodist women, where we gave our testimonies and answered their questions. They in turn shared with us, and taught us a very funny song about the animals in Zimbabwe. We taught them "His Banner Over Me Is Love," with accompanying motions. We admired their crafts, prayed together, and at the end took photographs. This was a lighthearted fun time, but it was also very important in building relationships. I know our Lord was pleased to see His daughters enjoying each other's company.

When Ron stopped by to walk with me one particular morning, he was telling how his hostess Naomi had prepared French toast for his breakfast. He had told her earlier how to do it, and she surprised him that morning. She said, "That's sharing, isn't it?" I saw her in the field with the ladies later that morning and told her how pleased he was; she was thrilled. This outstanding woman, president of the co-op, seemed to be everywhere we went; she said that she learned by doing and proved this by helping paint the co-op building.

As we were nearing the end of the mission, the team met to see how much money we had and what we wanted to do with it. When we pooled all our resources, we had enough to install a well at the primary school on the other side of the river, order the windows for the second story building on the compound, and pay for school for the three children of the local man whose ear had been cut off by the soldiers from Mozambique. That was one time in my life that I wished I were rich! There was so much to be done, but we did what we could.

There was a special program at the primary school where the children sang, read poems, and performed skits. I was so impressed; they were delightful! After the children went home, we adjourned to a classroom, at which time the chairman of the school board, the teachers, and the team were formally introduced. Ernest, a black man from our team, announced that we were giving them a well. This was so appropriate because of his heritage; he had joined this mission with his son to get back to his roots. One of the teachers gave a speech that was so moving. He said:

> *The voice of Jesus yells across the mountains, across the valleys, and across the sea. It's a voice of love. It isn't enough to say, "Makadini" (How are you), and go on your way. I have not seen love like I have seen in you. You are doing something—the way you speak to everyone. I have been touched and changed by what I have seen in your lives.*

And I thought to myself, "But, oh, the touch in our lives! The greatest witness is not in what we say, but how we live day by day."

Our farewell meeting with the 17-Ladies was a magnificent affair, and several men attended, including Willie, the carpenter who was there merely to repair a door but never left; Fiscon and Never, the other helpers; and the men from our team. President Naomi opened the meeting, and several of the ladies shared. Willie called us angels, and one of the ladies said we were Zimbabwans now, not Americans. Glenda gave out coins with scripture verses on them, and the one that she gave Fiscon read "Jesus is Lord." He said he had seen Jesus in us, and just as Jacob wrestled with the angel until he got a blessing, he wasn't going to let us go until he got a blessing. He wanted Jesus to be his Lord, so we led him in the sinner's prayer. He asked Jesus to be his Lord and to fill him with the Holy Spirit. He walked home with us afterwards, and I was able to share more with him about how to grow in his faith.

Glenda also gave one of the men some U.S. coins and a dollar bill, showing him the phrase "In God We Trust." He was so excited to be so rich, and he asked how anyone in America could steal money when it had "In God We Trust" written on it! The ladies presented a drama about a lazy woman who would not join the club, and there was more singing and dancing. They spread out their beautiful handiwork, and even the men bought some crocheted pieces to take home. Dorcas told me later they had made Z$150—which was quite an offering—and they were giving the money to Granny Miriam. President Naomi shared with us that the rainbow the Johnson kids had painted over the door of their building had all the colors of the Zimbabwe flag, making it even more special to them.

At our final formal church service Sunday morning, Mason preached at the early youth service, and Miss Charlotte gave her testimony. The team stood behind the altar rail and the congregation responded. There were approximately twelve young people lined up in front of me, all wanting salvation, with the exception of one who needed healing for a stomachache. One of the young men who prayed for salvation said he was so happy that Jesus was in his heart, and he was going to the hospital and pray for the sick. That afternoon, Dorcas and I met him and a friend he had brought (he was like the disciple Andrew, bringing his brother) as they came in to pray for Granny Miriam.

Ernie, the African-American man on our team, preached the last service, and his topic was love. I was honored to give my testimony. I told them about my vision of coming to Africa and that Jesus was the reason for it all; it was all about Him and His love. The following week, when I would be home in America, they would be there also because I carried them in my heart. That is still true today, many years later. I can lay my hand on my heart and feel their love there.

As Dorcas and I walked home, we reached a group of women who were singing, "Jerusalem Is My Home," and we joined in. This stirred me inside. Here I was a white American singing with black Africans about Jerusalem, our mutual home. There is only one Lord, one faith, one baptism, and one body of Christ. Suddenly, breaking the reverence of the moment, there came Ron in the back of a military truck with a load of soldiers, all laughing and making merry! Remember, we were not to associate with the soldiers, but not to worry, it was our last Sunday!

That night it turned cold, so Dorcas had a bucket fire in the kitchen, and Ron dropped by to visit. We had the popcorn that Barry, Ebbar's boyfriend, had brought. Kennedy had the visible signs of chicken pox that day, so I donated my baby powder to help with the itch. I could sympathize because my hands, sensitive to the malaria medicine, were still giving me fits, and my nose was red to the bone. We talked and enjoyed each other's company, and I didn't want it to end.

The next day, Monday, was our last full day, and we were at the high school at 7:00 a.m. for a ceremony. The headmaster presented each team member with a flag of Zimbabwe, a pin of the United Methodist Church printed with the phrase "The truth shall set you free," and a sticker of Zimbabwe to put on our cars.

In his speech, he commented that we had taught them the dignity of work. All whites they had ever seen did not work with their hands, but merely rode in their SUVs or horses and supervised, using blacks to do the labor. In that spirit, as we dismissed, he had the students go and take bricks from a pile to where workers were constructing the new library. We all helped them and then waved goodbye as we walked up the hill. I didn't think my heart could take much more.

But there was more. Nyika took us into Mutare for a short trip to see Thompson's Vlei, a game reserve. We drove the scenic road up the mountain and saw giraffe, zebras, monkeys, and wildebeests. Looking down into the valley, I saw a view of Mutare way below, and I sensed I had been there before–like déjà vu–that this was a part of God's plan for me. Then we drove down to the lake, where we saw elands, antelope, guinea hens, crocodiles, more monkeys, and two rhinoceroses. Surprise! We ran into two young students from Houston, Texas, brother and sister, who were visiting their father. We had fun sharing with them, and it was so good for me, as I was on the brink of tears at the thought of leaving.

As I walked home from Nyika's, I met Fiscon on the road, and he walked me to the house. I told him I was leaving a piece of my heart there and that the red dirt was in my blood, so I must return. We hugged goodbye.

I had my final meal of rice and kava and yams with Dorcas, and she let me skip the *sadsa* (like cold grits) as her goodwill gesture. Then it was time to pack. I divided my clothes, except the ones I was wearing home, into designated piles for certain ladies. I regretted I didn't have more to give; they had each given me so much! How could it be time to go home? We just got here! I prayed that night for courage and control to say goodbye.

Early that Tuesday morning, Ron, Earl, and Naomi came to get Dorcas and me. Nyika came in, and we had prayer together. Slowly the team assembled at Peter's house, where we had come in that first night. Neighbors came, and the ladies made a receiving line and started singing. We sang in Shona and in English. One of the ladies said they had been calling me by Dorcas's last name because I was living with her. As we drove away in our vehicles, they were yodeling and slapping their hips. Dorcas rode with me in the van, as she was going into Harare anyway, and she and her husband would come to the airport to see us leave. This extended our time together and made it easier for me to leave.

On our way to Harare, we stopped to visit the original mission in Old Mutare. We met Dr. Gail Johnson and her husband, who were to retire the following year. Our next stop was lunch at the "Teahouse of the August Moon," where we ate that first time on our way to Mutambara. Dorcas's niece worked there, and it was a joy to meet her. During our trip, Dorcas showed me the mountain where she was born, the area where her son had a farm, and later her daughter's farm. Dorcas seemed to have relatives all over Zimbabwe. When we arrived in Harare, she took a cab to her apartment.

The team then rushed to a dinner meeting with the Bishop and other leaders of the Methodist church. It was a grand affair, but stressful, as we were all panicky that we would miss our flight since, as usual, we were behind schedule. We said hasty farewells and departed for the airport. We had to board our plane at 8:30 p.m., and Dorcas, her husband, their daughter, and her family did not arrive until 8:15 p.m. As I left, I hugged my sister Dorcas and we made a covenant to pray for each other and for our children. I cried, "You are my sister; I shall never forget you."

And I boarded the plane.

I thought the mission was over, but the Lord had other plans. I sat between Esther, an Anglican from Mutare on her way to Canada to visit her son, and Carole, who was returning to college in Liverpool. Carole was backslidden, and as I witnessed to her, Esther encouraged her to get back into church. She confirmed her belief in the Lord Jesus as we prayed together. They were both fearful of flying, and as we landed, I took each one by the hand, assuring them that many people were praying for us to have a safe journey, and our Lord gently set us down in London.

From London to Atlanta, I sat next to Professor Winn, formerly of Saigon and now of Paris. He taught physics and chemistry, and was on his way to Fort Walton Beach, Florida, to visit his sister. He was a Buddhist, and I was trying very hard to share Christ with him. It became comical. He could not understand me, and I could not understand him. For instance, I thought he was trying to tell me about a gray Audi car, but he was talking about a Greyhound bus. I thought he was commenting about duck livers, and I was guessing everything I could think relating to ducks! I did give him a tract, and he promised he would read it. The Holy Spirit would continue His work, using other witnesses, because we were landing in Atlanta and it was time for me to finish. Family and home were waiting for me there.

I continued to correspond with Dorcas and Aunt Margaret, but in recent years they have not answered, so I lift them up to the Father's throne of grace, together with the courageous 17 Ladies. They made a tremendous impact on my life, and I miss them all. One of the songs we sang with the ladies spoke of "meeting again at the feet of God."

Heaven will be never having to say goodbye!

CHAPTER 5
SIBERIA, RUSSIA

MAY 1993

$\mathcal{I}$ first met Mike and Diane on a lay witness mission, and we served together many times after that. When the Lord called them to be missionaries in Siberia, I became a part of their support team, financially and prayerfully. Their home church, Mount Paran Church of God in Atlanta, was sponsoring mission awareness tours (MAT teams), so that as you served you could personally experience what was happening in that country and see if this might be a call on your life. I signed on to be a part of the third MAT team to Siberia. We would link up with another missionary from Mount Paran, Derryck, and his family, who were planting a church in Barnaul, Siberia, through a program called Operation Impact.

Our information packet contained the following statement of purpose:

> *It is the vision of Operation Impact to participate in God's redemptive plan for Russia by seeking to impact every strata of Siberian society with the gospel of Jesus Christ. One Operation Impact vehicle to accomplish this goal is the development of summer camps designed to evangelize, disciple and promote*

Christ-centered family values for children,
teenagers, and families.[1]

Mike and Diane were specifically working on the summer camp program, which was to be one of our focal points.

Our team was composed of seven from Louisiana, four from Atlanta, and one who met us in Amsterdam. We were split evenly—six men and six women. I was a bit nervous when I met the team at the airport in Atlanta because the only team members I knew were Mike and Diane, and they were in Siberia. The Louisiana folks knew each other and the other three from Atlanta all attended Mount Paran together and were acquainted. However, everyone was kind and gracious, and I could see immediately that this was going to be an exceptional trip.

The Lord had confirmed to me that I was to be on this mission, and that gave me confidence. Right before we left, I was short of money, and He provided just exactly what I needed at the very last minute! This had happened to me before, but it seems I never get accustomed to it. Also, I had specifically asked the Lord to give me my own special angel. I wanted the team to be covered as well, but I needed one of my own. I felt His response was, "Sure!" A friend had called me after I prayed, and said she had asked the Lord to give me an angel to watch over me and that I would feel his presence.

When we arrived in Amsterdam, I had an urgent need for my personal angel. Our family had hosted Anna, a foreign exchange student from Sweden, in 1981–1982. She had been to visit us a few times since returning to Sweden and was attending school in Holland at the time of my trip. She wanted to meet me at the airport in Amsterdam and spend some time with me during our short layover there. I checked with the information desk at the airport, but she was not there and she did not answer our page. The team had to leave and could wait no longer, so I prayed for my angel to get Anna and bring her to me. As we were on the platform and our train was pulling up, Anna came running. Thank you, my angel!

Anna went with us to De Poort, a youth hostel run by Youth With a Mission (YWAM), where the team was to attend an orientation meeting and spend the night. Anna even went to the meeting with me, even though she was not a Christian, and afterwards she was my guide for a short tour of the city. We took a canal trip, as that is the best way to see the city in a short time. A boat passed by, and I was amazed to see former Russian President Gorbachev waving at us. Anna didn't believe it was really him until another boatload of photographers came behind his boat, and that evening we saw him on the news. It was an exciting day, and while I was sad to say goodbye to Anna, she promised that she and her boyfriend, Branko, would meet me on my return trip.

The next morning we left for Moscow, but there was no time there because we had to rush to another airport on the other side of the city to depart for Novosobirsk, New Siberia. We did make a stop at McDonald's, the largest one I had ever seen. There were fifteen hundred employees! We were told that they had to be trained to smile and say, "Can I help you?" I could readily understand why, because the city was so archaic, like stepping back in time, and there was an aura of hardness that seemed to hover over it and the people. I could see no joy; no one seemed happy.

The airport was unreal—just a filthy place, with hardly any lights because they had all burned out. I was surprised to see a lot of Chinese people, and all around there were huge bales of some commodity that I could not identify.

We already had our tickets, but were charged an extra unexpected fee. We walked across the tarmac to board the plane, and I thought about the end of the movie *Casablanca*, where Ingrid Bergman leaves Humphrey Bogart, and it is sinister and foggy. No matter how it looked on the surface, I knew I was safe. After the team had boarded, the officials refused to let our guide, Svellana, come with us. There was more hassling, but finally she was seated. It was amusing just to look around the plane. There were some people who had chickens in a small cage, and a little dog was barking, plus the usual crying babies. Our flight attendant was a tough, tight-lipped woman, probably in her fifties, and she didn't put up with "nothing from nobody!"

I sat next to Anataly, thirty years old, who spoke very little English. He told me that his grandfather had been killed by Stalin because he was a Christian, and Anataly said that he was a Christian, too. The tray attached to the back of the seat in front of me kept falling and hitting my knees, and he was very concerned and tried to repair the latch. He gave me his card in the event he could be of help to me during my stay in Novosibirsk, where he ran an export-import business. He was very kind, and had such a lovely smile; he would have been a great asset to McDonald's.

Bradford, a young YWAM missionary, met us at the airport in Novosibirsk and drove us to our hotel. I was blessed to have my own private room, with a huge window (though there was no shade or curtain) and very cold water, which only ran at certain times of the day. It proved to be a bit hard to sleep because there was so little darkness at that time of the year, but I did well with covers over my head. And I used the early wake-up time for prayer.

That first evening, Derryck, our leader there, had supper with us and then took us by subway train to see the ballet *Gisele*. I was impressed by the Novosibirsk Metro because of all the magnificent art decorating the stations, and the trains were so clean! It was hard to stay awake during the ballet because I was so tired and the music so peaceful and calming. However, during the last act it was so cold that I started shaking, and that kept me awake. It was good to retire for the night, thanking the Lord and my angel for an exciting trip thus far, and anticipating getting down to the real mission the next morning: glorifying Jesus in that place.

We attended another orientation meeting the following morning where Derryck urged us to reflect, look inside ourselves, and see what God was showing us on this mission. He went into more detail about the method behind Operation Impact. Mixed teams composed of members with diverse gifts are used to establish self-sustaining churches. They would eventually be run by the locals, so that when the teams left there would be a thriving community with a world vision to go out and reproduce themselves. I was reminded how Literacy Action uses this same procedure in teaching people to read: each one teaches another, with the goal that in time illiteracy will be eradicated. Ideally, if each church reproduced itself, or if even each Christian would lead another person to Christ, the gospel would cover the entire world. Our Lord said Himself that this gospel must be preached to every people group before the end would come (Matthew 24:14).

The team, along with our translators, went to a local hospital that specialized in spinal cases. We gathered in a large room filled with children who were there for treatment, many of whom had deformed backs. The chief surgeon spoke to us and showed us a very impressive video of their work. Brandon and two lovely teenagers sang, and two young ladies gave their testimonies. Dr. Joe Ben (doctor of psychiatry) from our team gave his testimony. I was surprised that he had only known Jesus Christ as his Savior and Lord for ten months; he wasn't wasting any time in being about his Father's business. After this we were allowed to pray with the young patients for salvations and healings, and we gave out candy and tracts. Lowell took their pictures with a Polaroid camera, and gave the instant photographs to them, much to their delight. I was thrilled at this opportunity to freely share the gospel. This was why I came! At last we were actually doing the work and not just talking about it.

On the way back to the train, we gave out more tracts. The people seemed genuinely pleased to get them and started to read them right away. Back home, most people would have either refused the tracts or thrown them away. These fields were truly white unto harvest.

One incident on the train stands out in my memory. A middle-aged lady seated directly across the aisle from me held out her hand to receive a tract I offered, and then held up in her other hand a bouquet of flowers. I knew that she wanted me to give her another tract for the person to whom she was taking the flowers, so I smiled and gave it to her, and she smiled back at me. No words had been spoken; we had communicated spirit to spirit, and another bridge had been built.

We stopped at a bakery, and I gave a tract to a young male composer and his wife who both spoke English. They professed to be Spirit-filled Christians, and he wanted to talk to someone about his faith problems. He had a notebook with him full of questions. I invited him to the church and gave him a card with directions, but then I saw Brandon, introduced them to him, and he made an appointment to meet them at the church that Sunday. This proved to be a most productive divine encounter, because the couple did come to the church for a meeting with Brandon, became involved, and even served at the summer camp a few months later.

I woke very early the next morning because of the bright sun shining through my window. As I was reflecting on our first real day of ministry, the Lord told me that He had brought me here to be His love. The hugs at the hospital yesterday were His hugs, and I was His instrument. I was not here to gather scalps, but to be a channel through which His love could flow. Whether those fifteen to twenty kids the day before had sincerely prayed and accepted Him was His business, not mine, and the healings—they were also His business. He told me that He would work out the details regarding the composer and his wife to whom I witnessed at the bakery. "Do not reflect back on past works, either to be puffed up or to be pulled down if you thought you were not good enough. Leave it all in His hands; just glow with the flow," was the message spoken to me that morning.

The rest of the day was an extension of what the Lord had expressed during my prayer time earlier that day: just rest in Him and flow. After breakfast we had orientation and share time. It was interesting to hear what the others were experiencing. I knew where I was, but when they shared I was expanded and could see different perspectives. The YWAM team met with us, and then took us in small groups for shopping and free time. If the Lord had not given me that early morning pep talk, I am sure I would have been frustrated at shopping rather than ministering. However, it is most important that we do mingle with the local people, purchase their wares, and brag on their handiwork. It helps build relationships, and it is a vital part of ministry.

We went down by the River Opp, where many people were out enjoying the warmer-than-usual day, and rode the Metro to Gum department store—there are three floors!— where I bought my sons the traditional Russian fur winter hats. I still have some of the items I purchased that day:

three honey-bear wooden spoons, a ceramic reindeer, and a small slate cross.

After dinner at the Friendship Restaurant, we went to a meeting with the youth at the New Life Church, where we had a question and answer session. We then divided into small groups, and I was with two of the YWAM team, Marie and Mary Francis, and three teenage girls. We had a good sharing time, and I was touched by the sincerity of these teenagers who wanted more of Jesus, to be stronger in their faith, and to hear from Him. This had to be so pleasing to our Lord!

The rest of the team had already left for the hotel, so I rode back on the Metro with some of the youth and with our leader, Derryck. He impressed me with his leadership skills; he is a marvelous speaker, but he also jokes and plays. This is appealing to the youth and let's them see that being a Christian is fun.

On Sunday we went to the Russian Orthodox Church for a three-hour standup service. The music was beautiful, but you could not see the choir. The singing was continuous and simply surrounded you. The trappings were very ornate, with candles burning everywhere. It was so touching to see the devout older people. To know how they had suffered under communism and yet kept their faith made my faith seem a bit wimpy. I did give out tracts as we made our way back to the Hotel Novosibirsk for lunch—a little thing, but the Holy Spirit uses even the smallest deeds.

That evening we went to New Life Church for a joyous, energetic service. Just what the doctor ordered! Steve from our team spoke, and there were four salvations. It was good to see the couple from the bakery again and have more time to discuss his questions. They walked back with us to the hotel for our farewell banquet, and Peggy and Delbert, members of New Life who joined us, commented about this friendship being a lasting thing for the mission. It was a nice affair and each lady was given a red rose, but I was really excited that we were leaving the next day for Barnaul, as I was eager for new ministry.

Part of the team rode in a taxi to Barnaul, and the rest of us, including me, were on a bus. The countryside was lush and green, with birch and spruce trees, farms and lakes, horses, cows, goats, and sheep. The sky was clear and blue. Derryck said this was unusual because most of the time the pollution was so bad that you could only leave clothes hanging outside for a short time before they were covered in soot. Airplanes in the area have to fly at four thousand to five thousand feet before they can get above the pollution. This was not how I had pictured Siberia. I thought it stayed cold all the time, with snow and ice.

Barnaul was a beautiful city with wide, tree-lined boulevards. Apple trees, lilacs, and tulips were in bloom, and a sweet smell filled the air. It reminded me of home when the honeysuckles are blooming. The local Barnaul team met us at the hotel, and it was wonderful to see Mike and Diane, my dear friends. That evening the Barnaul team and our MAT team met for dinner at the Russian Tea Room. It was a quaint old house that had belonged to a wealthy merchant, and it was decorated with ornate wood carvings and large wool carpets. Unfortunately, the carpets smelled like wet dogs (the cleaners must have used too much water), and the odor was certainly in contrast to the fragrant outdoors. Nevertheless, it was a charming evening.

The next morning we had prayer and fellowship, with Derryck leading. He asked that the MAT team do devotionals for the rest of the week, so I volunteered for the next day. Immediately I was struck with fear—who did I think I was to volunteer? But it was too late, and then I recognized the source of my fear, rebuked it, and went on my way.

The team was split into three parts: one was to go to the medical college, another to a local Bible study, and the last—the group to which I was assigned—to the burn unit of a local hospital. Dr. Constantine, the director, gave us a tour, and it took all I had to hold back the tears. The facilities were so dilapidated and sparse. A little girl about two years old started to cry as we prayed over her; she was afraid of so many people who were speaking a strange language. A boy, about eight years old, and another girl, about ten, were getting along fine, but there were many adult men who were severely burned. We ended our tour in the surgery room, where Dr. Constantine testified that he was a Christian. This did not surprise me, as it was surely the love of Christ in him that enabled him to serve so compassionately in such heartbreaking circumstances. I was also pleased to hear that America and Holland were working together in a joint project to send them thirty beds. We stood in a circle holding hands and prayed for this doctor, his staff, the patients, and the hospital. I wanted to go off somewhere and have a good cry, a cry of sadness for the suffering of these dear people and a cry of joy for God's servants, who were doing all in their power to alleviate suffering. One purpose of a MAT team was to be made aware, and I for one was made aware through that experience.

That evening I was assigned to a Bible study called the New Believers. There were twelve in the group, ranging from age thirteen to sixty-seven, and three were *babushkas* (grandmothers). The study was on the Holy Spirit, and it was led by Andrei and Julia, husband and wife of ages thirty-one and nineteen, respectively. Andrei talked about the change in Russia. He said there were a lot of minuses but also a big plus—being able to worship with freedom and no persecution. He said they were like a dog on a leash that has been set free, but does not know what to do with its freedom. I could especially see this in the grand-mothers. For all their growing-up years the government had controlled them, and now they were at a loss as to their next step. They were very reticent to speak out, as if they might be reported; their freedom had not yet become a reality to them.

The following morning the devotional I led was based on Mary Magdalene coming to the garden on that resurrec-tion morning and meeting Jesus, her Lord. I was nervous with Derryck and Steve (real preachers) there, but God was faithful, and I didn't die! Actually, some of the ladies told me they were touched. My teammate, Virginia, had tears in her eyes as I spoke, and later said she especially liked Mary Magdalene's perseverance. I knew she was struggling with health issues, and I was pleased that the Lord had minis-tered to her that morning.

Our Lord does have His ways of keeping us humble. As the MAT team was in front of the hotel, waiting in vain for the bus to take us to the children's camp, we were making and giving out Polaroid photographs and also passing out tracts. An elderly lady became very agitated, saying we were too happy. It was a sin, she said, and we were making fun of God. I tried to convince her this was not the case and that God loved her, but as I touched her arm, she pulled away from me. She said we were too young to understand God. I wondered what kind of life she had to make her feel this way. We must continue to persevere, to keep on sharing His love even when we are rejected. Some hearts just require extra grace.

The next day was for me the best day of the entire trip. We went to the children's hospital, where the team divided to visit different floors. I was assigned to the cardiac unit, second floor. There was a shortage of nurses, so the mothers stayed in the hospital with their children. We met in a huge waiting room, with approximately forty-five in attendance.

Natasha from the Barnaul team spoke in Russian, Julia led us in singing, and then she sang a solo. I was asked to give my testimony, and at the conclusion, Lowell, our MAT leader, told me to lead them in a salvation presentation. I gladly complied. As I ended, I said that if they wanted to invite Jesus to come and live in their hearts, they were to hold up their hands, and then pray out loud after me (as Natasha translated). I was amazed to see almost everyone respond affirmatively, children and mothers alike. I knew that the Lord had honored the cry of their hearts, even as He did at the spinal clinic in Novosibirsk. Lowell started making Polaroid pictures, and we gave out all the candy, gifts, and tracts. They wanted us to sign their pictures, and some of the girls wanted their pictures made with me. I was so blessed! I was able to pray with some of the girls in small groups and with several of the mothers and their babies, anointing them with oil. I was told later that it was very important that I had stressed that they "invite" Jesus to come into their hearts, because in their culture it is rude to come in without an invitation. The Holy Spirit knew what He was doing!

Mike told us that one hundred beds would be there on June 27, some going to the burn unit (Dr. Constantine had claimed thirty) and the remainder to this hospital. We had also taken in medical supplies for both these facilities. Mike further said that Natasha had met with the KGB yesterday to explain our purpose for being here. They were observing us. That was funny, because we had observed them observing us.

That evening the two Susans from the MAT team and I had a late lunch with Kirsten at her flat before church. We shared our stories, and Kirsten, originally from Sweden, told us she would be leaving the following Tuesday for Colorado Springs to join the Living Bible Society.

She had been a widow for twenty years, and all her family was dead. She had led an exciting life, but something was missing. She left everything to discover what it was, even staying in monasteries on the California coast. Finally, she was introduced to Christ through a new Christian, started reading the Bible, and surrendered her life to Him. Her new job in Colorado would involve coordinating projects to get the Bible into other countries, and that was her heart.

What an interesting collection the Lord had brought together that evening, yet there was the common bond of love for missions. We came from different backgrounds, but each of us was uniquely fitted into the body of Christ. We would see even more diversity, yet unity, at church that evening.

Derryck preached that night on the treasure (Jesus) in earthen vessels. The congregation was excited because a local factory was allowing a weekly Bible study starting the following week, composed of approximately forty men. We again divided into small groups, and I was with Kirsten, Julia, and two babushkas (Anastasia, who sold fish, and Katsianna, a pediatrician), all of whom I knew, and also Gaddia and Oxanna. Tanya was our translator. We shared our joys and then we prayed for each other. One would say a need and another would pray. When we got to Oxanna, she said she did not have Jesus in her heart and did not understand. Tanya took her to the side, and after an explanation, she prayed for salvation.

The babushkas were sharing how they thought Americans were cold, hard people who wanted to hurt them, but, in fact, they are wonderful people. I replied how we had been told the Russians hated us and wanted to drop bombs on us and kill us, but all that was not true. If we could just get to know each other, we'd find that babushkas (grandmothers) are babushkas all over the world!

The following morning we drove out to Camp Krystal, the site of the project Mike and Diane were leading. There would be several two-week sessions during the summer set for different age groups, and the last one would be for handicapped children. This would be the first time handicapped children in Russia would be allowed to go to camp. The camp was set in the countryside, with green grass and birch trees. There was a soccer field and an auditorium with a screen so they could show movies. Volunteers were working hard to get everything in order for opening, and it was thrilling! We took many pictures to share with folks back home, and then we all gathered to pray for the camp. I was tickled to know that our "bakery couple" would be working there with the children. God is so good!

We had a farewell dinner that evening with members of the church, the Barnaul team, YWAMers, and the MAT team: about fifty-five people in all. There were small tables set up, and the order was to mix. I sat with Andre, Julia, the other Julia, Krista and Kristen. Andre and Julia shared how they had seen a gangster movie from America, and how much Joe Ben (on our MAT team) looked like a Mafia boss. Krista insisted that they tell him, but Andre and Julia did not want to offend him. I said it would just make him laugh. So we called Joe Ben over, and he did laugh, but then he shared his testimony with us. He had been an alcoholic, married to his first wife for sixteen years, then to a second wife for twelve years, and to a third wife for four years. Then he started dating another woman, and when he broke up with her, he swore off women. Subsequently, he came into a saving relationship with Jesus Christ. His second wife called and invited him to come with their son when he returned the son from a visit. They talked for twenty hours (she had recently come to Christ) and later they remarried.

After dinner the Russians got up and sang a song, the Americans replied with "The Star Spangled Banner," then the Russians again, and the Americans replied with "Dixie." Then the Russians sang Canada's anthem, and we all sang "Amazing Grace." It seemed there were representatives from countries all over the world. At the conclusion, there were hugs and I love yous, not the norm for Russians, but certainly the norm for Christians. As always, it was hard to say good-bye, but there was more to do and "miles to go before we sleep."

When we retired that night, it was not certain whether we would be leaving the next morning to return to Moscow on our journey home, but Lowell knocked on my door at 5:45 a.m., and we were off. We said hasty goodbyes and boarded the bus. There was the usual hassle at the airport because our tickets had been bought manually, and now we were on computers! I was unable to converse with my seatmates because they spoke no English, but I did give out tracts with a smile. When we were airborne, I could see from my window the neatness of the land below; no differences were discernible. Why can't we see each other that way? We really are all the same—only a bit different in language and customs, but that's such a little thing. Actually, it makes us interesting.

We had a longer layover in Moscow, for which I was so grateful. It is a beautiful city, with golden turrets rising up from the churches and historic old buildings, mixed with some new buildings that still look strikingly different from our skyscrapers in America. St. Basil's Cathedral, with its onion-shaped domes and spires, was inspiring. (No pun intended). It is just a stone's throw from the huge and stark Kremlin, with its brick walls and towers and soldiers all around. We were not allowed to enter the Kremlin because it was a historic day in Russian history when we visited:

they were meeting to draft a new constitution! *The Moscow Times* that day reported the following:

> *About seven hundred delegates to a Constitutional Assembly will begin to formally shape post-Soviet Russia on Saturday in a conference that President Boris Yeltsin intends to dominate... Delegates representing Russia's eighty-eight regions and leading social and political groups will gather for the opening plenary session at 10 a.m. to hear Yeltsin present his draft proposal for a new charter.*[2]

While history was in the making, life was continuing. I was amazed to see so many brides right there in the shadow of the Kremlin. Their tradition is to come to Red Square on their wedding day. Our driver drove us to a scenic overlook, and there were approximately twelve wedding couples having pictures made down in the park. In contrast to the beautiful brides, I was shocked to see so many women who looked like they had been beaten. Alcoholism is a major problem in Russia, as in far too many other places in the world, and men sometimes exert their rage on their women. I wanted to give one woman in particular some money, but our guide advised against it. The peddlers were very aggressive, and we were warned of groups of young boys who would single you out, gang up on you, and steal your purse.

Another historic event we attended was the last performance of the state-run Bolshoi Ballet. After that evening, it was to be privately owned and operated. We saw *Spartacus*, and it was spectacular. Our seats were not that good, as we were in the balcony and you had to lean way over to see, but then, nothing is perfect. I did get to share with a couple there. He was a businessman from Holland, and she was from a smaller city in Russia. They wanted to know the purpose of our trip, so this was a golden opportunity to witness. He was saying there were other ways to God, and I protested: "Oh, no. Jesus is *the* way!" He replied, "That's three crickets!" When I asked what he meant, he said it meant we would not argue about it. He told me that his girlfriend was unique in that she was a lawyer, and I replied that I also worked for a female lawyer in the States; I considered her the best in the firm because she was so well organized, not like the men. He started to protest, and I said, "That's one cricket!" We had a good laugh, and later as we said good-bye, I stuck a tract in his jacket pocket and said he might want to read it when he had time. He nodded his head in agreement.

We also went to the biggest flea market I had ever seen. There was booth after booth of everything you could imagine—capitalism at its finest! Some of the team bought antique items, such as icons and urns, and I wondered then if we might encounter some difficulty as we left the country (and we did). We had been warned not to take their artifacts. I was safe because I bought handcrafted angels to go on my Christmas tree. My financial situation kept me from temptation.

We also were able to see the circus, and it was delightful. Of course, we ate at McDonald's several times as a matter of financial necessity. So all in all, we had a most interesting and "wonder-full" time in Moscow.

When we went through baggage check at the airport, some of the treasures purchased at the flea market were confiscated, but at last we boarded the plane. The flight from Moscow to Amsterdam was over the Baltic and North Seas, Sweden, and Denmark. It was made more beautiful by the fact that it was in the direction of home. Anna and Branko met me at the airport and came back to De Poort with us. We had dinner together, and I was glad to meet this nice young man who had stolen my Anna's heart. (She later married Branko, and they have a lovely daughter). I was sad to say good-bye to Anna, but she promised to come to the States soon.

The team was de-briefed the following morning, and we gave our evaluations of the mission. I was very impressed with the YWAM program, and Amsterdam seemed to be the modern-day Antioch of church planting. All their workers had a zeal for the kingdom that was infectious. It had been an enriching experience, and it was my prayer that the Lord would erase our mistakes from the people's memories and just leave His good stuff.

There was just a little time before we had to depart for the airport, so I elected to do the canal ride again so I could spend more time with some of the ladies on the team. I knew that once we were on the plane, the mission would be more or less over.

At the airport, Lowell asked me if I felt a calling to go back, something called "mission awareness." I told him I had to go home and pray, but I appreciated his confidence in me. I've been around the block a few times, and I know it is not wise to make decisions when emotions are running high. After all, it is God's call as to where we serve. Our part is to be obedient, to go where He says, when He says.

Home! My son Scott collected me at the airport, took me out to supper, and let me talk his ears off. When I got home, I called my daughter Stacey, and she announced that she was pregnant with her second child. She told me to be prepared because Steve, my other son, had been offered a big promotion with his company, which would mean a move to Chicago. That was quite a welcome home! I came off the mountaintop real fast and hit reality.

Not to leave you hanging, dear reader, I will report that my daughter gave birth to a beautiful baby girl on Christmas Day, 1993. She has already decided she wants to be a missionary. My son Steve declined the promotion and is still living in the Atlanta area and prospering with the same company. In addition, my son Scott still patiently listens to me talk about my life and travels.

I am blessed indeed!

CHAPTER 6
MY FIRST JOURNEY TO ISRAEL

APR 1995

$\mathcal{M}$y mission to Israel consisted of three trips, each one complementing the other. The first visit was supposed to be as a tourist. However, I quickly learned that every trip to Israel is a mission trip. One of the saints said that the Holy Land is the fifth gospel, and I believe that our very presence there is a witness for Christ. Our group was led by Adis from Pennsylvania, who had conducted many Israeli tours. My friend Clara worked with her daughter, and that is how we got into the mix. Adis is a devout Christian, and I was blessed on this first trip to see Israel from the perspective of her guidance.

Clara and I met our fellow travelers at JFK Airport in New York City, and after security clearance we boarded El Al for our flight to Israel. I sat next to a young man from London who was a musician and composer and who wanted to come to America to live. As we talked, he said he believed that God is everywhere (I agree) and whatever anyone thinks is OK (I don't agree; most of us suffer from "stinking thinking"). He was not receptive to my testimony, so we just engaged in pleasant conversation for the rest of the flight.

Approximately ten hours later, we arrived at Ben Gurion Airport in Tel Aviv ("Hill of Hope"). I had the strangest sensation that I had come home, that this was not a new place to me, and that I was not just a tourist! I did not know then I would come back two more times, and each time I would feel the same way—like I was coming home. There will be a day when all of God's children will worship Him in that New Jerusalem (Revelation 21:24,26). I was just a bit early.

Our hotel was by the Mediterranean Sea. There were many sailboats, but it was too cold and breezy to spend any time on the beach. It was nice just to enjoy an elegant dinner inside, where many Jewish families were celebrating Passover, and to get a good night's rest for the journey ahead.

Breakfast in Israel is an event. There is so much food spread out, from fresh fruit to varieties of bread to cereals to eggs, boiled or cooked to order; pastries and yogurt; plus hot tea, coffee, milk, and hot chocolate. Clara and I would take little bags and load up for lunch. The fruit in Israel is incredibly delicious and beautiful. It is easy to believe that the Garden of Eden was in the Middle East.

Our first stop was Jaffa, or Joppa, one of the oldest cities in the country. It is only a fifteen-minute drive along the coastline north from Tel Aviv. It is said to have been founded by Japheth, Noah's son. Jonah sailed from here as he was running from the Lord, and was swallowed by the great whale (Jonah 1:3,17). Jaffa was a fortified Philistine city, which fell to David. It became the country's main seaport, through which King Solomon imported the cedars of Lebanon for the building of the temple (1 Kings 5:9–10). We saw the house of Simon the Tanner, where Peter had the vision of the sheet and was sent to Cornelius to share the gospel with the Gentiles (Acts 10). It was there that Peter raised Tabitha from the dead (Acts 9:36–41). Alexander the Great conquered Jaffa in 332 B.C. and made it one of his principal mercantile centers. Napoleon used St. Michael's

Cathedral as a hospital for his wounded soldiers. Even today the residents have blue and purple shutters on their houses to keep the devil out. This is a Muslim superstition, but many Jews observe the tradition because "It wouldn't hurt!"

On the way to Caesarea, we saw construction everywhere. Ezra, our guide said, "The building crane has become the national bird of Israel." In 1948, the population was six hundred thousand, and in 1995—the time of this trip—it was 5.5 million. From 1992 to 1995, approximately seven hundred thousand Russian and Ethiopian Jews had immigrated into Israel. At that time 85 percent were employed and none was homeless.

Caesarea was founded by Sidonite merchants in the third century B.C., and they called it Migdal Straton. In 22 B.C. the Roman emperor Augustus awarded it to Herod, who renamed it Augusta Caesarea. Herod enlarged the city, deepened the harbor, and built an aqueduct that ran for five miles from Mount Carmel. A five-thousand-seat theater had been reconstructed by archaeologists and the acoustics were remarkable, as the sound bounced off the echo wall built behind the stage. Several tour groups were there taking turns singing, so we joined in with our renditions. Ezra said archaeologists had recently discovered an even larger theater. We saw a stone at the main entrance with the name Pontius Pilate engraved on it, the first written record of his existence. There was a large tamarisk tree, which the Bedouins call "the manna tree." The branches have bubbles on them, and insects burrow in, leaving a hole covered with sap that tastes like honey, but it only lasts one day.

Caesarea became the Roman capitol, and only Romans could live there. It was the governor's residence, and that is why Herod was there at Passover during Jesus' time (Luke

23:7–12). I was walking through the Bible; it was becoming more alive!

We proceeded to Haifa, which means "pretty." The name reminded me of our Siamese cat named Pretty. She was a gift to our son on his seventh birthday, and he called her by that name because she was just so lovely. So is Haifa. In the Talmud, it is said to be a place where wise men dwell. It is the third largest city in Israel and is called the San Francisco of the Middle East. It is built on three tiers and overlooks the Mediterranean Sea. We went into the Stella Maris ("Star of the Sea") Carmelite Monastery, supposedly built around the cave where Elijah lived. Haifa is a center to the Carmelite monks and nuns, a Catholic order founded during the Crusades. Ezra pointed out the connection between Jesus and Elijah, as symbolized by their meeting on the Mount of Transfiguration (Mark 9:4–12). It is interesting to note that Mount Carmel is not just one mountain, but a range of mountains.

We passed through the Zebulon Valley, where the desert bloomed like a rose. We could see Lebanon in the distance. There were fields of brilliant green in sharp contrast with the brown sand, and we saw large groves of banana trees and row after row of pineapple plants. The banana trees were referred to as "spoiled" plants because they require fresh water, which is so precious, and only live one year. Israel uses a system called drip irrigation. Pipes with holes punched into them are laid on the ground so that the water goes directly to the roots and none is wasted. The system is computerized so that the plants get only what is needed. Ezra said that the desert is now filling with Jewish immigrants returning to Israel from every corner of the globe. Now the desert is Israel's breadbasket. Israel is a large exporter of produce as well as fresh flowers, all in fulfillment of Isaiah 35:1–2.

Our next stop was Acre, or Acco, which the tribe of Asher co-inhabited with the Canaanites (Judges 1:31). It was later held by the Assyrians, then by the Persians, and was finally conquered again by Alexander the Great, who restored its harbor and renamed it Ptolemais. Acts 21:7 records that Paul visited this city on one of his missionary journeys. The Romans used the city as its main port of entrance to bring in its troops to quell the rebellion of 66 A.D. We saw more ruins from the Crusades, Turkish mosques, as well as the walls built by the Ottomans to protect the city, which prevented Napoleon from capturing it in 1799, stopping his advance to the north. This city is over six thousand years old, so it was amazing to see modern solar heating units on the roofs of all the antiquated buildings. We were told that modern updates such as those units are the law. You can't stop progress!

Next we visited Tiberias, located on the western side of the Sea of Galilee. It was built about 18 A.D. by King Herod Antipas to honor the Roman Emperor Tiberias. The Sanhedrin met here, and it was here that the Talmud was completed in about 500 B.C. The entire city was destroyed in 1837 and was not rebuilt until the Zionists started to reclaim the land.

We stayed in Tiberias that night at the Jordan Hotel, where there was much festivity because Passover was ending and because it was also the Sabbath Day. Many families had come to the hotel to dine and celebrate, all dressed in their finery and in pleasant moods. There was a carnival atmosphere in the area behind the hotel where the shops were located, and music was blaring out over loudspeakers. You could buy all sorts of souvenirs, of course, as tourism is their biggest industry. Ezra said that there were approximately two million tourists per year, bringing in about $4 billion. I could believe it, because the hotel, the shops, and the streets were packed with people. It was a fun-filled, lighthearted time, and the scenery was beautiful with the Sea of Galilee and the boats in the background.

The next day we went out on the Sea of Galilee, which is not a sea but a lake. Jewish legend has it that an rabbi once said, "After God created the seven seas, He made the Sea of Galilee for His own pleasure." In the Bible it is also called the Sea of Chinnereth, or Chinneroth, Gennesar, Lake of Gennesaret, and Sea of Tiberias. Jesus' ministry took place on the northern side. It is 8 miles wide by 16 miles long, is 150 feet deep, and lies 680 feet below the level of the Mediterranean Sea, with its bed forming a part of the Great Rift Valley. The winds generally blow in from the Mediterranean, but they can quickly reverse and cause sudden storms. I remembered the story of Jesus asleep in a boat in the midst of one of those storms, as related in Matthew 8:23–27. There was a great tempest in the sea—the word *tempest* being translated from the Greek "seismos," which describes an earthquake.[1] The disciples woke Him, asking Him to save them. He rebuked the winds and the sea, and there was a great calm. The veracity of the Bible was being pounded into my spirit. I was seeing it firsthand!

The Sea of Galilee is the only freshwater lake in Israel. Ezra shared that another lake had been unearthed in the Negev but it contains brackish water. Researchers have discovered that this brackish water can be used in desert agriculture, helping preserve the area's precious supply of drinking water.[2] Many see this development as a fulfillment of biblical prophesy:

The wilderness and the wasteland shall be glad for them, And the desert shall rejoice and blossom as the rose...For waters shall burst forth in the wilderness, And streams in the desert. The parched ground shall become a pool, And the thirsty land springs of water. —Isaiah 35:1, 6-7

We sailed on the *Mark*, a replica of the boats used in Jesus' time, and we flew the flags of Israel and the U.S.A. One of the mates demonstrated how the disciples would have fished in those days, casting a net into the sea. I thought of how Jesus had said He would make us fishers of men (Mark 1:17). On the shore to the right, we saw the Golan Heights and the region of the Gadarenes, where Jesus cast demons out of a possessed man and the demons entered the herd of pigs, which ran down the steep bank and plunged into the sea (Mark 5:1–13). To the left we could see the village of Magdala, the home of Mary Magdalene, from whom Jesus had cast out seven devils and to whom He appeared on the day of His resurrection (Mark 16:9).

We landed at Ginosar and went on to Capernaum, the headquarters of Jesus' public ministry (Matthew 4:13–17). We saw the remains of the synagogue, and in the eastern yard, games were etched in the stone pavement. Very close by was Peter's house, where He healed Peter's mother-in-law (Matthew 8:14–15). This is also where Jesus healed the servant of the Roman centurion by granting to the centurion what he had believed in faith (Matthew 8:5–13). Excavations here unearthed remnants dating from the era of the Second Temple, including a star of David and a wine press. Capernaum was on the Via Maris road. A caravan station was there where people would meet and share stories. Don't you know that Jesus was the talk of the town?

A short distance away was Tabgha, the Church of the Multiplication of the Loaves and Fishes, located at the foot of the Mount of Beatitudes, where Jesus fed the five thousand (Matthew 14:15–21). Some Christians believe this is the location described in John 21 where Peter was appointed as leader of the disciples and where Christ met the disciples after He had risen from the dead.

At the top of the mountain, we visited the Church of the Beatitudes, with its copper-domed chapel and beautiful gardens. It was built by the Italian architect Bertalozzi, and is octagon-shaped. It was easy to visualize at least five thousand people on the hillside leading down to the Sea of Galilee. It is a natural amphitheater, so Jesus could easily be heard as He taught the Beatitudes and gave His Sermon on the Mount (Matthew 5–7).

Then we came to the ruins of Korazin, one of the most authentic sites in Israel. This was a wealthy community in Jesus' time, and the people would not listen to Him. Jesus spoke woe upon their city because of their failure to repent in spite of "His mighty works" done there (Matt. 11:20–21). Years later, the city was destroyed by an earthquake and never rebuilt. In that city, we saw the remains of a ritual bath, a synagogue, and a U-shaped table where Jesus could have sat with His disciples. I had prayed before leaving on the trip that the Lord would show me the places where He really had been, because many of the sites are just guesstimates. However, I felt His presence very strongly in Korazin, confirming to me that He had been there. There was much sadness in my heart to think that He had been rejected in that place.

Our next stop was Zippori (Sepphoris), supposedly the city where Anne, Mary's mother, was born. It is located six miles from Nazareth, and in 63 B.C. was used by the Romans as the capital of the Galilee. Ezra said that this was where Jesus spent His silent years. It was an educational center, and Jesus was probably schooled there. *Rabbi* means "learned man," and since Jesus was called a rabbi, we know that He was educated. A mosaic of a beautiful woman containing fifteen hundred tiles was unearthed there. Like da Vinci's famous painting, when you look at the woman in the mosaic, she seems to look back at you, no matter where you are standing. Because of this, the woman is often called "the first Mona Lisa." A rich man's villa was also discovered here. They knew he was a rich man because they found a toilet in the villa.

In Nazareth we went to St. Joseph's Church, supposedly the site of his carpenter shop, and the Church of the Annunciation, where Mary received the news that she would bear a son and name Him Jesus (Luke 1:26–31). The Greek Orthodox Church is built on the site of Mary's Spring, where Mary returned after the death of Herod (Matthew 2:19–23). The priests seemed to be annoyed by our presence, and when we came out on the street, a shopkeeper poured out a bucket of water so that it splashed on Ezra. He did it on purpose because the locals wanted to be the exclusive tour guides in the city, and the Board of Tourism required that guides be registered. There were many beggars and aggressive souvenir sellers. I thought of Nathaniel's statement, "Can any good thing come out of Nazareth?" (John 1:46). Well, Jesus did!

We traveled on to the Jordan River, Israel's longest river, running from the foot of Hermon through the Sea of Galilee and the Jordan Valley to the Dead Sea. The Israelites crossed the Jordan to enter into the Promised Land (Joshua 3:17). We went to a very popular tourist site, and many people were baptized here. My friend Clara and I had our own private ceremony, which was especially meaningful for us. We know that Jesus was baptized in the Jordan (Matthew

3:13), but probably in another location. Still, it was the Jordan, and we had to take some water home.

The following day, we passed by the Hot Springs of Tiberias and could see the steam rising. This was where Naaman, the king of Syria, received his healing after obeying Elisha's instructions to dip seven times in the water (2 Kings 5:14).

We stopped at Bet Alpha, where an ancient synagogue was discovered in 1928 when a man on a tractor, digging a drainage ditch for a kibbutz, hit a stone. It was unusual to see a Greek zodiac in a Jewish synagogue, but this was a center of Greek influence and the zodiac was used as an agricultural calendar. Rabbis allowed it to be used secretly until the end of the fifth century, and after that, openly. There were more mosaics on the floor, including one of Abraham sacrificing Isaac.

Close by was Bet She'an National Park. Bet She'an is one of the oldest cities of the ancient Near East. It was the town of Manasseh in Issachar, and was on the main caravan road from Egypt to Mesopotamia. The Philistine rulers of Bet She'an displayed the bodies of Saul and his sons upon its walls after they had been killed in the battle of Mount Gilboa (1 Samuel 31:10). At the time of Herod the Great, the city had a population of fifty thousand, and it had a hippodrome and a theater. Josephus named it as the chief city of the Decapolis.[3] The remains of some eighteen layers of settlements going back to the fifth millennium B.C. have been found here. The city was destroyed by an earthquake in 749 A.D. and became mosquito-infested marshland. In 1953 the city was rebuilt, and the theater was discovered. It has a seating capacity of approximately seven thousand and is being used today. Archaeologists have so far unearthed Byzantine bathhouses, two other smaller theaters, colonnaded streets, a Roman temple, an elaborate fountain building, a pottery workshop, forty complete statues, and life-sized mosaics of animals. An entire city is being uncovered, and the parts of artifacts are numbered and put to one side like giant jigsaw pieces ready to be reassembled. It is an intriguing sight.

Next we came to the Valley of Jezreel, also known as Armageddon. The Tel of Megiddo was discovered here, containing twenty-five layers of the ruins from ancient cities. A tel is a hill of dirt, and to the archaeologists in Israel it means there is the probability of buried history. From the top of the tel, we looked down into the valley, and I had to fight back the tears. In Revelation 14:20, we are told that this is where the Battle of Armageddon will be fought, and blood would flow up to the horses' bridles. It was more than I could fathom. This is a vast plain, surrounded by Mount Carmel, Mount Tabor (the Mount of Transfiguration), the Samaritan Mountains, and the Mountains of Nazareth; it is the meeting point of the Jezreel, Harod, and Jordan valleys, a beautiful vista. It is very fertile, and is aptly called The Bread Basket of Israel, but one day it will once again be a battleground, a field of blood.

Megiddo was an ancient royal city of the Canaanites, and they were not driven out by the Israelites, but were forced to pay tribute to them (Judges 1:27–28). It was made famous in the song of Deborah when Barak defeated Sisera, recorded in Judges 5. It was one of Solomon's chariot cities, and the ramps into the city were zig-zagged to slow advancing enemies. The seal of King Jeroboam was found here. There was a water tunnel that took 183 steps to descend. An interesting story is that it was dug from both sides in order to save time, and when the two sides met, they could hear each other digging, and the space between them was less than one inch. The workers sang, "We hear the hammer, the voice of the people, one stone to go!"

At last, we were scheduled to go up to Jerusalem! We traveled the Via Marisa Highway ("Way of the Sea"), passing by an Arab/Muslim village; through the Plain of Sharon; the Ajalon Valley, where Joshua fought the Amorites and the sun stood still (Joshua 10:12-14); the city of Latrun, home of Saint Dismas, the good thief on the cross,[4] and the ruins of Emmaus, where Jesus walked with Cleopas and his friend on the day of His resurrection (Luke 24:13–35). We saw the remains of trucks and tanks from the 1948 Israeli War of Independence scattered over the hillsides as memorials of Israel's miraculous victory. Indeed, we did go up to Jerusalem, which is 2,500 feet above sea level.

When we came within sight of the city, we pulled over to the side of the road and celebrated communion. We prayed to "Blessed God, Almighty God, who brought us to this moment," and we ended with the traditional phrase "Next year in Jerusalem," the last words of Passover. That is one communion I shall never forget!

We checked into the Laromme Hotel, and while Clara rested, I went to Liberty Bell Garden Park up the street. Moroccan-Jewish families were out enjoying the last day of Passover, and soldiers were everywhere. I could see the walls of the Old City and the golden Dome of the Rock. I was raring to go, but that had to wait for the morrow because it was late and everyone was tired.

The next day we went to an olive factory located in the orthodox community of Mea Shearim. The men wear black coats and hats, and the women wear dark dresses. The girls under age seventeen wear their hair in two braids, and over seventeen in one braid, signifying they are ready for marriage. In some Orthodox sects, married women shave their heads and then wear wigs and scarves as a sign of modesty.[3] Matchmakers arrange marriages, like in *Fiddler on the Roof.* There is a bit of strife between this orthodox group and the rest of the Jews because the orthodox brothers claim exemption from the draft. At age eighteen, Israeli men are drafted into the army for three years, and women for two years; men serve in the reserves from age twenty-one to fifty-four. The women are not allowed in combat because Israel will not allow their women to be subjected to capture; they are used as teachers.

We went into the open market and its stalls were filled with lemons, strawberries, melons, radishes, dates, olives—just every kind of produce imaginable. It was an artist's picture. I exclaimed, "Wow! Look at that!" and an elderly Arab man sitting in a chair started laughing and repeating what I said, over and over. I knew he was pleased that I was pleased with his country, and that is very important in building witnessing relationships.

We visited an agricultural kibbutz, named Mitzpeh Ramat Rachel, after Isaac's wife. This kibbutz was on the front lines during the 1948 Israeli War of Independence. Ironically, we met Ezra's son here, who was in the army at that time. Several years later I would learn that he had been killed in an attack by the Palestinians. Even to think of it today brings tears to my eyes—such a fine young man.

All Christian tour groups go to Bethlehem, the birth-place of King David and later Jesus Christ. The Church of the Nativity, one of the oldest churches in the world, has been built over the proposed site of the manger. The church is shared by three denominations—Armenian, Greek Orthodox, and Roman Catholic—each having its own entrance. It is actually a complex, divided into several parts. The central hall contains the manger, with an altar made of cedar from Lebanon. Below is a fourteen-pointed star, representing the fourteen stations of the cross. This is where God fulfilled His promise. Later, time was divided into B.C. (before Christ) and A.D. (Anno Domini, or After Christ), thereby acknowledging His birth.

St. Catherine's Church is another part of the complex. Upon Catherine's conversion in Egypt, she was tortured and martyred on a wheel for her profession of faith. The church is decorated with golden wheels at the archways along both sides of the ceiling in her honor. Close to it are several grottoes. The first is dedicated to the children Herod killed at the time of Jesus' birth (Matthew 2:16). I placed my hands on the rock wall and prayed for my children, thanking God that they were alive. A second grotto commemorates the angel who warned Joseph to flee to Egypt (Matthew 2:13–15), and the third is alleged to be the cave of St. Jerome, who translated the Old and New Testaments into Latin, the version called the Vulgate.

We saw the fields of Ruth and Boaz, known as the Shepherds' Field, where angels announced the birth of Jesus to the shepherds. It was my turn to lead the devotion, and I talked about us having two possible responses to this trip: we could be like Mary and "ponder these things in our hearts" (Luke 2:19, author's paraphrase), or we could be like the shepherds and go and tell others (Luke 2:17). I knew I had to "go and tell."

The next day we proceeded into the old city of Jerusalem, entering through the Dung Gate. Ezra told us to stay close, but I got lost in the moment; all the sights were overwhelming me, and suddenly the group was gone. It didn't take long for Ezra to find me, but he was very upset, so I faithfully promised to heed his warning in the future. He took us to the temple steps where Jesus found the moneychangers (Matthew 21:12), and in my imagination I could see Him chasing them with a whip. We saw the pinnacle of the temple, where Satan tempted Jesus (Matthew 4:5), and the Church of St. Peter in Gallicantu, built on the location where Peter denied Jesus three times before the cock crowed (Mark 14:66–72). We actually heard roosters crowing across the street! Archaeologists discovered here the crypt of Caiaphas, the High Priest, and we saw the stone dungeon where Jesus was kept. Barabbas would also have been kept there, as that is where hardened criminals were incarcerated. This was another one of the sites where I felt His presence, and it was hard to stop the tears. Imagine, our Lord made those rocks, and yet He submitted to being held there. Jesus was led from the dungeon to the northern corner of the temple, then taken to Pilate, who had Him scourged. From there He walked the Via Dolorosa to the cross of Calvary. We saw the Field of Blood, where Judas killed himself (Matthew 27:3–5), and the Mount of Olives.

We re-entered the Old City through the Zion Gate, and took a break to have some fun because all we had seen that morning was spirit-shaking. We rode camels, called "the ships of the desert," and as they started galloping, we started screaming—and the soldiers started laughing. It was a merry time, and it made for good relationships and precious memories.

In the outer court of the Dormition Abbey, there was a statue of Mary lying in sleep. Rails formed a circle around the statue, and people were praying there. Some traditions say that Mary fell into eternal sleep and was taken to heaven, while others believe she was buried near Gethsemane at the base of the Mount of Olives. Inside the chapel you could hear people singing, and the acoustics were phenomenal. Our group went in, and we sang some hymns. The sweetness of the Lord was in this place, and I prayed, "Lord, make me a mother of grace, as Mary was and is."

We went to the Upper Room, the proposed site of the Last Supper, described in Luke 22:10–20. There was nothing to prove this was an authentic site, except the location. There is a cross from the Crusades in the room and the remains of a mosque with a stone emblem showing the directions to Mecca. It was just a big empty room, but with your imagination, you could picture Jesus and His disciples seated around the low tables. I could almost see Jesus washing their feet (John 13:4–5). This was also the proposed site of Pentecost, where fifty days after His resurrection the Holy Spirit filled those who were gathered, just as Jesus had promised (Acts 1:4–5, 8; 2:4). Our group, His disciples today, held hands and prayed together.

We left the Upper Room and went downstairs to visit David's tomb. The Bible says in 1 Kings 2:10 that David was buried in his own city, Jerusalem. He had chosen Jerusalem as his capital so the tribes would not fight; it was a neutral site. The shrine was opened to the public after the Israeli War of Independence. There is a huge sarcophagus dating back to Herod's days, and below it is a burial chamber. It is decorated with three images of the Torah and crowns and is covered with a royal blue velvet coverlet with gold fringes. On the wall is an inscription that says, "David King of Israel is alive."

Once again we departed the Old City, and looking down into the valley we saw the village of Ein Karim, alleged to be the birthplace of John the Baptist. Our destination was the synagogue at the Hadassah Medical Center, with its famous Chagall Windows. The windows are freestanding, and you are struck by the vivid colors. An information sheet from the hospital describes the windows:

> *The synagogue is illuminated by a hanging lantern and by sunlight, which streams through the magnificent Chagall Windows... The creation of the windows*

was a labor of love for Chagall and his assistant, Charles Marq, both of whom worked on the project for two years. Marq, developed a special process of veneering pigment on glass so that Chagall was able to use as many as three colors on a single uninterrupted pane of glass, rather than separating each colored pane by a lead strip... The windows represent the twelve sons of the patriarch Jacob, from whom came the Twelve Tribes of Israel. Chagall's windows are populated by floating figures of animals, fish, flowers and numerous Jewish symbols... But it was the Bible which provided his main inspiration... The dominant colors used in each window are inspired by these blessings as well as the description of the breastplate of the High Priest in Exodus 28:15, which was colored gold, blue, purple and scarlet.[4]

Strangely though, there are small white pieces in some of the windows. The hospital is on the border between Israel and Jordan, and during the war in 1967, two bombs fell, and four windows were damaged. Ezra said the story is told in Israel that a telegram was sent to Chagall to inform him of the damage, and his response was that they should take care of the war, and he would take care of the windows. These white pieces stand in the windows to represent the war.

We continued on to Yad Vashem, the Museum of the Holocaust, with documents and films of life in the ghetto, the death camps and gas chambers. The construction of the museum was sponsored built by Abraham and Edita Spiegel to honor their child, who was killed in the Holocaust.[5] The Children's Memorial is dark, with mirrors on the walls reflecting the light of five candles, giving the appearance of stars. The Germans kept precise records, and names are read out loud from the lists of those who were killed. It was very sobering to know that each name represented a life that was lost, and one and one-half million of those were children under the age of fourteen. Two statues on the grounds were especially touching, one of a teacher being led away with his students, not willing to leave them alone, and the other of Rachel crying for her children. Two boats were on display from Denmark that fishermen had used to smuggle out 7,200 of the country's 8,000 Jews to Sweden. The entry into the museum is called the Avenue of the Righteous, dedicated to non-Jews who dedicated their lives to save the Jewish people. Trees had been planted with plaques in their memory, and number sixteen was Oskar Schindler's tree. There is another memorial wall containing six million mosaic tiles, representing all those killed and listing the names of the twenty-two camps. It is mandatory that Jewish soldiers come to Yad Vashem for eight days as a part of their training. On the last Thursday in April of each year, sirens blow for two minutes all over Israel to commemorate the Holocaust, and people stop wherever they are and keep silent. (This happened while we were at the Garden Tomb).

Ezra told us that when his mother-in-law, a blue-eyed blonde, was fourteen years old, she and her parents were forced into a line of Jewish people destined for a concentration camp. A nun passed by and pulled the young girl out of the line. When a soldier stopped her, she said, "This girl doesn't belong. She's not one of them." To save her child's life, the girl's mother said, "She isn't my daughter." His mother-in-law survived; her parents were killed.

The Shrine of the Book is a most unusual building, shaped like the lid of an ancient jar. It contains some of the oldest manuscripts found at Qumran, Masada, and other places. They are kept underground so if the building were bombed, there would be no damage. We saw the Dead Sea Scrolls, plus the scrolls of seven more psalms that have been found. Ezra called on me to read Psalm 151, and I was thrilled! Israel is trying to buy back all the scrolls that have been discovered, but some countries will not sell. Unfortunately, not all of the countries are preserving them correctly, so the scrolls may be lost. Ezra's eyes filled with tears as he shared this information, and so did mine.

At the Holyland Hotel, we saw a scale model showing Jerusalem from the period 40 B.C. to 70 A.D. The owner of the hotel had the model built to honor his son. At that time five archaeologists were working on it based on the Talmud, the writings of Josephus Flavius, and daily excavations being made in the city. It is said to be the most accurate in the world today. Ezra pointed out to us that the path from the Mount of Olives, through the Eastern Gate (where Messiah will enter at the end times), and on through the Inner Court of the Temple and the Holy of Holies (where the curtain was torn from top to bottom when Christ was crucified), and to Calvary's hill, is a straight line. This appeared to me to be another confirmation that the Lord was saying just to connect the dots.

The next day we went to the Western Wall, or the Wailing Wall. This is the only part of the Temple that remains, and the poor paid for it in Herod's time. It is also called the Wall of Tears because dew collects on it at night, giving the appearance of tears. Legend says it will stop when the Messiah comes. Also, the Jews face the Wall and lament over the destruction of the Temple. This site is most holy to the Jews because the Holy of Holies lies just beyond the wall. The men and women are separated by a fence; they do not pray together. In the Jewish tradition, you are to cover your head and remove your shoes. The men wear their prayer shawls, holding together the four corners, which are the four corners of the world and represent unity, while the 613 knots in the tassels represent the law. There are cracks in the wall, and they are stuffed with written prayer requests. It was difficult to find an open space for my three lists of names for salvation, healing, and blessing. As I prayed over each name, I started weeping, sensing so strongly the presence of the Lord.

We walked up to the Temple Mount, also called Mount Moriah, where Solomon built the Temple. It was destroyed and ultimately rebuilt by Herod, then destroyed again by the Romans in 70 A.D. The Arabs of the seventh century took possession of the site and built two mosques there, the Al-Aqsa and Dome of the Rock.

The Al-Aqsa Mosque, where we were neither allowed to wear shoes nor take pictures, was built in 705 A.D. It was later demolished by an earthquake and rebuilt by King Farouk of Egypt. As a result of the Six-Day War in 1967, it became a part of Israel. In 1969 an Australian pyromaniac burned a large part of the Mosque, and the fire damage was still visible. The Mosque is a huge, rather empty building, with prayer rugs over all the floor. The beautiful stained glass windows were the only adornment.

Upon exiting the Al-Aqsa, we proceeded up some steps to the Dome of the Rock, on the very top of Mount Moriah. Muslim legend says that Adam was made from the Rock of Moriah. Jews and Christians believe this is where Abraham brought Isaac to be sacrificed (Genesis 22:2). However, Muslims believe he brought Ishmael, not Isaac, and that it is from here that Mohammed ascended into heaven. There are four entrances: David's gate in the east, Paradise Gate in the north, the Women's Gate in the south, and a nameless gate. Inside the Dome, the top of the mountain is exposed, and it is circled by marble columns. The gold-covered dome is encompassed with porcelain and marble plaques in shades of blue and white, and each plaque tells a different story. There is a wooden booth containing the Jasmine Rock, and when you rub your hand on the rock, it smells like jasmine. My nurse friend was upset when I did this (because of all the germs), but I could not resist. Ezra called the Dome "the yellow thing." I asked him why Israel did not destroy it when they captured the city in 1967. He replied that it would have caused a third world war, and Israel will not destroy anything that is sacred to another religion. God will destroy it in His way and in His time, he said.

We went to a smaller dome, located next to the Dome of the Rock, called the Dome of the Chain. This was where the people were judged when accused of a crime. Ezra explained that the defendant would sit in the judgment seat under a chain coming down from the ceiling. One was proven innocent and set free if he or she were able to touch the chain. If the accused could not touch the chain, it was considered an indication of guilt. Being a short person could present a real handicap.

We saw the Golden Gate, or the Eastern Gate, where Jesus had entered the city prior to His crucifixion. The gate is now sealed, but tradition says it will be supernaturally opened when the Messiah returns. Then we went to the Lions Gate, or St. Stephens gate, where Stephen, the first Christian martyr, was stoned to death (Acts 7:58–59).

The Church of St. Anne honors the mother of Mary and contains her alleged birthplace. There was a sweet, sweet Spirit there, and you could feel the presence of the Lord. While we were there, a group was singing "I Am

Thine, Oh Lord," which is one of my favorite hymns. It was a time of refreshing.

The Pool of Bethesda, or Bethsaida, which means "House of Healing," was actually empty. Caves on the mountain fill with water from springs, and they suddenly spill the water out, down the hill, and into the pool. The pool then drains out, and the process is repeated. The man Jesus healed in John 5:1–15 was waiting for the waters to be "stirred up" because no one knew when the water would come. Jesus gave him the Living Water that does not go in and out, but remains forever. Again, I felt the Lord's Presence there and knew it was an authentic site.

We walked the fourteen Stations of the Cross on the Via Dolorosa, "The Way of Sorrow." This number is significant because the Bible tells us that there were fourteen generations each from Abraham to David, from David to the Babylon exile, and from the exile to the coming of Christ (Matthew 1:17). Our Lord has a way of underlining His evidence. The Via Dolorosa itself is not mentioned in the Bible but was used to illustrate certain details of Christ's sacrifice for those who were unable to read or write.

1. The first station is the Church of Condemnation, where Jesus was found guilty by the Sanhedrin, as recorded in Matthew 27:1–2.

2. The second station is where He was scourged (Matthew 27:26), and located here is the Church of Flagellation. On the original stone floor is carved the game the soldiers played— Push the King—and on the ceiling is a circular metal sculpture of the crown of thorns.

3. The third station is a stone carving over a doorway depicting the first time Jesus fell. On that day, the city would have been packed with people who had come to celebrate Passover. Standing there, I could easily imagine the noise, the pushing, the crowds.

4. The fourth station is another stone carving that shows Mary reaching out and touching Jesus (according to tradition).

5. An inscription and the Roman numeral V mark the fifth station, where Simon of Cyrene took the cross from Jesus (Mark 15:21).

6. The sixth is a wooden door with markings to show where Veronica wiped His brow (also according to tradition).

7. The seventh is another stone carving on top of an archway, commemorating the second time Jesus fell.

8. The eighth, marked by a metal sign and a carved out niche in the wall, is where the women of Jerusalem were weeping (Luke 23:27–28).

9. On the site of the ninth station, which marks the third time Jesus fell, is a chapel built by the Egyptian and Ethiopian Christians, called Coptics. The priest here read to us from a cross-shaped Bible the scripture concerning Phillip carrying the gospel to

the Ethiopian eunuch (Acts 8:26–39), and then he pronounced a blessing on us.

Lastly, we came to the Church of the Holy Sepulchre, built three hundred years after the Crucifixion, which contains the last five Stations of the Cross.

10. The tenth station is the rock where Abraham offered Isaac as a sacrifice, but God intervened and provided Himself, the Lamb (Genesis 22:8).

11. The eleventh station is where Jesus was nailed to the cross.

12. The twelfth station marks the location where the cross was placed in the ground. It was from here the earthquake started, the rock split, and the curtain in the Holy of Holies was ripped from the top to the bottom (Matthew 27:51).

13. The thirteenth was where the body of Jesus was laid and wrapped in a shroud.

14. The fourteenth and last station is the tomb of Jesus, which is divided into two sections. One section is dedicated to Joseph of Arimathea because it was his tomb and he offered to allow Jesus to be buried there (Matthew 27:60), and the second is dedicated to Jesus.

As we were waiting to enter the tomb, people were breaking in line, fussing, murmuring, and complaining. One woman was furious that she had to wait. There were services simultaneously by all the denominations, so it was very noisy and smoky from all the incense being burned. The trappings were very ornate. Nothing had changed since Jesus' time. I did get to briefly touch His assumed tomb, and I thanked Him for dying for me. I also prayed that He would keep me quiet inside so I would not miss His presence. There was no peace in this place, and I was happy to leave. I did not believe this was an authentic place.

We came back to the Cardo, which would have been the main street back in Roman times. There was a corridor of columns that reached all the way to the Damascus Gate. The stones on the wide street were grooved so that the horses would not slip as they pulled the chariots, and there were many shops along the way. It was like going to the mall, but in Roman times.

Our last stop of the day was the Burnt House, which had been destroyed in 70 A.D. when the Romans burned the city, including the Temple, leaving "not one stone…upon another" (Matt. 24:2, NKJV). It was a large house and is believed to have been used to make perfumes because of the many bottles found there. A weight stone indicates that Katros was likely the name of the owner. Ezra told us that the arm of a young woman had been found in the kitchen. Here was tangible evidence of the destruction, and it was sad to see it so personal; these were real people.

Our first stop the next day was the Garden Tomb. To my heart, it seemed like the real thing. The tomb itself was uncovered by accident in 1867 as the land was being cleared to install a water system. Ezra told us that General Gordon from England was looking from his hotel room and saw the hill that looked like a skull, as described in

John 19:17. He noted that it was near the city and located along a major road. The land had been left undeveloped because it was thought this was where Stephen was stoned and was therefore unclean. The large amount of water found there indicated a garden had been nearby, and a winepress was also discovered. The tomb itself is a first-century tomb, man-made, as indicated by chisel marks, not natural. The Bible says in John 19:41 that "there was a garden; and in the garden a new sepulchre." The tomb was large enough for a person to stand and contained a weeping chamber and two tombs. There was a groove in front of the tomb that the stone would have been rolled into to seal it. The person who owned all this had to be wealthy, so Joseph of Arimathea qualified. When I entered the tomb, I felt a sadness because He had died, but then I was filled with joy because He was not there. He is risen indeed! Our Lord is alive!!

We proceeded to the Chapel of Ascension on the Mount of Olives, which had been renovated by the crusading men and women. I touched the rock from which Jesus ascended into heaven and prayed, "Even so, come quickly, Lord Jesus!" This is also the site to which it is believed He will return (Acts 1:11–12). There is a mosque located next door to the chapel with a sign posted that says No Entry. I had to laugh at the comparison. Jesus is the entry: the Door, as He called Himself in John 10:7. A cemetery is also located on the Mount of Olives, where people have been buried from the time of Christ to date. It is outside the wall of the Old City because this is where the Messiah will come first. From this point, we could see the straight line Ezra told us about earlier that runs from the Mount, to the Garden of Gethsemane, through the Kidron Valley, through the Eastern Gate, and finally to the Temple.

Coming down from the Mount of Olives on our way to the Garden of Gethsemane, we stopped briefly at the chapel of Dominus Flevit, a Franciscan church built in 1954 in the shape of a teardrop. This is where Jesus had wept over the city, and in the chapel is a touching mosaic of a mother hen with her chicks (Matthew 23:37).

In the Garden of Gethsemane we saw gnarled olive trees, some over two thousand years old. Matthew 26:36–57 paints a vivid picture of Jesus praying there, sweating drops of blood as He surrendered His will to that of the Father. The disciples would have been leaning against some of these trees, sleeping. Judas Iscariot entered the garden with a multitude of soldiers, betraying Jesus with a kiss. There was a scuffle here, and Peter cut off a servant's ear. However, Jesus, being Jesus, healed him. Then the disciples fled, Jesus was arrested, and taken to the Caiaphas, the high priest. The Church of All Nations has been erected over the Rock of Agony, and there are magnificent paintings depicting scenes from that event, including the disciples asleep (wouldn't you hate to be a disciple and have that recorded?), the kiss of Judas, and Jesus praying. This seemed to me to be an authentic site; Jesus had been here.

From the Jewish Observatory, we looked out over the Valley of the Cross, where the wood from Jesus' cross came. Then we drove past the Knesset, the Jewish Parliament, which has 120 members who vote for parties, not for individual presidents. It was not in session, so we did not stop.

We concluded the day at the YMCA, where we tremendously enjoyed a performance by the Tzabarim Folklore Ensemble, composed of young men and women born in Jerusalem. The program we were given explained the reason for the name of their ensemble, which is the pluralized form of the Hebrew word *tzabar* or *sabra* (cactus) "which, like the native Israeli, is rough on the outside but sweet inside."[6] The last dance, the Israel Hora, was described as: "A young and dynamic dance, full of the pioneering spirit which filled the hearts of the first Jews coming to Israel, and which has become the national dance."[7] It was an enriching experience.

The next day was a free day, and Clara, Adis (our leader), and I had quite an adventure. Adis had a friend named Hannah who lived in the Windmill Village close to our hotel. Adis had misplaced her address, and upon questioning a man in the general neighborhood, he said that both Hannah and her husband were dead. However, he showed us where Hannah had lived. We knocked on the door, and Hannah opened it! Adis was jubilant! Times had been very hard, but Hannah was doing much better now. Adis had purchased art from her before, and she was pleased to show us her work. There was a print of the Wailing Wall that spoke to my heart, and I had to have it. She shared how her grandfather had doubted God, but on going to the Wall, he wept and said, "Yes, there is God." I got a bonus there—not just the lovely painting of the Wall, but a true story of how God had used it to touch another heart.

Clara and I then went to King David's Tower, the Citadel, located in the Old City. There were breathtaking views from the top of the tower, and in the museum there we saw a short film about the history of the city. As we stopped to eat our lunch on some rocks at the Citadel, we saw a man with a gun (not a soldier), who was apparently guarding two young girls. This is quite common in Israel, as their children are considered very precious—their future—and they protect them from kidnappers. They have not forgotten the Holocaust.

On our way back to the hotel, we stopped in the Windmill Park to admire the roses, which came in every color you could imagine, even black. It rained; just little drops for a few minutes. When we asked Ezra earlier about the possibility of rain, he said that if it rained during the time of year in which we were visiting, it meant Messiah would come! He thought we were teasing when we told him at dinner that night about the brief afternoon rain in the park.

Our dear waiter, Kamed, promised that I would have hot chocolate for breakfast the next morning, our last morning. How sweet! He told others in our group at breakfast that morning that he was reading the Old Testament and New Testament in the Bible, plus the Talmud and Quran, trying to find God, and they had prayed he would find the truth. This is being a witness for Jesus, just loving people into the Kingdom. It really was a mission trip.

The next morning we left Jerusalem, moving south and east into the Judean Desert. We went through an area where eighty thousand Bedouins live. The basic Bedouin unit is the family, several families form a tribe, and the tribes represented by a sheikh. Several sheikhs have been elected into Israel's Knesset. They are Israeli citizens and serve in the Army. Ezra told us that the men are allowed to have four wives, and the heavier, the better because skinny ones are gone with the first windstorm. Camels sell for five thousand dollars each, and Ezra jokingly said Adis, our leader, was worth three camels, making her very valuable indeed.

We passed through the wilderness where Jesus was led by the Holy Spirit after His baptism by John the Baptist (Luke 3:21; 4:1), and we saw the point at which the River Jordan enters into the Sea of Galilee, the most likely place of His baptism. In the distance we could see Mount Nebo, where Moses viewed the Promised Land (Deuteronomy 34:1), and probably where Ruth and Naomi returned to Israel from Moab (Ruth 1:22). The wise men from the East coming to visit Baby Jesus would have entered this way also.

Herod the Great constructed the mountain fortress of Masada. He built two palaces there, plus warehouses, baths, a pool, and reservoirs. It rose 440 meters above the Dead Sea, and the only way up was by the Snake Path, a narrow, winding trail. We went up by cable car, but the stout-hearted still walk the path.

After Herod died, a Roman garrison took over and held it until 66 A.D., the year of the great rebellion. Jewish zealots came to fight for Jerusalem but could not get in the locked gates, so they came to Masada, picking up more people along the way. They built another wall parallel to Herod's wall. In 70 A.D., the Romans conquered Jerusalem and headed for Masada. The siege lasted three years. The Roman commander Silva built a great ramp to cross over the chasm between the walls using ten thousand troops, plus Jewish slaves. It took seven months to build. Finally he stormed in, but his soldiers found that of the population of 967, only two women and five children were alive, the rest having committed suicide to avoid capture. An archaeologist said that one of their greatest finds had been the pieces of pottery found at Masada with numbers, indicating that there was a "lottery" for the suicide mission. Everything had been burned except their provisions, which showed they could have lasted another five years. Masada has become the symbol of the Jews' will to be free and their unconquerable spirit. It is mandatory that all Israeli soldiers come to Masada, and the war cry is: "Masada shall not fall again."

We left Masada, an unforgettable experience, and went over to the Dead Sea, which is a part of the Jordan Rift. It is the lowest point on earth, 412 meters below sea level, and has the highest concentration of salt and minerals in the world at 33 percent. There are salt formations along the shore, and one is named "Lot's Wife" because this is where the Lord destroyed Sodom and Gomorrah. Lot's wife was warned not to look back, but she did and was turned into a pillar of salt (Genesis 19:26). It is fun to swim in the Dead Sea because you cannot sink, but the water tastes awful! People come here to take the mud baths and to buy the many skin products.

Ezra told us that Jordan, bordering the Dead Sea on the east, had a treaty with Israel to mine potash and magnesium from the sea, and accused Israel of using more than its share of the water. Israel denied the claim, and investigators found that the sea has tilted in favor of Israel. They are still the "apple of [God's] eye" (Deut. 32:10).

As we went on through the desert area to the Ein Gedi Reserve, we could see the desert blooming with bright fields of green in the middle of the sand. The Ein Gedi is an oasis that contains four springs, and it is abundant with wildlife, birds, and fruit-bearing trees. Artifacts have been found dating back to 4000 B.C. This is the place where David fled from Saul (1 Samuel 24:1), and later from his own son, Absalom (2 Samuel 15:14).

At Qumran we viewed the ruins of a Jewish collective community, where the Essenes and, most likely, John the Baptist lived. The Essenes led an austere life, and they copied and wrote scrolls; they were preservers of the Scripture. Many view them as the first Christians because of the similarity of their teachings to the preaching of Jesus. We saw the cave where the Dead Sea scrolls were found in 1947 by a Bedouin shepherd. The find included eleven full scrolls and over eight hundred fragments, including the book of Isaiah, the Scroll of the Temple, the War Between the Sons of Light and the Sons of Darkness, the Essenes's Manual of Discipline, and a commentary on the book of Habakkuk. Ezra said that two professors working on the book of Isaiah found only four letters that were different. The scriptures that have been found there and in other caves include almost all of the Old Testament, with the exception of Esther and Nehemiah, and are almost identical to our Bible today. Perhaps Esther is not a part of the treasure because it does not mention God. It was amazing to me to see how our Lord watches over His Word and carefully preserves His truth from generation to generation, just as it says in Psalm 100:5. This was a fitting final stop.

We had a farewell dinner at the Hotel Laromme, and Adis asked each of us to share his or her favorite part of the trip. The majority said the Garden Tomb. I had to agree, but the Wailing Wall was a very close second. Also, I was deeply moved at Korazin and at the Pool of Bethesda because of the quickening in my spirit at each of those places that Jesus is the Living Water—just a simple thing but very personal and dear to me. Ezra gave a sweet speech and encouraged us to be ambassadors for Israel. I was sad that he didn't acknowledge that Jesus was the Messiah, as I had prayed so hard for him and planted my little seeds as we went along; maybe next time. We closed with hugs all around.

The next morning we left for home via New York City, where the group dispersed. Clara and I had another leg of the trip to get back to Atlanta. I came home with a greater appreciation of His Word, for I had seen it come alive. I had walked where Jesus walked! It was an incredible, unforgettable journey that left me aching to return to my spiritual home.

Shalom and lehitra'ot. Next year in Jerusalem!

CHAPTER 7
MY SECOND JOURNEY
TO ISRAEL

NOV 1997

My second tour to Israel was sponsored by David and his wife Marcia, Messianic Jews who lived in Orlando, Florida. My traveling friend, Clara, had seen David's brochure, and we both got excited about a second trip. One time to Israel simply isn't enough! He had led fifty-seven trips previously, and this one was unique. He brought together thirty-two people from different races and denominations, coming from all over the United States—Florida, Georgia, New York, Ohio, Oregon, Texas, and Minnesota—plus one young lady from Ghana. We went to many of the places covered on our first trip, but this chapter will talk only about the new sites I saw, including those visited on our long layover in London.

Upon our arrival in Tel Aviv, I again had that feeling of coming home. We went by bus to Netanya, eighteen miles north of Tel Aviv, and gratefully checked into the Moriah Hotel on the Mediterranean coast. The next morning we had that wonderful Israeli breakfast experience and met our guide, Charles, who was originally from France and had immigrated to Israel. He became just as great an asset on this second trip as Ezra had been on the first one. I believe all guides must have a wonderful sense of humor, a lot of patience, a passion for his/her country, and a wealth of knowledge.

That first day we headed north for twelve miles along the coastal highway to Caesarea, the City of the Emperor by the Sea. As on the first trip, we sang in the amphitheater, but this time we had in our group George, who had sung with the New York Opera. He had toured with Howard Keel, so we had a real concert! Rosa Elena, our new Spanish-speaking friend, powerfully prayed at every stop. Already this was shaping into an exciting adventure. We did see more of the harbor, the ruins, the moat, and in a vault we found fleur de lis (a floral symbol sometimes used to represent the Virgin Mary) carved into the stones.

El-Muhraqa, the site on Mount Carmel where Elijah had the contest with the four hundred prophets of Baal, recorded in 1 Kings 18:20–39, was impressive. On this clear day, we had a magnificent view of the Mediterranean Sea on one side and the countryside of Israel extending into the distance on the other side. Just imagine Elijah scampering down this mountain and outrunning Ahab to Jezreel (1 Kings 18:46)! He had to have done it in the strength of the Lord.

The Valley of Jezreel still made me sad. This is the valley where the nations will converge for the last battle in history, and it is a sobering sight. A short distance away we saw a tomb that had been discovered when the road was built, and it had a huge rolling stone like the one where Jesus was buried at the Garden Tomb. It was reassuring to know that this Jesus who rose from the dead will be the conquering King at the Battle of Armageddon.

Continuing east, we came to Nazareth, where Jesus grew up. We went into the Church of Gabriel, built on the spot where Gabriel allegedly announced to Mary that she would give birth to the Messiah (Luke 1:26–33). I recalled that on our first trip the Church of the Annunciation claimed that site to mark the authentic location of this event, yet here was another guesstimate. Nazareth means "branch," and Charles said that you must "will," or make a conscious decision, to come here because it is off the beaten path.[1]

We drove through Cana, where Jesus performed His first miracle at the request of His mother by turning water into wine at the wedding feast (John 2:1–12). There was just a small monument to mark the event.

Safed, the City of Air, is an artist colony situated on the top of Mount Canaan. It is one of the four Holy Cities of Israel, the other three being Tiberias (the City of Water), Hebron (the City of Earth), and Jerusalem (the City of Fire/ Eternal Energy). The Kabalistic movement started here in the sixteenth century by Jews coming from Spain. In the seventeenth century, the city started to decline and suffered from famines, plagues, and finally an earthquake in 1837. By 1948, only two thousand Jews remained. It contains many synagogues and has become a place of pilgrimage. Charles told us that in the synagogue, there must be three elements: the Torah, which is put in the highest place; the ark, where the Torah is kept; and the light, which is directed toward Jerusalem. We saw huge stacks of old books, which are never destroyed, only buried. Jews are forbidden to draw images of faces or creatures, so they created a system whereby images are formed by using printed words. I bought a picture of an outline of the face of Ruth with one long braid, a two-strand necklace, and a small crown sitting off by itself. As you look closely, you see that the picture is actually a composite of the words of the entire book of Ruth. Amazing! Also amazing was the glorious sunset we saw as we left this mountaintop City of Air.

Our final destination that first day was Tiberias, the City of Water, by the Sea of Galilee, which would be our base for the next two nights.

The next morning, we revisited the Mount of Beatitudes, the traditional site of the Sermon on the Mount; Tabgha, where Jesus fed the five thousand; and the synagogue at Capernaum, which means "City of Mercy." The Bible says that a leper was healed here, as well as the centurion's servant, and Peter's mother-in-law. It is in this city that "they brought unto him many that were possessed with devils: and he cast out the spirits with his word, and healed all that were sick" (Matt. 8:1–17). Capernaum was a major city on the Via Maris road near the Syrian border, and taxes were collected here. This is where Peter got his tax money from the fish's mouth (Matthew 17:24–27), and it was here that Jesus called Matthew, the tax collector, to be His disciple (Matthew 9:9).

We crossed the Sea of Galilee by motor launch. While many of the places we had visited were traditional sites, we knew that Jesus, called Yeshua in Hebrew, had sailed on the Sea of Galilee and had even walked on it (Mark 6:45–51). We could see the Golan Heights that we hear so much about in the news. The Golan is a high plateau, and probably Abraham passed through here on his way to the Promised Land. It was awarded to the half-tribe of Manasseh, but no cities were built here until the reign of King David. A famous battle was fought there in the great rebellion of 66 A.D. against the Romans, where the Jews fought with unprecedented courage.

Next we went to see *The Galilee Experience*, a documentary film about Israel and the region of Galilee. I found that the more I learned about my spiritual homeland, the more I appreciated it and the more I wanted to know.

We proceeded to the southernmost part of the lake, where the Jordan River enters. This is a popular tourist site, and familiar to Clara and me from our first trip. Twelve of our group chose to be baptized, and we were given the choice of either the Christian or Jewish way. I had been sprinkled as a Presbyterian at my conversion, and had been immersed as a Baptist when I joined that denomination, so I chose the Jewish way. This means that you are prayed for on the shore by the person baptizing you, then you walk out into the water, give your testimony, and then immerse yourself. You are *mikva*-ed. It was a heartwarming experience that I shall never forget!

That evening we attended a concert by one of our group, Alyosha, a classical pianist originally from the Ukraine and then from Florida. He played, among other things, a song from the Ninety-first Psalm and his own "Dry Bones Concerto." We were joined by other Messianic Jews from that area, and they knew how to praise the Lord! The only thing that could have made the evening better would have been me not being so tired. My spirit was overflowing with all I had experienced thus far, but my flesh was calling for a break. "Stand in awe…commune with your own heart upon your bed, and be still," the psalms say (Ps. 4:4). Amen!

The next day we headed south toward the Dead Sea area. Our first stop was Bet She'an, where massive excavations were continuing to uncover a temple of Bacchus (the Roman god of wine), hot baths, and more of the streets and buildings. We sat in the amphitheater, where George again sang for us. There was a Japanese group there, and they exploded into applause when he finished; we shared greetings with them (building relationships). There is a huge mound across from the present excavations that contains the ruins of twenty-four cities, all piled on top of each other. Some were cities of refuge in Yeshua's time. Charles told us that this great city had once been destroyed in seconds by an earthquake, and it could happen again. Here's that courageous Jewish spirit—you get knocked down, you get back up, and build again.

We passed through the desert, which was blooming like a rose. I was again surprised by that contrast. It made me reflect upon how our lives before Jesus are like the desert, but when He comes in, we bloom and produce fruit. Israel truly is the "fifth gospel"!

We were in the Jordan Valley, which lies on the eastern border of Israel, embracing the Jordan River from Bet She'an in the north to Jericho in the south. It covers an area of 1,300 square miles, and at the time of our visit there were seventeen communities in the region. Jericho had been turned over to the Palestinian Authority, so the safety of the communities to the south had been compromised. We visited the immigrant community of Yafit, which was established by a group of young French immigrants. To be an immigrant, you must be two generations Jewish and approved by the government under the Law of Return. Aviv and Charles had both fought in the 1967 war, plus Charles was from France, so they had much in common. There were thirty families living there and trying to live in peace with their Arab neighbors. Their leader, Aviv, said they get along fine, but in time of war, they must fight. They took us into their massive greenhouse, where we saw beautiful long-stemmed roses that they ship all over the world. They gave one to each of us. We also saw their bomb shelter, and when we entered the settlement, we passed through a security post. They are confident that God has called them here and asked that we help them by correcting media distortion, joining in an exchange program, giving financial aid, writing to them, and above all, praying for them. These were real-life pioneers!

We passed by the Mount of Temptation, where Jesus was tempted by Satan. Jesus defeated the enemy with the Word of God, replying to each temptation: "It is written" (Luke 4:1–13). In like manner, we are overcomers by the blood of the Lamb and by the word of our testimony (Rev. 12:11).

We came to Jericho, the first city to be conquered by Joshua (Joshua 6:20–26), and the first one to be given away— to the Palestinian Authority through the Oslo Accords. There was a big concession center there, and some of the group took camel rides. We saw the sycamore tree that Zacchaeus climbed so he could see Jesus (Luke 19:1–10).

Coming through the Judean desert, we encountered the Bedouins. The largest clan is related to King Hussein. They are known for their hospitality because they believe and live by the motto "Tomorrow it could be me." A guest is limited, however, to a stay of three and one-fourth days. That time period was not explained to us, but I assumed it was similar to another saying: "Visitors, like fish, start to smell after three days." The desert has a striking beauty all its own. We passed by the Inn of the Good Samaritan, written of in Luke 10:29–37.

We entered Jerusalem from the east, which our leader said was the traditional way. We passed by Bethany, the city of Lazarus, Mary, and Martha, which has been enveloped by Jerusalem. Then we continued past the Mount of Olives, Gethsemane, and the sealed Eastern Gate. George started singing about Yeshua coming back into the city.

We toured the Church of the Nativity in Bethlehem, six miles from Jerusalem, supposedly located on the actual spot where Jesus was born, but I felt here that it was like Bet She'an—covered with layers of rubble. Christ's birth was simple and authentic, but man had laid on all the trappings. A mosque had been built across the street. Charles said the Arabs build their mosques near the holy sites and build them higher. We saw that in all the cities; the mosques were the tallest buildings.

Bethlehem was now under Palestinian control; the Jews had left the city. The Bethlehem Hotel was our home base for the next four nights. There were huge portraits of Yasser Arafat hanging in the lobby and small paintings in the hallways depicting scenes of Palestinian women carrying water pots and various other scenes. Written on the paintings were the words: "We shall stay as the everlasting Walls of Jerusalem," and, "As the olive trees, we are here to stay." Arafat's mother-in-law lived in a personal suite on the sixth floor. We were gone most of the daytime hours, but in the early hours of the morning, we were awakened by the call to prayer of the Muslims. The area around us was like a war zone, so desolate, and we had to pass through a checkpoint to enter Jerusalem. Rachel's Tomb was a short distance away, and we had to detour past it one day because of a riot. One reason our leader wanted us to stay here was because he wanted us "to see Bethlehem from the inside and know exactly what is happening here." He also wanted to make a statement that "Bethlehem still belonged to Israel, even though the accursed Philistines (Palestinians) were in temporary control." It made for a very interesting, but unsettling trip.

The next day, Thanksgiving Day, we visited some of the sites I had seen on my first trip, but with a different slant because of our Messianic Jewish leader. We viewed Jerusalem from a scenic overlook on the Mount of Olives. Legend has it that when the temple was destroyed, the Holy Spirit went to the Mount of Olives to wait for the sons of Israel, and when they did not come, the Spirit moved to heaven. Charles, pointing to the cemetery, explained that 150,000 people were buried there, including Muslim warriors on their horses with their weapons. When the dead arise, he said, they are going to cross over the Kidron, which is now a dry river course called the Valley of Jehosophat, and enter the city through the sealed gate. Yeshua will arrive via the Mount: "And his feet shall stand in that day upon the mount of Olives, which is before Jerusalem on the east, and the mount of Olives shall cleave in the midst thereof toward the east and toward the west, and there shall be a very great valley..." (Zech. 14:4). What a day that is going to be!

We went down into the valley, passed by the tombs of Absalom and Zacharias, and entered the city through the Dung Gate. We went to the Western Wall, also called the "Wailing Wall." During the Byzantine period, Jews were forbidden to come to the Wall, which is the closest to the Holy of Holies and, therefore, most sacred to them. The Jordanians also barred them from the Wall, and it was not until the Six-Day War that the Wall was made accessible to all. I was so happy that I could go there once again to pray and insert my requests. A dear friend had given me three pennies dated with the births of her sons, and I put those pennies in the wall and prayed for her special requests. We walked through Wilson's Arch, located at the northern end of the Wall, where we saw fourteen of the Wall's strata, leading to the rock on which the Temple's podium was erected. We were looking at layers of history.

Charles told us that Jerusalem has eight gates, and each gate has three names. At St. Stephen's Gate (also called the Lion's Gate or St. Mary's Gate), I saw again the Pool of Bethesda. Jewish soldiers entered through this gate in the Six-Day War (1967). Each gate has a pool where the animals could be washed for sacrifice in the temple.

We walked the Via Dolorosa, covering the fourteen Stations of the Cross. Our leader called the Church of the Holy Sepulchre, where the last five stations are located, "...a religious supermarket containing everything from the slab on which the body was embalmed to the hill of

Calvary and not one but two tombs. We visited this place only to compare it to what is probably the real tomb of Yeshua…the Garden Tomb."

At the Garden Tomb, we did the usual tour, but this time we had a communion service in the garden area, using a serving set that David had donated in memory of his father fifteen years ago. The officials in charge had it there for us to use. This was especially meaningful to David. It was special to me because it was Thanksgiving Day, and I was spending it in this sacred place. My cup was running over!

We went to the Garden of Gethsemane, which means "olive press,"[2] and saw the old olive trees. The olives had to be crushed to bring forth the oil that was used for light, and I thought of how Yeshua had been pressed here to the extent that He sweat drops of blood (Luke 22:44), so He could bring light to a dark world. He told us to also be lights: "Let your light so shine before men, that they may see your good works, and glorify your Father which is in heaven" (Matt. 5:16). I prayed at the Rock of Agony asking forgiveness for all the times I, like the disciples, had slept, not watching or praying.

The Lord gave me a rich opportunity to be His light just a short time after that prayer. We had returned to the city, and as Clara and I were sitting on a little wall eating lunch, I overheard a young woman and a young man discussing the divinity of Jesus. I excused myself from Clara and walked over to them, introducing myself. The woman was originally from Pittsburgh, had come to Israel sixteen years ago, and was a tour guide. She had changed her name to Tovar. Her friend was an Israeli student named Elot. I said that I had heard their conversation and wanted them to know how I met Jesus. I gave them my testimony, told them of my love for Israel, and assured them that many Christians were praying for them. Tovar said that if this Yeshua did not come soon to intervene on their behalf, there would be nothing left; Iraq was able to destroy the whole world. I was confident that the God of Abraham, Isaac, and Jacob would not fail them and told them that I would never stop praying for them by name and for Israel. This was a tender moment, and I was so sad to have to leave them, but David, our leader, was calling. We exchanged hugs, and I have kept my promise to pray for them by name. This was a God-ordained encounter, and I know He followed up on Tovar and Elot. I look forward to seeing them one day in the New Jerusalem.

We proceeded to the Upper Room, then downstairs to the Tomb of David, and on to the Cardo, which seemed to be one of the favorite spots for our Jewish friends. There were many shops here, and it was a good place to get prayer shawls, shofars, jewelry, etc. On the way back to the hotel we passed the Knesset, Israel's Parliament, but once again there was no stopping. I put it on my list for "next year in Jerusalem."

That evening Alyosha held a concert at Christ Church (the Jerusalem Anglican Church). The pastor and his wife refused to collect him because it was too dangerous for Jews to be in Bethlehem. This was another concert that seemed to be just for me, although I could see how others were being blessed as well. He played music based on Isaiah 40:31: "But they that wait upon the LORD shall renew their strength; they shall mount up with wings as eagles; they shall run, and not be weary; and they shall walk, and not faint." He closed with a song from Psalm 91, and the word of the Lord—how He sees our tears, loves and cares for us, and will be with us always. A perfect ending to a golden day!

The next morning we departed for the Dead Sea. We stopped at Ein Gedi, which is an oasis and means "spring of the kid."[3] We could see the Moab Mountains and

Jordan in the distance as we swam in the sea. While it is called the Dead Sea, it is actually good for life. A sunbath here is actually good for the skin! In Ezekiel 47:1–12 and Zechariah 14:8 it is prophesied that a new river will flow from Jerusalem dividing into two parts, one flowing into the Mediterranean and the other into the Dead Sea, which would then teem with life. Alyosha told us that the Dead Sea has been dividing during the past ten years. And in fact, from the top of Masada, the site of the last stand by the Jewish zealots against the Romans, the split was visible.

At Qumran, we saw again the cave where the Dead Sea Scrolls had been discovered by boys looking for a goat. That evening I made this notation in my journal:

> *Really feel the Lord brought me here for a purpose. Perhaps it is to love Israel more and be more diligent in my prayers, to be in what He is doing, to come to know more personally my Jewish brothers and sisters. Even this [diverse] group—…we are all one in the Lord with no races, no denominations, even no genders; just one in Him. Plus, what Alyosha has taught me—speak to the dry bones, stay close to the Lord—things I know but need to be reinforced. Surely I was born for such a time as this! What did I see today, or where did I see God today? At Ein Gedi, an oasis in the desert; a Dead Sea that is good for life; [at] Qumran, how the Lord preserves and authenticates His Word; [at] Masada, man's inborn desire to be free, and God's provision.*

The next day was "free for rest" according to the itinerary, but who wants to rest in the Holy Land? You can do that when you get home. Many of the group chose to go with Clara and me to visit Hannah, our artist friend from the first trip, but sadly, her home was boarded up. We left her a note. Then we went to the Montefiore Windmill, which is the first settlement built outside the city walls. The windmill faces the wrong way, so it cannot catch the wind and therefore cannot be used to grind wheat and corn. It seems very out of place, making it a popular tourist photo spot. Here our group split, with just a few of the ladies going with us to the King David Hotel. This is the place where all the dignitaries stay, and it is grand indeed, as the name suggests.

Across the street is the YMCA, and we climbed the tower to get a panoramic view of the City. We saw more stairs and went up to a small rotunda, which had stars painted on the ceiling, and my verse: "They that wait upon the LORD shall renew their strength" (Isa. 40:31). We could feel the presence of the Lord in that place, so we held hands and prayed, closing with the Lord's Prayer. Etris, one of the ladies, said she had been wanting the group to pray the Lord's Prayer together, but we had not done it. This prayer was an answer to her prayer.

We walked back to the Old City, entering the Armenian Quarter, and then we saw the arch of The Hurvah Synagogue, which had been restored after the Six-Day War. Legend claims the holy vat of oil and the shofar are hidden there, which only the prophet Elijah may use to light the eternal flame in the rebuilt Temple and announce Israel's freedom.

Murphy, our van driver, had offered to guide us that morning, but we declined because once he let us out at the Jaffa Gate, we were in walking distance of the places we wanted to visit. He had given us directions to his store in the Christian Quarter of the Old City, in which he said there is "no push, no shove." Murphy was a Palestinian Christian; they constitute only 2 percent of the population. He shared with us his testimony of being healed of a brain tumor and took off his cap to show us the scars. His doctor told him he would have no more children after his surgery, but his wife was expecting their third child very soon. He gave us some very good deals and walked us up to the Jaffa Gate. As we were leaving, rain began to sprinkle briefly, and when it stopped we saw an incredibly big rainbow! How appropriate to see the sign of God's covenant promise here in the Holy Land at the end of another golden day. He is so good—all the time!

We returned for our last night at the Bethlehem Hotel. While our group had been having a lovely day in Jerusalem, Bethlehem had been experiencing outbursts of violence. Some prisoners were scheduled to be released that day, but they were not. Children were throwing stones, shots had been fired, and many people had been hurt. Our Lord had kept us safe thus far; surely He would keep us one more night. A sign of encouragement was that our roses from the settlement were still beautiful, so Clara gave them to the receptionist.

We left the Bethlehem Hotel early the next morning and went to the LaRomme Hotel in Jerusalem, where Clara and I had stayed on our first trip. David had arranged for Jan Willem van der Hoeven of the International Christian Embassy (also a good friend of Benjamin Netanyahu) and Stan Goodenough from the *Middle East Intelligence Digest* to speak with us. Mr. van der Hoeven said the reason Jerusalem is so important is because the Temple Mount will be the site of the third temple; that Yeshua did not come to start a new religion, but that when we become believers, we become Jews. He predicted that the time is coming when

Jews everywhere will be persecuted, and the only safe place for them will be Israel. They had prayed for seven years for the Berlin Wall to fall, and are praying even now against the lying spirit that has blinded the Muslims. Mr. Goodenough told us that God Himself will save Israel, not America, because God will not share His glory with anyone.

At the end of the meeting, I asked Mr. van der Hoeven why I had that strange feeling of being home in Israel. He replied that there is one tree, and I had been engrafted. He was referring to Romans 11:1–27, wherein Paul speaks of Israel's rejection of Yeshua and how the salvation of the Gentiles would provoke them to jealousy. They were the natural branches; the Gentile believers were engrafted as wild branches. Each person receives a call, either come home or be an intercessor. Then he prayed for me and spoke these words: "You have been through so much, but God has a purpose for your life. You are an intercessor." Truer words have never been spoken. I carry Israel in my heart and pray for her daily, especially for the peace of Jerusalem, and I travail in prayer as the Holy Spirit directs. This was the highlight of the trip for me; the Lord had spoken so clearly into my life—one of those light bulb moments.

After this monumental meeting, we had just a short time before we had to board the bus and go to the airport. The majority of the group went to the Cardo for shopping, but Clara and I were headed for the Temple Mount, as our leader had not taken the group there. Five of the group wanted to come with us (you can't come to Jerusalem and not see the Temple Mount). These were our special friends who had prayed in the YMCA rotunda with us, plus Sidney. We went into the Dome of the Rock, and when we came out we held hands and sang "Standing on the Promises." We prayed against the falsehood of Islam and claimed the Temple Mount for the third temple. We were obedient to

Jan Willem's challenge to "do prophecy," not just talk about it! That was a fitting end to our Jerusalem journey.

On the way to the airport, we made a quick stop again at Yad Vashem, the Museum of the Holocaust. I was so glad the group did not miss this historic and poignant monument to the suffering of the Jewish people. Since Clara and I had been there on our first trip, we spent a quiet time in the outside gardens prior to our mad dash to the airport in Tel Aviv.

Clara's seatmate on the flight to London was a young man who was separated from his wife. She was living in Scotland, and he now lived in the States working in a hotel very close to the Atlanta airport (small world). His wife was coming with their two children to visit him for Christmas, and if they reconciled, they would come back in the spring to live in Atlanta. I could overhear the conversation, and I prayed as Clara talked. Also, I happened to have a *Decision Magazine* with the cover featuring an article entitled "How to Come to God," so I quietly handed it to her. She handed it to him, and he took it and said he would call her; he wanted Clara to be a friend to his wife.

London was foggy and cold! We made a quick bus tour of the city and drove by Trafalgar Square, the Secret Service building, the River Thames, Parliament, Westminster Abbey, Big Ben, Buckingham Palace, and Piccadilly Circus. We actually stopped and went into the British Museum. Our leader had lived in London, so he was not that excited about being there, but it seemed he loved the museum. Clara and I went in, but then we ducked out. We wanted to be in the city, so while others looked at the exhibits, we did a little walking to see the shops and returned to the museum, with none the wiser! The rest of the group wanted to go to the hotel and chill, but a very sweet couple, Brian and Linda, went with Clara and me to eat fish and chips (of course). They were from Minneapolis, and he was in his last year of seminary. The Lord gave us this couple so we could have this added joy in London. After dinner we went to St. Martin's Theater to see *The Mouse Trap* by Agatha Christie, the longest running play in the world. At that time, it had been running for forty-five years. The saying is that as long as there are ravens at Buckingham Palace, there will be a monarchy, and as long as *The Mouse Trap* runs, there will be a London. Linda, Clara, and I kept falling asleep during the first act because we were exhausted and so cold. At intermission we went to the ladies' room and doused our faces with cold water, so we made it through the second act. The audience makes a promise not to reveal "who done it." Brian's father had acted in the play, so Brian knew, but he didn't tell us.

It was exciting to see London all lit up at night and to see London's night life. Some guys were playing drums and singing in Leicester Square, two girls were singing while sitting on the floor in the Tube (London's subway), and a man was playing a trombone. We rode the Tube to Victoria Station and then had a long train ride to our stop, but we enjoyed chatting with the local people, once again building relationships. It was a long walk in the rain to the hotel, and after thanking Brian and Linda we collapsed into our beds! I did pray a quick prayer: "God, save the Queen and England, and please send revival. Amen."

We left London in the snow! The plane had to be de-iced, so I had an opportunity to share my testimony with the young, married lady seated next to me. She was Methodist, and her mother had been a missionary. I told her about Israel, all the things we had seen and learned, and that I felt in my spirit Jesus was coming soon. Her eyes filled with tears and so did mine. This is an integral part of the mission—sharing the story.

As I reflected back on the trip, I could see the Lord's hand of blessing. He taught me a lot about my Jewish heritage, how I was engrafted, circumcised in my heart—hence my love for Israel and my call to intercede. Prophecy was fulfilled before my eyes. He showed me signs of His reality and His return. There were the pioneers in Yafit and the divine encounter with the young people (Tovar and Elot) in the Old City; there was Jan Willem van der Hoeven explaining my identity and calling and what was happening in Israel; finally, there was the mixture of our group and what I learned from them, especially the Jews. Even on the plane coming back, I heard the news about Arafat's claiming Palestine as a separate state, and the ostracism of the Jews in Switzerland, so I could see God's plan rapidly unfolding. What a time to be alive!

Even so, come quickly, Lord Jesus.

CHAPTER 8
MY THIRD JOURNEY
TO ISRAEL

JUNE 1999

A couple from our church, Atlanta City Church, had a strong calling to go to Israel, and many of us in their care group caught their vision. We called ourselves the Shalom Jerusalem Mission Team, and we coordinated with Operation Mobilization (OM). The purpose of the trip was to pray and intercede for the city of Jerusalem, the nation of Israel, and all the citizens of Israel, whether Jewish, Arab, or Christian. We would prayer walk the Old City, worship with the saints, and encourage and support OM's missionaries living there.

It was exciting to see how the Lord put the team together and to see His timing. One entire family—Mimi, Steve, and their four children, Matt, Jack, Kelsey and Leigh— established at the beginning that they wanted to go, since it was the heart cry of Mimi and Steve that started the ball rolling. I actually got down on my knees and begged Billy, Cheryl's husband, to go with us, so he jumped on board toward the end. David of OM was to be our leader, but he had passport problems at the last minute, so his wife Terri became the new leader. A donation was made so that Bonnie, co-leader of our care group, could go. We were to leave at 2:15 p.m. on June 19, and her passport came in at noon on the day of departure. Another member of the care group, Sharon, also joined us.

When we departed from the Atlanta airport, God had His team, and it was good. Actually, it was very good!

As a footnote here, Carla, another member of our care group, came to the airport to pray for us. She had scriptures for each of us, and mine was Isaiah 58:11, "The Lord will guide you always; he will satisfy your needs in a sun-scorched land and will strengthen your frame. You will be like a well-watered garden, like a spring whose waters never fail" (NIV).

We flew into London, but there was no time to leave the airport. We encountered an additional delay because the co-pilot failed to report, but at last we departed and arrived in Tel Aviv that evening. I experienced that familiar sensation of having come home. We rented vans and drove into Jerusalem; it was beautiful to see the city at night with all its lights.

Christ Church was our home away from home during our stay in Jerusalem. A "Welcome Christ Church" pamphlet gave us a brief history of the church and its concerns for the Jewish people. It was the first Protestant church in Jerusalem, built by the Anglican Missionary Society, now called the Church's Ministry Among Jewish People (C.M.J).. It is the oldest Anglican church in the Middle East, consecrated in 1849, and is based on Romans 1:16, "I am not ashamed of the gospel of Christ, for it is the power of God to salvation for everyone who believes, *for the Jew first* and also to the Greek" (NKJV, author's emphasis). The founders believed that before Jesus returned, the Jewish people would be restored to their own land and many would acknowledge Jesus as their Messiah. They felt that Christianity had:

...strayed far from the simplicity of its Hebraic origins. Jesus was a faithful Jew. All of the original apostles were Jewish...the New Testament itself was a Jewish document, written by Jewish followers of Jesus, with the possible exception of Luke [and] Acts...The question then was not could a Jew believe in Jesus as the promised Messiah, but could a gentile believe in Jesus without first becoming a Jew....The founders of the Christ Church in Jerusalem wanted the Jewish people to be able to enter the church and see the Christian faith...as it was in the beginning—Jewish. The church was built to be a Protestant place of worship with similarities to a synagogue. These included Jewish symbols and Hebrew writing on the stained glass windows, the reredos at the very front of the church, and the Holy Table. The original founders came to Jerusalem over 150 years ago to proclaim Jesus Christ as "the Passover Lamb and the final sacrifice for sin." They are still preaching this message of salvation today.[1]

At our team devotional the next morning, the Lord said our job here was to know Him; He was to be our agenda. This really freed me because I could just flow with Him and not feel I had to meet certain requirements, such as passing out x number of tracts and witnessing to x number of people each day. We could just glow with the flow.

Christ Church is situated at the Jaffa Gate, so we started there and prayer-walked the ramparts surrounding the Christian Quarter. It was sad to see so much trash and debris in this Holy City; it seemed shameful. We descended at the Zion Gate, walking through the Armenian Quarter into the Jewish Quarter and the Temple Mount area. We came to the massive Western Wall, built on the foundations of Solomon's temple. Members of our home church had given us names for whom to pray and put in the Wall (affectionately called "God's Mailbox"), so we spent time here, interceding and weeping over those precious requests. This was my third visit to the Wall, yet it still provoked much emotion. On the men's side, there was dancing and joy as a young man was celebrating his bar mitzvah. On the adjacent side, the women were quietly praying with their heads covered, some kneeling on the hard stone pavement, while others were standing to touch the Wall. A few had chairs to sit, but as Cheryl was warned, women must not cross their legs!

We ate lunch at the Cardo, and continued our walk through the Roman ruin to the Muslim Quarter. I gave a tract to a young Jewish man in exchange for one of his, plus a tract to a trumpet player out on the street, and I put a tract on a public bulletin board. The Jewish tract I received claimed that Christians were trying to destroy them and their heritage, all in the name of love. This was thought provoking and helped me to see their viewpoint. The founders of Christ Church were right! The Jewish heritage is vital to the Christian faith; it is not to be destroyed, but embraced.

We walked through a bazaar, which was a heady experience of pungent spices and noise. Everyone wants to make a deal; it's like rushing to a blue-light special at K-Mart. We proceeded to the Christian Quarter, but I was unable to locate my old friend Murphy, whom I had met on the second trip. His brother told me that he had died in

November. I recalled his victorious testimony and rejoiced that now he had an even more precious victory—he was with Yeshua, and he left precious jewels here on this earth, despite what the doctors said!

We ascended the wall at the Damascus Gate, prayer-walked our way to the Jaffa Gate, and then went back "home" for dinner. That evening we attended a service at Christ Church, where we joined in glorious praise and worship. Some of the team chose to sit outside for a while, and as we were talking, a fifty-five-year-old woman came to us. She shared her testimony about how God called her name from heaven and how He sent her a Christian to mentor her. She was originally from Germany, but the Lord told her to come to Jerusalem. She had been working spasmodically and had a little money, but she did not want to stay in the hostels because of the clientele. She was waiting for a lady from the church who played the violin to assist her with a place to stay. The others retired for the night, but I stayed behind. I prayed for her, she prayed for me, and I gave her a little more money. Three other team members arrived, so we talked a little more, and then it was goodnight as she continued to wait for her friend.

As I reflected in my bed, I thought that if I had been home I could have offered her a place to stay, but I had no material resources here in this foreign land. It was frustrating, but then I remembered the Lord's word to us that morning—we had no certain job to accomplish; it's all His agenda. I lifted her up in prayer, committing her to His tender care. Thus ended our first full day in Jerusalem.

The next day, Steve took his two sons to walk through King Hezekiah's tunnel (2 Kings 20:20), while the rest of the team went to the Upper Room for prayer and intercession. When we left the Upper Room and came out into the sunshine, we had flecks of gold on our hands. This phenomenon had been happening in our home church, so we were especially pleased that the Holy Spirit saw fit to bless us that same way here in the Upper Room where Jesus had shared the Last Supper with His disciples. We went downstairs to visit David's tomb, and then started our walk down the Via Dolorosa. We only covered a few Stations of the Cross because Sharon had an opportunity to share with a local shopkeeper. That was more important. We then were out of time.

After lunch at Christ Church, the entire team went to the Garden Tomb. No matter how many times you go there, it is always a heart-touching place. I knelt in the tomb in gratitude to my Lord and rededicated my life to Him and His service. We came back into the Old City and went to the Lion's Gate, where Stephen, the first Christian martyr, was stoned to death (Acts 6:8–7:60). At St. Anne's Church, we sang, as everyone does because the acoustics are so marvelous, and prayed at the altar. Then we walked to the Pool of Bethesda, where the lame man was healed (John 5:1–15).

We recommenced our walk down the Via Dolorosa, stopping at each station of the cross. It was a precious, holy time for us, until we got to the Church of the Holy Sepulchre, which contains the last five stations. The team felt the same distaste as I had on my previous visits. This church made me think of the money changers at the Temple with all the hustle and bustle, compared with the gentle, sweet spirit at the Garden Tomb.

That evening we met with the OM Jerusalem team—five beautiful young women. They shared with us their testimonies, their mission, and sang for us. At the conclusion, each one sat in a chair, and we gathered around to pray for them individually. The Lord had words of encouragement for each, until the last young lady. As we prayed, she began to weep uncontrollably. She had to lie down on the sofa because she was so spent. As we continued to intercede, there was a breakthrough, and she was delivered from the curse of abuse she had suffered as a young girl. At last she realized it was not her fault, and she was able to fully receive the Lord's great love for her. Now she could serve Him in and through love, not guilt. This had to be one of the main reasons the Lord brought us here—He wanted her to be free. He says in His Word: "And you shall know the truth, and the truth shall make you free" (John 8:32, NKJV).

The next morning we went to the girls' apartment to take them all the gifts we had brought for them from home. It was like Christmas! We visited just a little while and sadly said our farewells. There were many more miles for us to go in just a short time and, we hoped, more God-appointed meetings to keep.

The Kenneset was closed again, and I accepted that maybe I was not to visit there. We did get to Yad Vashem, the Museum of the Holocaust, which is heart-wrenching no matter how many times you see it. The children had their pictures taken with some of the soldiers there as we visited the gardens. Their parents believed the museum was too harsh at their age, so they did not go inside. Actually, it's too harsh at any age, but it is reality.

We returned to the Western ("Wailing") Wall in the Old City, but this time we went through the Western Wall Tunnels. Shortly after the Six-Day War of Liberation in 1967, the Ministry of Religious Affairs began the project of clearing the Western Wall area. They wanted to expose the full extent of the hitherto-concealed Wall. These excavations revealed the entire length of the Western Wall—all 488 meters—in all its glory. Rooms and public halls were also discovered, along with a section of a second Temple road, a Hasmonean water tunnel, a dam, a pool, a staircase from the Roman period that ascends to Bab al-Ghawanimah Street, and an exit tunnel dug in the mount that exits on Lions Gate Road. We went through the secret passage built as a substructure to support the Street of the Chain above it. The stones of the master course area of the Wall were huge, and people were putting their prayer requests into the cracks. We still had requests we had not been able to put in the exposed Wailing Wall. A kind guard nodded to us in agreement and even held his flashlight for us to see, so we deposited more of our God-mail. This was that part of the Temple area that contained the Holy of Holies, and there was an awesome reverence in this place. I strongly sensed a validation of God's Word, the Jewish heritage, and my own faith.

After dinner that evening at an Armenian restaurant, we returned to the Wailing Wall to deposit and pray over the last of the prayer requests from home. A rabbi was praying with some soldiers, and then the Muslim call to prayer came over the loudspeakers, so I prayed louder and harder. There were wildflowers growing out of the Wall, and the lights shining on it at night made it an unforgettable scene. There is life in this world, and I rejoiced to be a part of it.

The next day we went to the Temple Mount. Part of our mission was to pray over the areas and sites we entered, taking back ground the enemy had taken. In the Al-Aqsa Mosque, Mimi and Steve were holding hands, walking and praying silently. One of the Muslim attendants was quite upset, and he ran up and yelled, "Don't touch!" Steve tried to explain that Mimi was his wife, but in their culture, that did not matter—she was a woman.

There had been talk since we arrived in Jerusalem that unexplained water had been found in certain sites, and because of the prophecy in Ezekiel 47:1–12 concerning the river flowing from the Temple, it was stirring up some excitement among believers. We did not see any water accumulation in the Dome of the Rock, but there were two big water vacuums next to one of the walls. We went outside and continued praying over the entire Temple Mount. Then we gathered together at the point leading to the Eastern Gate, which the Muslims had sealed in 1187 A.D. to prevent the Messiah from entering. We formed two lines facing each other, extending our hands toward the gate to form a welcoming corridor for *Yeshua Ha'Mashiach* (Jesus, the Messiah). Come quickly, Lord Jesus!

We departed for Qumran, where the Dead Sea Scrolls had been discovered. I was blessed to see an exhibit that had been added since my last visit, including a short movie on the Essenes and John the Baptist. We took a dip in the Dead Sea and then went over to a different area of the Ein Gedi. We took a nature walk and saw many ibex along the way. A number of descriptions of the Ein Gedi are found in the Song of Songs by Solomon, such as, "My beloved is to me a cluster of henna blooms In the vineyards of En [Ein] Gedi" (1:14, NKJV). We splashed in a Shulamite pool and played under a small waterfall. Our fun was cut short because Matt, Mimi and Steve's oldest son, fell and hit his head on his way to the big waterfall. We returned to Jerusalem, and he required five stitches. We told him that he must return to Israel someday, because his blood was left there. (I must return because my heart is there!)

That evening at Christ Church, Rabbi Henry Noach, a member of the Conservative Sect of Judaism (not a Messianic Jew), was giving a lecture on Zionism, and our group was invited to attend. He told us that the world is like a human eye: the white part is the ocean, the iris represents the continents, and the pupil is Jerusalem, which reflects the Holy Temple because the eye is focused on Jerusalem. Zionism is a nation with an identity, while Judaism is a religion and a way of life. The Law of Return of Israel states that a Jew is one whose mother is a Jew and not converted to another religion; if they have converted, they no longer want to be a Jew. He said that the firstborn is responsible for the family, and that made me think of Jesus, the firstborn of many brethren (Romans 8:29; Hebrews 1:6). Here was another nugget of truth: Jesus certainly accomplished His responsibilities for the family of God, of which I am a member! He said that God created Adam from the dust of Mount Moriah, and the world developed from that site, making it the navel of the earth. I recalled that Isaiah 51:22-23 says that Jerusalem would be a -cup of trembling- to the nations, and suddenly I could see that Jerusalem actually hits at the world's belly; thus all the contention and strife. The Lord was doing a deep work in me with respect to Jewish heritage and beliefs, helping me understand and showing me new truths. I also experienced another one of those light bulb moments: I should be praying for the rabbis! Once they knew Jesus as Messiah, they would teach their congregations. As we left, I sensed that I had been there before, déjà vu, and I was simply walking God's plan at that moment in time. I was so excited that as I was thanking the rabbi, I impulsively gave him a big hug! I wondered later if I had made him unclean by hugging him on the evening before the Jewish Sabbath.

The team had been keeping a list of faux pas our group had made. Cheryl had been in the lead for crossing her legs at the Wailing Wall, but Mimi and Steve unseated her for holding hands in the Al-Aqsa, and now I was the undisputed champion because I hugged a rabbi!

We hired a guide for a walking tour of the city. He explained the meanings of the various markets and took us to the rooftop of one building, pointing out the significance of the various surrounding buildings. As we walked through the city, the guide showed us places where battles had been fought in the war between Israel and Jordan. Bullet holes pitted the walls. I remarked to the guide that God did a miracle for them in the Six-Day War, and he replied, "Work from below and God sends miracles from above."

Mea Shearim is that section of the city occupied by the ultra-orthodox Jews. They are exempt from military service because of their religion, and this was causing a big controversy since there were at that time thirty thousand who could have been serving. The guide said that these Jews do not want Israel to be a nation because they say God must do it without man's intervention, yet they are protected and subsidized by the government. There are no televisions or magazines, and women must wear their dresses or skirts below the knee. They must follow the rules of their particular rabbi. We saw a huge house they had prepared for the Messiah, but after one year when He did not come, they converted it into a school. It was surprising to me that they were so short on patience.

That evening we participated in a lovely Shabbat ceremony with fellow believers at Christ Church. Scripture was read, songs were sung, the wine and the bread were blessed, and then we had a lovely dinner. After the meal, there was a prayer of thanksgiving, and we were instructed to give "handshakes and hugs! Extend the peace of Yeshua to everyone! Shabbat Shalom!" Our team ended the day with a private time of sharing on our last night in Jerusalem.

After checking out the next morning, we went to the Mount of Olives for camel rides and a last spectacular view of the city. We descended to the Garden of Gethsemane and then proceeded to the Church of St. Peter in Gallicantu ("Cock Crows"), where Peter had denied Christ three times.

We left the city in our van for a beautiful drive to the Stella Carmel Center. I was so glad Billy had come on this trip because he knew the names of every plant, tree, and flower, and Bonnie knew about the historic places, so we had our own tour guides. After lunch at the Center, we went to Muhraqa, situated at the northeast angle of the Mount Carmel range, and the site where Elijah slew the 450 prophets of Baal (1 Kings 18:16–40). On an observation deck, we viewed the Valley of Armageddon, the site of the last battle of the ages. I had an opportunity to share with a man there and gave him a copy of *More Than a Carpenter* by Josh McDowell with the prayer that the Lord would reveal Himself to that man.

We had supper at the Center and then attended the worship service at the Mount Carmel Assembly there on the premises. The sermon was based on Elijah and the Baal prophets, which was most appropriate for us in light of where we just visited. The main point I drew from the sermon was that I must daily die to self, that I must be as a dead woman (Romans 12:1).

After the service, some of us went to Haifa to visit Rosie, a friend and next-door neighbor of David and Terri when they lived in Haifa. She was the only member of her family to survive the Holocaust. When she was eleven, she sat by her mother's dead body for two weeks until an uncle came to get her. She had written a book about her experiences, which I gladly bought, and she autographed it for me. We prayed for her, but she was not a believer. I corresponded with her after I got home, and she wrote me that she had accepted Jesus as her Messiah!

The next day we proceeded to the Galilee. We went to Tabgha, where Jesus fed the five thousand with five loaves and two fishes; and to the Mount of Beatitudes, where Jesus preached His Sermon on the Mount; and then to Capernaum, His base of operations. These were repeat visits for me, but sharing them with the team made it extra-special. Plus I was seeing new things with each visit.

We stopped on the eastern shore of the Sea of Galilee so Jack could swim while the rest of us waded in the water. Steve found a ring on the beach, and while it turned out not to have great monetary value, it was priceless because of the circumstances.

We continued to Yardenit, a popular baptism site on the Jordan River. My special friend Billy baptized me, a spiritual highpoint for me. We went to Tiberias for *The Galilee Experience*, and we put out tracts in strategic places, such as water closets and car windshields. We had dinner by the sea at Marina Sunrise, where we ate a type of fish called "St. Peter's fish." This is the fish Peter caught when Jesus told him to take the money out of the mouth of the first fish and pay his taxes (Matthew 17:27). The fish is served whole, eyes and all, and it is a bit unnerving to eat because the fish seems to be looking at you!

We returned to the Center at Mount Carmel for packing, and to get ready for a 3:30 a.m. departure time. As I reflected on the trip that evening, I realized that if we had just come for the deliverance and freedom for the OM missionary, it would have been worth it. I could also see that Terri had been expanded, shown her leadership capabilities, and she had been especially blessed by the gold in the Upper Room. Bonnie had gotten a taste for missions, and Sharon had received more healing. For Mimi, Steve, and their family, was this a launching out for them?

Surprise! We did leave on time, and upon arrival at Ben Gurion Airport in Tel Aviv, we encountered no problems and had an uneventful departure, all on the same plane. Praise the Lord!

On the flight to London, I made this note in my journal: "My heart carries a sadness today—that loneliness that creeps in on me occasionally. I find that I want to be home."

I read in Matthew concerning the places we had been the day before (Tabgha, the Mount of Beatitudes, baptism in the Jordan). In Matthew 3:3, John the Baptist is described as "the voice of one crying in the wilderness" to prepare the way of the Lord. I felt that as a team and individually we had done that on this mission. We had been all the way around the Sea of Galilee, even swam and waded in it. Jesus was there, and He called us to be fishers of men (Matthew 4:19). I thought about the Mount of Beatitudes and the church there on top of the mountain. We are to be like that—a light that cannot be hidden, shining for Jesus. As I read Matthew 6:25, He confirmed that I am not to worry about my life, but to follow His call in Matthew 6:33 to seek first the kingdom and His righteousness and trust that all the things I need will be added. I also read Matthew 7:24–27 again, "my" scripture about the house on the rock. The Bible becomes so vivid and real once you've walked where Jesus walked!

When we arrived in London, Dick from OM met us and took our luggage to the Manna House in Brownley. We rode the Tube to Piccadilly Circus and had fish and chips for lunch. We took a double-decker red bus tour around the city, but there was no time to get off and visit any of the famous places. I felt no great loss since I had been there before. I did wish my friends could have seen more of the sites, but we were all at the point of exhaustion. We rode the train from Victoria Station to the Manna House for a light supper. This was our last time for sharing, and it was good to hear each person's views. Sharon was especially encouraged when we reminded her of the way she witnessed in the Cardo in Jerusalem.

On our last morning, Steve brought us scones from the local bakery. Then it was off to the airport and our long journey home. I was seated between Steve and Sharon, so there was no need to witness, just relax and enjoy the ride.

We arrived home on June 29, 1999, what would have been my forty-seventh wedding anniversary, but that was dwelling on the past. The Lord had given me beauty for ashes, and my cup was running over (Isaiah 61:3; Psalm 23:5).

Our mission had been accomplished—to His Glory and my delight!

CHAPTER 9
ESTONIA

APR 1996

This mission was the special undertaking of Kathy, worship leader at Atlanta City Church (ACC). She had a close relationship with Dan and Hai, who were missionaries in Estonia. Kathy dreamed of taking a small youth team there who could teach and preach the gospel and be of assistance to the missionaries in their ministry. When the project was presented to the ACC congregation by Alan, the youth pastor, my spirit started jumping up and down, and I knew I was to go on this trip. I certainly was not a youth, but I was graciously accepted by the rest of the team. In addition to Alan and Kathy, Cheryl and I completed the team of adults, and our five teenagers were Scott, Brent, Terée (Kathy's daughter), Christiana, and Jessica. These teenagers were not "kids" but young men and women of God, and I was honored to be serving with them.

On the flight from Atlanta to New York, I sat with Alan, our leader. I first met Alan in the early nineties at a zoning meeting where he was representing ACC and trying to get approval of a neighborhood location for their church. I was impressed then by his integrity and could see the love of Christ in him. When I later joined ACC, my first impression was confirmed.

As we departed New York City, we were leaving behind us dusk (sunset), moving toward light. My prayer was that the Lord would move us closer to the true Light of the World and that His light would shine through us on this mission so that many souls would be saved. I also prayed for the manifestation of healings, signs and wonders. Peter described Jesus as one "who went about doing good" (Acts 10:38). I wanted to be like Jesus, so I covenanted with Him to do all the good I could, trusting Him to do all the good He could through me. Then I praised Him in advance for a glorious mission!

Estonia is the smallest and northernmost of the three Baltic states. It borders on the Gulf of Finland in the north, the Russian Federation in the east, Latvia in the south, and the Baltic Sea on the west. As we flew over the Baltic Sea, huge blocks of ice were beginning to melt and break up—a magnificent sight. We landed in Helsinki, Finland, and took a small plane over the Gulf of Finland into Tallinn. I sat next to a mechanic from Finn Air who said he believed in Jesus. He said that while he didn't go to church much, his wife did, and he was glad we had come. I gave him a tract to read later.

Hai and her son David met us at the airport. We stopped for a lunch of pizza with pickles on top—an Estonian delicacy—and proceeded to Tartu, where we exchanged some money, bought some groceries, and saw some of the city. When we settled into our apartment in Laeva, the teenagers immediately crashed, while the adults talked and shared, focusing on the message of unity in Psalm 133. Two girls from the apartment complex, Kristi and Rita, brought us pussy willows and a box of cookies as welcoming gifts; they would need to meet the youth the next day. Before I fell asleep, I reflected on the beauty I had seen that day—the seas, the ice and snow, and forests of birch and fir trees. It was so different from the warmth of spring and green pine trees I had left back home.

The next day the youth went out with Kristi and Rita to call on the neighbors and invite them to church, while the ladies went to what we called the local "Wal-Kroger-Mart." We walked around the neighborhood greeting the people and playing with the children. Hai and David took us to lunch at TarBurger, and I was beginning to see that Estonians love fried foods. This was not to be my healthiest trip, food-wise. Beside the TarBurger was a huge hill that Jessica and Scott slid down. The snow was a delight to our kids, especially Scott, who originally came from Florida.

Hai took us to her house for a briefing. They were starting a Bible college that September with thirty students, but it had to be under government control. She told us that our beautiful Kristi's mother, a teacher, was an alcoholic with three children, each of whom had a different father, and she was now married to seven-month old Martin's father. Her teaching salary was $7.50 per month. Hai said that many children go all day to school with no food and cry from hunger. Parents have no money to pay for three meals, served at a cost of eighty cents per day. That information put a new light on the value of the pussy willows and cookies Kristi gave us as welcome presents on our first night in Estonia!

Our first church service was in the auditorium of the primary school in Laeva, and we had approximately fifty people in attendance. Our youth did a mime presentation, Jessica gave her testimony, and Scott sang "After God's Own Heart," preceded by his short testimony. Alan spoke about how we are blessed to be a blessing to others. At first it seemed there would be little altar response, but as we lingered, several came for prayer. The Holy Spirit sweetly ministered to their needs through us.

Then it was back to TarBurger, where I had hot dog soup. Hai gave us more insight into the histories of the different people we were meeting so we could understand their plights. The youth were pepped up, so there was dancing and more playing in the snow to let off steam.

Our next day was Saturday, and we had three church services scheduled. Our first stop was Kauski, the poorest of the churches, with 80 percent of the congregation unemployed. They had no pastor and have to wait for Hai and Dan to come when they can. Jessica shared first, and then I gave the message, giving my testimony and stressing that they must never quit, because our God does come in the fullness of His time. We had been told that Estonians were stoic, but I was touched by their emotional response. I prayed with several ladies for healing, and as I looked around, the team was praying for others as well, so that almost every person present received ministry. No one wanted to be left out. These precious people gave us gifts of flowers and chocolate candy, and one lady for whom I prayed gave me a beautiful dyed egg! I knew this was a great sacrifice for them and prayed the Lord would give them a hundredfold return.

Our next stop was Aarna, where approximately thirty people packed into a small room. Their pastor played a mean guitar. This was a charismatic bunch, so there was a lot of praise and worship. Christiana shared and Kathy gave a timely message on worship. At the conclusion, several wanted prayer for healing, and we ministered as long as time permitted.

We proceeded to Krootuse, where we visited a church that met in a school and had the same pastor as Aarna. Terée and Brent shared, and Cheryl spoke on the ability to hear God. Many children were walking around during the service, so Hai had them come to the front and sit with her. She started to address their parents about this lack of discipline, but discovered they had no parents there. They had been sent to the church to get them out of the house so their parents could continue their drinking. Alcoholism was an epidemic in this country! The team ministered to those who came forward; a lady for whom I prayed said she felt "warmth" all over her body. If ever a people needed miracles, signs and wonders, it was these people. It would take the mighty hand of God to stop this vicious cycle of poverty and attendant alcoholism.

It was Easter Sunday! I had felt in my spirit that I was to speak at the first service, but during our morning meeting, Alan did not give me that assignment, so I kept silent, especially since I had spoken the day before. Kathy, Cheryl, and I rode in the car with Hai, while Alan and the youth were in a separate van. We were almost at our destination when Alan signaled for us to stop. He ran to the car and asked if I would give the message. Of course I would! This really bolstered my faith, as it confirmed that I had heard from God, and so had Alan. The service was in a home in Toolama, which our host and hostess (husband and wife) inherited from the wife's mother. The wife, who also served as the pastor, said her mother had shared with her a vision of people worshipping God in her home. The house was filled with mostly older women and only one man, our host. After Kathy read scripture, I taught on John 20 about Mary Magdalene coming to the tomb on that first Easter morning, focusing on how very special we are to our Lord. Many of the women wanted prayer for salvation for their families, especially their sons; another wanted her marriage restored; another asked to be filled with the Holy Spirit, and, of course, He obliged! A mother there with her two children said she needed strength. The Holy Spirit revealed that she and the children had been abused by her husband, so she received intensive prayer and was filled with the Lord's peace. Sadly, there were two other women who were in abusive, alcoholic relationships, and they were covered in love and prayer. We even had one salvation! The Lord moved in resurrection power that Easter morning; the tears and the love flowed to His glory. I would say unequivocally that it was one of the best Easters I ever had!

Lunch was in Tartu, and it was interesting. The people were very friendly, and outside amidst all the snow, lovely flowers were being sold by vendors on tables lining the streets. Alan presented Hai with a rose bouquet, a continuation of our blessed Easter Day.

Jakko met us when we got back to the apartment; he wanted us to visit the center where he lived with approximately fifteen other men, who were all active members of the Laeva Church. Two families served as house parents. The men were recently released from prison, and they were trying to learn job skills, overcome alcoholism, and speak English. One clever way they were learning English was by singing worship choruses.

Our youth had been teaching three of the local girls, Reeleka, Kristi, and Sveta, along with Jakko, how to mime. They came to our apartment to get into their mime makeup for church that night at Laeva. We discovered that Aljonas was actually Sveta's sister, and that their relationship was not very cordial. Kathy did a makeover on Aljonas (a little mascara, lip gloss, and a feminine hairdo) and the transformation was miraculous; she was shining inside and out! Also, Sveta was feeling very good about herself, with her mime makeup and all the attention she had received from our youth. These girls' parents were alcoholics and had been removed from their home, so these young ladies were carrying quite a load.

The worship service was awesome. Jakko and the girls performed flawlessly, to the delight of their congregation. Christiana sang the "Heartbeat of Our Mission," Jessica read scripture and gave a short testimony, and Terée spoke poignantly about hurts she had experienced. There was good response to the altar call, and Sveta, Kristi, and one of the men from the ministry center received the baptism of the Holy Spirit!

After our TarBurger supper, we returned to the apartment to be gloriously entertained by Brent and Scott, a very joyful and hilarious ending to a glorious day.

We had no scheduled services the next day, which was Monday, so we had more time for a team devotional, Bible study, and prayer. Brent shared how the Lord had changed him, enabling him to love his father despite all the pain he had caused him. The way adults injure their children must surely grieve the Holy Spirit; I know it grieves me.

We drove into Tallin, the capital of Estonia, for some sightseeing. We had flown into Tallin on our arrival but did not have time to visit, so this was a treat. We went to a park on the Gulf of Finland, where we saw huge ships, ferry boats, swans, mallards, and little sea gulls, and there was still a lot of ice and snow. The city dates back to the eleventh century, and there are massive rock walls, fortress spires, historic churches, and, of course, the big city plaza. I had to laugh when I saw McDonald's, but I did give them some business! The team continued to divide, and I found myself with Alan, Cheryl, and Leihold, who was an excellent guide. He gave us much insight into the history of the city, especially that section called, quite appropriately, the Old City. I bought a watercolor print of birch trees from a local artist, and I still love looking at it today and remembering the beauty of Estonia. I considered it a golden day, a gift from God. I wanted to do something for Him, so I handed out lots of tracts!

We collected Dan at the airport, and he shared with us glowing reports of his very successful trip to the U.S.A. Hai was thrilled to have her husband by her side once more. She carries a big load when he is not there.

Back in our little home, everyone was a bit punchy and it didn't take much to set off the giggles. The washer was broken, so Scott and Brent were taking their jeans out to put them in the dryer. Alan was videotaping, and he zoomed in on the bathroom floor, which was covered in black hair from Kathy's haircut. Brent joked, saying that it was where she had shaved her legs! I wondered what our folks back home would say when they saw all these antics. Is this what missionaries do? Yes, among other things!

It was Tuesday and back to work! Our devotional was led by Christiana, and the other girls read psalms about the brokenhearted. I was amazed at their spiritual depth. We traveled to Viljandi and had a very nice lunch with Ester and Peeter, who together pastor the church where we met later that night. The team split into two groups, one to do street ministry and invite people to come to the evening service; the other, including Pastor Ester, David (Hai's son), Maia (our translator and guitar player), the teens, and me, to minister in the handicapped children's hospital. The youth did their mimes and gave their testimonies, and I used the Wordless Book, a book with pages of different colors, to present the gospel. At the conclusion, I gave them the opportunity to invite Jesus into their hearts, and many little hands were raised. I prayed they understood, but only the Holy Spirit knows and He'll take care of the details. The youth concluded the service with more songs, at which time the children got up, danced, and sang with them. We were inundated with hugs; one little boy put his arms around me and actually lifted me off the floor. Simultaneously to our ministry in the hospital, the other team was ministering to people on the street. Five young boys accepted Christ as their Savior. Jesus was showing us how He loves the little children!

After finishing at the hospital, David, the teens, and I went to the school, the site of the evening service. In the gym, some Estonian youth were playing basketball, so we watched, and after the game the female coach came over and invited our youth to play volleyball. She put some of the Estonians on our side as well, and they had fun playing together. Afterwards she gave me enough Olympic pins for everyone. Talk about bridge-building! There is a saying that goes "Make a friend, be a friend, and bring your friend to Christ." We made friends that day in the hospital, in the gym, and on the streets. We extended our hearts to them, and they extended theirs to us. The kingdom had been advanced.

At the service, Kathy and Maia sang "I Sing Praises to Your Name." The congregation requested that they sing it again, and as they sang, the people stood to their feet and lifted their hands in praise. After our youth did a mime skit, Alan preached. When he gave the altar call, many came forward for prayer to be saved, healed, and delivered from bondage. A glorious ending to a glorious day!

The following morning, Scott led our devotions, focusing on the mercy of God. We had praise and sharing time in preparation for two services that day in Viljandi.

The first service was actually in a real church building! Pastor Reio and other Spirit-filled members of the congregation had left another church and planted this one. We recognized some of the members from other meetings we had, and it was good to see old friends. The church was in a new building, with a wooden altar, candles burning, and a very high lectern; there were big windows with sunlight bringing the outside indoors. Pastor Reio even wore a robe, so I felt like I was in "high church." Brent shared his message so eloquently, and pastor told him later that he had a call on his life to be a preacher—a bridge between America and Estonia. This was an encouragement to this wounded young man, and, I am sure, the words came straight from the mouth of God to the ear of the pastor.

I was amazed when I was asked to preach—me, standing in that high and lifted up position! I talked about Paul's shipwreck; how our Lord carries us through the storms of life in order to accomplish His purpose in us. I stressed that we did not come to them as Americans, saying they had to do things our way, but we came to preach Jesus Christ and Him crucified. The altar call was tremendous! We didn't have enough translators, but many in the congregation spoke English, so ministry was everywhere. One woman who was deaf in one ear received her hearing. There was a lady in a purple coat who had arthritis in her left hand, and I asked if she had unforgiveness in her heart. Gozelle translated for me as I shared scriptures, and then the lady prayed, forgiving a certain person who had offended her and asking forgiveness for herself. Then I prayed and asked the Lord for her healing; however, the van was about to leave me, so I had to give her a quick hug and run. I wanted so desperately to stay, but I trusted the Lord to finish what He started and what only He could do.

On the way to our second service at the Word of Life Church, we passed by a logging truck that was stuck in the snow, so our men helped while the youth played in the snow (they did that at every opportunity). The day started off rather warm and pleasant. However, the temperature was dropping, and it was beginning to snow. We met Pastor Reio at the church, which was located on the second floor of an old building, and we divided into small teams for street ministry. We were to minister as the needs dictated, give out tracts, and invite people to the evening service. I was with Christiana, Scott, and Enno. Some of the people refused to talk with us, but one elderly man prayed for salvation! We had an interesting conversation with a man who had fought in Afghanistan, and he asked, "Where was God then?" He said his mother and grandmother were believers. He did not want to pray with us, but he promised he would come to the evening service—and he did! He also brought his wife and a friend. When he saw me that night, he came to me and kissed my hand! Kathy and Maia sang, the youth did their mimes, and then Kathy preached on the love of God. It seemed everyone in the room wanted prayer, and one young man wanted Jesus to come into his heart. Several women came to me who had problems similar to those in my past. I was able to comfort them by the same comfort I had been comforted by God (2 Corinthians 1:4). One lady asked about why I was anointing them with oil, so I explained and then gave her my oil to use when she prays for others. The Holy Spirit moved in this upper room, and it was exciting to be a part of it.

Jessica led our devotions the next morning, sharing about abiding in the Vine. It was an encouraging word as we were nearing the end of the mission. I, for one, needed the reminder that as we continued to abide in Him, He would bring forth fruit in our lives (John 15:5). Blessed assurance!

We went to Tartu, the second largest city in Estonia, for shopping. The market was unique in that all the meat was exposed, not prepackaged, like at home. There were pigs' heads laid out on tables, snouts and all, plus eggs, fruit, and vegetables. After the market we went to the department store, which had three floors, and there I purchased souvenir gifts for my family. Most of the team ate at

McDonalds, but Hai, Alan, Gozelle, and I ate an Estonian meal. Our youths were too tired, so instead of going into the old part of the city, we returned to the apartment for some rest. This was a very wise decision in light of what we encountered that evening.

Hai ministered regularly at the men's prison in Viljandi, and she had received permission for us to hold a service that night. When we walked in, I was hit with a burden of intercession. There was such oppression in this place. There were approximately forty men in attendance. The youth sang and did mimes, but the men were not interested in their message; they only wanted to glare at our girls, making them very uneasy. Alan had the girls move to the back of the room and over to the side. Brent spoke first, pouring out his heart, and a few men tried to leave, while the rest were laughing and talking. He then introduced Scott, who was very concise and to the point. At the end of his message, he knelt down on the floor and prayed for them. This act of humility turned the tide. The men got quiet and the jesting stopped. The team divided into small groups, including the girls now, and we went to talk with the men. In my little group, I asked if they had questions about America, which broke the ice. One young man asked about the cross I was wearing, and that opened the door for the gospel. One man prayed for salvation, and the one who was listening so intently behind him prayed also. Some of the men tried to intimidate the ones who were making decisions, but I would keep praying and standing between them. One young man was Russian, but one of the guards could speak Russian, so he translated for me. The man said he believed in evolution, and I replied, "Then why are there still monkeys?" The conversation continued, and then the guard, who was a believer, began witnessing directly to the young man. The young man concluded that we had a point and that he wanted to think about these things, and he walked away. The girls said the men were asking why Jesus was important to them, and they were bold and sincere in their responses. Hai was especially encouraged, for this was the first breakthrough she had seen with the men, and now Maia and Gurlie, who also had been trying to get permission to minister there, agreed to work with her. By the time we left the prison, hostility had turned into hospitality, and doors had been opened.

However, the Lord wasn't finished. We went to a coffee shop that was packed with more teenagers. Some of us handed out tracts, and then our youth started talking with them about Jesus. Three of the locals could speak a little English, and we stayed a couple of hours. Some of them walked (or slid) with us to our van, as the street had turned into a sheet of ice. Here was more bridge building!

Some of the team had been praying and singing songs about snow in hopes that we would be snowed in and could stay longer. I confess I was not a part of that group. I wanted to complete the mission, do all the Lord had called us to do, and go home to springtime in Georgia, my family, and my oasis in the woods. On the way home, we had a snow detour! A strong gust of wind blew our van off the road, causing us to slide into a bank of snow. Our guys tried to dig us out, to no avail. People were stopping to help, and finally a big truck came, and those drivers, plus our guys, got us back on the road. We had some minor bumps and bruises, but so much for which to praise the Lord at the end of that day!

I wrote in my journal that night:

Each day we've said, "This has been the best one," but each day has had its own particular flavor. Each part has been an important part of the whole. The more dramatic [experiences] were the children's hospital and the prison, but the Lord also loves the lady with unforgiveness and arthritis in her hand and the little old ladies who are concerned about their children being saved. Each one is a concern of the Father; each one is important. I feel this team is a body of Christ. Sometimes we're used as a main part that can be seen, other times an uncomely part that cannot be seen, but nevertheless, important. It takes all the parts working together to make the body function properly and fulfill its mission. My heart's desire is that our Lord be pleased, well satisfied, with this mission.

Kathy cooked us a scrumptious breakfast the next morning, and then Alan led us in a debriefing session. He posed some questions that provoked emotional responses: Do you feel this mission was a success? What's going to happen when you go home? What needs did you see here? What has God done in your life? Undeniably, we had all been stretched, and our hearts had been through a grinder. For many of the group, especially the youth, this was a launching pad.

The plan was to go out into the streets and invite people to come to our evening meeting at the church there in Laeva. Instead, the neighborhood youth came to our apartment to eat, of course, and sing and practice mimes for their drama that night. These kids were like thirsty flowers, soaking up all the love they were missing at home, and then opening up, blooming, and flourishing. It was beautiful to behold!

After an early supper at the TarBurger, we went to the school for our third and final service in Laeva. Jessica sang, and then the local youth did their mime skit to the delight of all, especially their own congregation. They were pleased with themselves, and rightly so. Christiana shared and Scott preached.

We had a smaller group that night, but many came forward for prayer. After the ministry ended, the church gave us a love offering of twenty-two dollars. Knowing what a sacrifice this was for them, we were overwhelmed. Dan had us form a circle, holding hands and singing "I Love You With the Love of the Lord." What a lovely way to end our time with these new brothers and sisters in Christ who were outstanding examples of agape love!

The youth, ours and theirs, went back to the TarBurger, while Kathy, Cheryl, and I returned to the apartment. Jakko, Rita, and Sveta came with us for soup and cookies. We enjoyed a chill-down time and exchanged addresses so we could keep in touch.

Terée led our devotion the next morning, encouraging us to use our talents to move forward the kingdom of God and not lose our focus on this last day of ministry. Dan collected us early for a long ride to Valga, situated on the Latvian border. The local pastor and some members from his church met us, and we divided into small teams for street ministry. I was with Alan, Hilga (local), and our translator, Reite. Alan prayed with a young boy named Mark while I prayed with Nicolai, eighty-seven years old, who was lonely and wanted to talk; his eyesight was failing and he was unable to read, so he needed a special blessing. I was delighted to pray with Larisa, in her sixties, who accepted Jesus as her Lord and Savior and who also came to the service that night. Alexandrais, also in her sixties, was gloriously saved that night also. I felt especially close to these two ladies because they were my age, and they didn't need to be wasting any more years. I talked with two young ladies, but they wanted to pray when they were alone. However, the one with the beautiful red hair had tears streaming down her face, so the Holy Spirit was doing a work in her heart. I was sad that her friend was holding her back. One man said he was a Pentecostal preacher, and another man, who came on a motorcycle, did not want to talk at first, but then his heart melted and we had a good conversation. We gave out many tracts, and some said they would come to the service, while others declined our tracts, much less talking with us. I refused to be daunted by the rejections because there were two for sure who had come into the kingdom, and our Lord wasn't finished with the other seed that had been planted.

After lunch at the Conspirator Baar (I never understood that name), we drove to the border to make a short excursion into Latvia. Meanwhile, Scott, Terée, and Leigho responded to the invitation of an official with the border guards to visit in his home and talk with his son about Jesus. There was a lot of hassle at the border crossing, which consumed a lot of our time, so we decided Latvia would have to wait.

Our translator, Reite, said that we were bold, and Estonians are not accustomed to that. We had prayed for boldness, but we had to be careful not to be arrogant or rude. We wanted to catch fish, not repulse them.

The best word to describe our service at the Valga Word of Life Church would be wow! Two of the local young ladies led in worship, then Christiana sang, Terée shared, and our youth did two mimes (without their makeup, which they forgot to bring). Alan spoke, and at the altar call, the spirit of laughter fell. The worship leaders, plus three of our teens, were doubling over with joy. I prayed with a woman for healing, and she wanted strength to live victoriously for Jesus. Larisa, the Russian lady who accepted Christ that afternoon on the street, wanted prayer for healing of her arthritic hands. Marika, a young woman who had throat problems and trouble speaking, was slain in the Spirit and laughter fell on her. She got up, and when I reached out simply to touch her, she fell out again and started saying over and over, "Iteh [thank You], Jesus! Praise the Lord; Hallelujah!" Dan then prayed for the team, giving us words from the Lord. I had secretly wondered if this would be my last mission because of my age, and part of the word for me was, "The Lord isn't finished; you are not at an end, but there are more nations to visit…a triple anointing…to minister to the lonely and broken hearted." These words penetrated my spirit to the core. My Lord knew my heart, and He cared. Wasn't it just like Him to end our mission with His stamp of approval?

The local children and Gozelle came to the apartment at 6:00 a.m. to eat breakfast with us and say final goodbyes. This was extremely difficult, and to say there were a lot of tears would be an understatement. All of these children had empty love tanks, and they were in desperate need of nurturing. I just kept praying over and over in my heart, "Lord, please send people to love them. Please touch their parents and save them. Oh, Lord, help!"

When we pulled away in our vans, they ran behind us waving and shouting. I remembered a similar departure in Peru, and it hurt just as bad.

The ride to Tallin was a bit subdued. We saw several storks on a pond, and there were some nests on chimneys, signaling that spring was on its way. At the airport, I felt a sadness as we left Estonia. They were the only Baltic nation to gain their independence without war. I wondered what the future had in store for them. Was their freedom only temporary? What about the children? What about this epidemic of alcoholism and hopelessness? "Lord, send more laborers. Do you want me to return?"

The short hop to Helsinki was uneventful, and at last we were on the plane for the long flight home to Atlanta, via New York City. So much had happened during the past eleven days, and there was much to ponder in my heart.

We arrived in Atlanta to the hugs and cheers of our families and friends from ACC. While it was good to be home, I was not quite in sync. I remembered a story about some missionaries in Africa who hired some tribesmen to carry their supplies through the jungle. The missionaries were in a hurry and kept rushing the men, until one day the men abruptly stopped in the middle of the trail and sat down. When asked why they had stopped, they replied that their spirits needed to catch up to their bodies. That was how I felt—my spirit was in Estonia, and my body was in Atlanta. I needed some time for them to connect.

CHAPTER 10
MY FIRST JOURNEY
TO REYNOSA, MEXICO

JUN 1998

My dear friend David founded Looking Unto Jesus Ministries Inc. after his retirement, and one of his main mission projects has been Maranatha Iglesia de Dios in Reynosa, Mexico, a church pastored by the Reverends Daniel and Adamina. They were pastors in a Protestant church for thirteen years, but were asked to leave because of controversy with respect to their preaching topics. The Lord instructed them to build another church in Reynosa, and in six months they had the money (six million pesos, equivalent to seven thousand dollars). However, the seller swindled them, selling them land that belonged to his sister and then running to the United States. Thereafter they bought two lots and a house for 60 million pesos, the money coming in from people who had earlier wanted to help them when they were ready to buy a home. After they had been there for nine years, they tore down the wooden church they had built and sold the lumber, which was quite timely because one week later a hurricane came and leveled the buildings all around them. At the time of this mission, their new building was less than one year old and still under construction; they hoped to have the first floor completed by the following September. Members of their congregation were helping with the work and doing various projects to raise money.

They are an amazing family. Danny sings, plays the guitar, preaches, and has a local radio show; Adamina is a mover and a shaker, as well as a dynamic speaker, full of enthusiasm and great wisdom. I just wanted to sit at her feet. Their son David and daughter, Abigail, also sing and play the guitar, and their eldest son, Elijah, plays drums. They are all fluent in English and are excellent translators—not just with the words, but with emotions.

David takes small teams to Reynosa, usually only five or six, because housing is limited to the pastor's home. Our team consisted of Sammy, Jeff, Julie, Seth, David, and me. Julie and Seth had just graduated high school, and they were filled with that vibrant excitement of youth. We flew from Atlanta into Houston, where we transferred, and then had another hour flight into McAllen, Texas, where Adamina met us with the van. When we walked out of the airport, we were hit with one-hundred-degree heat. There had been no rain for six months, and the hot wind was blowing dust that covered everything and everyone. The people were very warm and friendly, and the children were exceptionally beautiful. They more than compensated for the hostile weather conditions.

Our first service was held that evening. Due to the construction work, all services at Maranatha were held in the front yard of Danny and Adamina's home, which was next door to the church. The worship music was awesome. In some supernatural way, the Spanish language lends itself to glorious praise. Jeff, who doesn't like to fly but came anyway, preached while Adamina translated. At the altar call, many came forward for prayer. Several were slain in the Spirit and just laid out on the ground. There were at least four salvations, and one lady for whom I prayed received healing of her arm. The team was ministering to what seemed to be the entire congregation of approximately thirty-five people. They had come expecting, and they were not disappointed.

Our next day (Friday) was a full day of ministry. We started out with communion and breakfast, then hit the streets of the neighborhood. It was very hot, and the wind was blowing; David said it was like being sand-blasted! In one home, a father and his daughter accepted Christ, and later we met the son on the street, and he also was saved. In another home, a woman named Fostina was ill, so we prayed for her healing. (She came to church that night and testified that she was well). At a little grocery store, we prayed with Nicholas for his salvation, a wife wanted prayer for her husband to be saved, and another woman needed deliverance. The Holy Spirit had certainly preceded us and gave us a fruitful morning.

We went to the mall for lunch and to get some groceries. Jeff pointed out a pregnant lady who seemed to be nauseated. He bought her a drink, and I sat with her while he went to get Adamina because we were having language problems. I speak *muy poco* ("very little") Spanish. Adamina came, led her to the Lord, and arranged to get her a ride home.

I had the honor of preaching that night, and once again the altar was full. One situation in particular was very painful. A little girl, maybe ten years old, was heartbroken because her father had left home two months previously. As we talked, I found myself crying with her. Afterwards, her mother shared with me, and we prayed together. After service each night, the youth moved all the chairs and set up for volleyball, so we invited them to stay for supper and games. After three tortillas and a lot of fun, the girl was laughing and playing.

It was Saturday, so after communion and breakfast we went to the market. The park was full of vendor booths and the streets were packed with people shopping. It was colorful and joyful, just like the people of Mexico. My cup was running over!

On our way to the children's jail for ministry (ages 7–17) that afternoon, Adamina told us that there would be nothing for their supper, so the team put together some money and stopped at a local grocery store to get food for sandwiches, cookies, and drinks. I already had some candy and David had Bibles, so we were in good shape. We prepared the food, ate, and visited with the kids. Julie and Seth, our teenagers, gave their testimonies, and I presented the gospel to approximately five girls and nineteen boys. Nine came forward for salvation, and we prayed with them individually. I had to fight back tears when we left!

At the evening service back at the church, Julie and Jeff shared and Sammy preached. He had formerly been a pastor, and there was a dynamic altar call and response. I could sense the heavens opened above us, and the glory came down; I was staggering as I ministered. People were delivered, saved, and filled with the Holy Spirit. Even little children were laying out on the ground under the power of the Spirit.

We had a Father's Day party after the service with balloons, games, prizes, and supper for all! One mother was raising money for their building fund by selling mollies (frozen juices). I was one of her best customers because it was so hot. They only cost one peso, and it was a very good cause!

On Sunday, the only ministry scheduled was the evening service. After breakfast and communion, we had prayer for Adamina, who had a sore throat, and Seth, who had a fever, nausea, and sinus congestion. The team rested all day—reading, praying, napping, and sweating! The heat seemed to sap our energy; I could see why our friends south of the border take siestas.

We had a powerful evening service! A local group played and sang, including David and Abigail. There were fifteen guitars, which made the praise glorious. I wondered, are all Mexicans born with the gift to play the guitar and sing? It seemed so! After testimonies by some of the locals and our team and a time of preaching the Word, there was again that warm response at the altar. An entire family came forward together. The husband and wife wanted wisdom in raising their children, two boys and a girl, ages three, eight, and eleven. We prayed for them all, and they were all slain in the Spirit. This was our last night, so we made sure all who wanted ministry received, and they did. We had supper at midnight!

Suddenly it was Monday and time to go home. Pastor Danny gave each of us an audio cassette of his music, and then Adamina drove us to the airport in McAllen. Thankfully, we got through the border with no inspection. On the trip from McAllen to Houston, I sat next to Mary, a young lady from Portland who was very active in her church. From Houston to Atlanta, I sat next to Julia, a young woman on her way to Atlanta from Los Angeles for a seminar. As I shared with her about our mission, she said she felt a strong conviction that she needed to rededicate her life to the Lord and get back into church. I asked, "Why not now?" She agreed that it was time, so I prayed with her. She was so happy, thanking me over and over. I reminded her that the Holy Spirit was the one who arranged this divine appointment.

It was good to be back home, as always, yet I was sad to say farewell to this anointed team. We had been about our Father's business, and the more He used us to bless others, the more blessed we were—an endless cycle of love. Still, there was so much more we could have done if we just had more time. Surely the cry of every missionary's heart is for more time.

CHAPTER 11
MY SECOND JOURNEY
TO REYNOSA, MEXICO

APR 2000

Almost two years had passed, and I found myself returning to Reynosa, Mexico. David was again our leader, and the remainder of the team consisted of George and his fifteen-year-old son Caleb, sixteen-year-old Eden, and two pastors, Louie and Robert. As on the first trip, we met at the Atlanta airport, flew into Houston, and from there went to McAllen, where Pastor Danny and Eduardo collected us for the drive across the border into Reynosa.

We roomed at the parsonage, but Pastor Adamina arranged for us to have our meals in different neighborhood homes so we could build closer relationships with these warm, loving, generous people. We knew it was a sacrifice for them, but they took joy in giving.

Our first stop was lunch at Gloria's house with some of her friends. After a delicious meal, we had a time of sharing and prayer. Adamina and George were slain in the Spirit—laid out on the floor—and my left arm was shaking uncontrollably. I was so excited! If just lunch was this powerful, what did the Lord have planned for the rest of this mission? I wrote later in my journal: "I thank You, Lord, for the shaking, the visible sign that You are in me! All these guys are mighty men of God. I want to be a vessel for You, not to glorify me, but that Your children can be totally saved—

body, soul and spirit. That this would be a jubilee weekend to Your glory to advance Your Kingdom."

The church had completed their first floor, so we were able to hold services there instead of in Danny and Alamina's front yard. We had young ladies who played tambourines, plus gifted musicians with their guitars, and the worship was precious each time we met. At the service that evening, David had the team introduce themselves. Eden sang a song in Spanish, Caleb gave his testimony, and George preached. When the altar call was given, the people quickly responded. The entire team was ministering, and I prayed with one lady whose daughter was in an abusive marriage; another woman needed healing in her shoulder and the Lord graciously did that for her. We also prayed that her two sons would come to Christ. There were so many needs, but we have a great, big God!

Supper was at the home of Ignacio, who had been saved the week before. He was not wasting any time! Maria walked us there. The house was full, and our host and his lovely wife made sure we were fed first. I felt like royalty! This was New Testament Christianity, there was always prayer and we enjoyed "breaking bread from house to house… [eating] with gladness and singleness of heart" (Acts 2:46).

Friday, our first full day, was a blockbuster day.

Gerardo Sr. brought his two sons, Ramon and Gerardo Jr., to the parsonage to have communion and eat breakfast with us. The boys had run away from home, but after some sharing, George led them to the Lord and then prayed with the father, who rededicated his life to the Lord. After they left, George, son Caleb, and Eden went to play *béisbol* ("baseball") with the neighborhood kids. George was a youth leader in his church, and his heart was especially soft toward their needs; the kids understood this love connection.

Meanwhile, David, Robert, Louie, and I made two house calls. The first was to visit Salía, who was grieving over the miscarriage of her baby just four days earlier. Robert shared how he and his wife had also lost a baby, and I shared about the loss of my grandson, Jason. Salía prayed to come back to the Lord, and we also prayed with her mother-in-law, Maricela, who was already a Christian. It never ceases to astonish me how our Lord matches people up in ministry situations, just as is described in 2 Corinthians 1:4. I've seen Him do it again and again, but still it is amazing each time.

Our second visit was to the home of Arnulfo and his sister, Celanna, who were also Christians. His problem was hypocrites in the church. They said they would come to church that night, but Robert had an excellent word for him from John 21 right then.

Then we had another awesome lunch experience. This was as good as church! We had a delicious meal at Marie Luisa's home with her and several friends. After we ate, Adamina shared some great healing stories. We prayed with six people to receive Christ, and almost everyone there was slain in the Spirit. Artamio had back surgery several years earlier and was still having pain. We prayed over him, he was delivered, and the pain left; he could not stop crying for joy. We also prayed for Lubénia, his wife, who was healed of headaches. Their daughter Lisetta had prayed for salvation, so this entire family was healed, delivered, and saved!

It was thrilling to see Caleb and Eden, our teenagers, leading people to Christ and to the infilling of the Holy Spirit.

Eden shared at the evening service, and Robert preached on the resurrection. Artamio gave testimony about his healing and deliverance that afternoon. The altar was filled with people who were already saved but wanted more. The Holy Spirit filled them up and then laid them down! How I prayed that our churches back home would experience that move of the Holy Spirit. Oh, Lord, let the walls come down!

We had a very late supper at Manuel and Lipido's home in Reynosa. She is Adamina's sister, and they are on-fire believers. It was good to have a nice meal, sharing time, and to just unwind from the incredible day.

We began our Saturday with breakfast at the home of Raquel, a lawyer and special education teacher. She was a beautiful woman, inside and out, and the mother of two sons, one of whom had Down's syndrome. Her husband was a doctor, but he could not cope and had left home; she was heartsick. She had been saved only a short time, and this was a challenge to her faith. I was able to share my similar testimony with her and encouraged her to persevere and stay close to her family of God. We had a sweet prayer time with her, and I could feel her pain—been there, done that— and it still hurts. She was very faithful to attend the services at church, where she was covered in hugs, love, and prayer each time she came.

Then it was off to the youth jail, and I was pleased that the population was down in number: only eleven boys this time. Eden and Caleb shared, and George spoke. All eleven prayed the salvation prayer, but there was one that seemed questionable to me. When I asked him, he said that he didn't have Jesus in his heart. Adamina came over and I told her the situation. She explained in detail to him the gospel message, and I told him that I wanted to see him in heaven, so then he prayed in earnest. He seemed pleased that someone really cared about him, and I was so glad the Holy Spirit gave me discernment to see the truth. This was one Satan would not get!

We had lunch at a lovely member's house, whose name I did not record. Three of her daughters were there, plus their many children, and we had such fun. One daughter had never accepted Christ, so she prayed for salvation; another daughter thought she was pregnant, so we had special prayer for her; and the third daughter also wanted prayer, and as we prayed, they all received the baptism of the Holy Spirit. This precious mother blessed us with her hospitality, and the Lord in turn blessed all of her daughters. You can't out-give God!

That evening I gave a longer version of my testimony per David's request, and then he preached. There was tremendous response at the altar. Everyone wanted prayer, a touch from the Lord. We had to step over people in order to minister. Adamina fell out, and the congregation came to encircle and pray for her; she stayed out for a very long time. She had been suffering from kidney stones and said she knew they had been removed. Raquel, our hostess for breakfast that morning, came forward for prayer and encouragement, and I was delighted to see her commitment to walk this out to victory.

It was very late, but we went back to Manuel's for enchiladas. We were all pumped up, and it was such fun to celebrate with these special friends. They never seemed to run out of energy.

It was Sunday, our final full day of ministry. The team helped clean the church for the morning service and prepared the elements for communion. My job also was to heat tortillas and mash avocadoes for the guacamole for breakfast. (Mexican food is so yummy!) This kind of practical ministry is just as important as the spiritual ministry.

George, Caleb, and Eden had to leave for home at noon, so David had them share first during the service so they could take their leave quietly. Poor Eden didn't want to leave, so it was a very "wet" goodbye. We had communion and then Robert preached. There was a good response at the altar, and I was glad to see Raquel come forward again; she was continuing to press into the kingdom, and I knew that the Lord would not fail her. She could not come back that night for the evening service because one of her sons had a ball game (sounded like America), so I told her good-bye and promised to keep her in my prayers.

Pastor Danny drove us to Norma's house for lunch, and his daughter Abigail served as our interpreter. Norma had a beautiful baby girl named Genesis, and Hortensia, her mother was there, along with a few other friends and neighbors. Norma was contemplating leaving her husband because he was physically abusive and would not work. She wanted her husband to be saved and delivered, and she needed wisdom and guidance. We had a sweet time of prayer for everyone, but we especially centered on Norma because the need was so great.

At our last evening service, David, Robert, and I shared briefly, and Louie preached. Again, the altar was full, and our team of four was very busy. I personally prayed for two people for salvation, one for healing, and many for the infilling of the Holy Spirit. The harvest was great!

Supper was a continuation of the church service. We went to Maria Louisa's house for the second time, and there were lots of people. Three neighbors and their two daughters had been invited, and they prayed for salvation and also asked for the infilling of the Holy Spirit. Another neighbor wanted to pray for that "power," and the children, who had been filled at church, wanted prayer again. As a friend of mine says, "The Lord showed up, and the Lord showed out!"

A young mother named Heidi had come to help Adamina while we were there. Her sons were Adrian and Danny. She ate breakfast with us that morning at the parsonage, and shared her story with us regarding her living arrangement with her boyfriend. She could now see clearly, and she wanted to repent and rededicate her life to the Lord. As she prayed, the Holy Spirit fell, and she stayed out for over twenty minutes. She had served us so faithfully, and now it was her turn!

We were putting our baggage into the van when Norma and her husband Gustavo arrived. We prayed for her on Sunday and now here he was! He was upset over a dream he had that night. He was in a fire and his skin was falling off; he was terrified. He asked, "What does it mean?" David told him that he needed to come to the Lord. I awakened that morning with a burden for heavy intercession, but I did not know for whom; apparently it was Gustavo. I told him the Lord was saying that in His mercy, He was firing a warning shot across the bow of his boat; that he was to be the priest of his home and was responsible for his wife and daughter; that it would be better for a millstone to be put around his neck and he be cast into the sea rather than lead them astray; and that the Lord was calling him to repent and do what was right, or he was heading straight to hell. As I was speaking, my left arm was shaking violently, so I sat on my left hand, but then my right side started shaking as well. The Lord was very serious! Louie spoke to him, and Robert shared with him about a man he knew who had a similar dream about a fire. The man lived for the Lord for a while, but then fell away and died in a house fire. Gustavo was convicted, prayed the sinner's prayer, and then asked to be filled with the Holy Spirit. When he got up after about ten minutes, Adamina ministered to him and his wife Norma while I held baby Genesis. They had to forgive each other, and then they were hugging each other, laughing and crying at the same time. What a dynamite ending!

Adamina took us to the airport. I learned so much from just watching this vessel of honor, and I was already looking forward to a return trip. I witnessed to my seatmate on the last leg of the journey from Houston to Atlanta. He was Roman Catholic and his son had been baptized the week before. I shared my salvation testimony, and we both agreed that our relationship with Jesus is what counts.

There is something special about coming home to my oasis in the woods. As I was unpacking, I felt the Lord's presence. I just sat on the floor, and my left arm started shaking again. What is this? I poured out my heart to the Lord, asking for His wisdom. Before, when His presence came on me, my heart would pound. But now there was more, and my body was trembling. My earthen vessel could not withstand the power. The Lord reminded me of the Superman movie I had gone to see years earlier and how He had promised to be my Superman and fly me higher. This was that time—He was taking me higher—but I was to rest. We rest, we work, we rest, we work, repeating the process until our assignments on earth are completed. Nonetheless, it was while He was resting at the well that the woman came to meet Him as Messiah, and then she went and told her village (John 4:4–26). After this He sweetly filled me with His Spirit afresh and anew, and I rested, waiting for His call to work again.

CHAPTER 12
MY THIRD JOURNEY
TO REYNOSA, MEXICO

DEC 2000

I had been to Reynosa in the spring, but David wanted to send a team in for the post-Christmas and New Year holidays. This time he had five members from Byron United Methodist Church: George and his thirteen-year-old son Daniel, Whit and his son John, fourteen years old, and Miss Mickey. We had the same flight plans as the previous trips: Atlanta to Houston, then to McAllen, Texas; and the schedule was the same—Thursday through Monday. Pastor Danny and his daughter, Abigail, collected us for the border crossing and drive into Reynosa.

Our first stop was at the home of Lipido and Manuel (Pastor Adamina's sister and brother-in-law), one of our regular places to hang out. We introduced the new members on the team, had a delicious Mexican lunch, and then went by the market to get a piñata for John's fourteenth birthday, which was that very day. Finally, we arrived at the parsonage, and we met Autón, Pastor Danny's brother, who was living with them. He had suffered a stroke but was recovering nicely, contrary to the doctor's terminal prognosis.

The evening service at the church opened with that powerfully anointed music. It was so good to be back with my sisters and brothers in Christ who knew how to enter His courts with praise and worship. That has to be a major reason that the Holy Spirit moves so mightily among them! John shared about discouragement; he was so young, but so mature in the Lord. George preached on the Ninety-first Psalm, and from Mark 5 about "going to the other side." Many came to the altar for prayer. Among them was my special friend Raquel from the previous mission, whose husband had left her and the boys. The latest news was that he had come home but had since left again. Her hopes had been up and then dashed. My heart ached for her, and we joined together in prayer for her, her husband, and the two sons, who missed their father.

Supper was at the home of Juan and Patricia. Juan was a former lieutenant in the army and had attended West Point Academy. He had suffered cancer of the thyroid and went through surgery to remove some of his vocal chords. The cancer was gone, and his voice was returning. His father, Juan Sr., was there. We prayed for this entire family, and for Juan Carlos, the youth pastor. They were all slain in the Spirit!

We returned to the parsonage to celebrate John's birthday. There was ice cream, cake, and the piñata. He was blindfolded and given a big stick, and at long last, he gave it a good whack and candy flew all over the place. This had to be one birthday he would never forget!

We started our first full day with breakfast at the parsonage. Then we went for visitation. Our first visit was held in the front yard of Walberto, one of seven brothers. He had recently been released from jail, where he had accepted Christ. He had tuberculosis and asked that we pray for his healing and that he, his wife Olga, and daughter Marisél be filled with the Holy Spirit. His brother Antonio and Antonio's Claudia prayed for salvation and for the infilling of the Holy Spirit. We held an outdoor mini-service, and the Lord did His stuff!

We went next to the home of Walberto's youngest brother Fortunato and wife Susana. We found the three children at home alone: Eric, seven years old, watched them; Michelle, age six, did the cooking; and three-year-old Jaziel was the little one. The parents were at work. They said that their relatives checked on them, and we had a little prayer with them for their protection. We returned later in the day and met Fortunato and Susana, who were Christians. They said they worked all the time and had no time for church. They were concerned that their faith was growing cold, and so we prayed for them. Their hearts were hurting and they needed wisdom and encouragement. We certainly did not want to be judges over them, so we showed them our love and concern and welcomed them to return to fellowship. We prayed for the Holy Spirit to empower them to live victorious lives.

Then we proceeded to the ICU at the local hospital to visit Pastor Adamina's nephew, Reuben, who had pneumonia. His mother, Marta, was also visiting him at that time. The entire team could not go inside, so Whit and Adamina went. Whit was able to share the gospel, and both Reuben and Marta accepted Christ! Meanwhile, in the waiting room, I was sitting with Raul and Marie, whose seventeen-year old daughter had been admitted for injuries she sustained in a car accident. In my very limited Spanish, I tried to witness to them. In error, I thought they both were saved, so I gave them two Spanish bookmarks and prayed in English with them. The wife started crying. Pastor Adamina approached, and as they conversed in Spanish, she learned that only the wife was saved. The woman's husband prayed for salvation, and she prayed to be filled with the Holy Spirit. Then their three cousins arrived, all Christians. A hospital worker named Sylvia saw what was happening, and she asked for prayer for her daughter. There in the waiting room we had church, and Adamina led all of us in prayer.

We had lunch again at Manuel and Lipido's home—tacos and beans! ¡*Deliciosa*! They are such people of faith, and it was a joy to share with them the events of the morning because it struck them personally.

At the evening service, Lipido shared with the congregation the news of the salvation of her nephew Reuben and sister-in-law Marta. Daniel gave his testimony, and I preached a message called "Glory to Glory." There was a good crowd, and their faith level was high from hearing the testimonies, so the altar was full. As the team ministered, people were being healed, saved, and filled. They were "expecting," and the Holy Spirit was faithful. Ask and receive!

We had supper at Maria Luisa's home, another old friend. It is always fun to go to her home because she invites so many of her neighbors who are not members of the church. The food was so tasty! We had worked hard all day and had great big appetites. Maria Luisa was having upper respiratory problems, so we prayed for her healing, and, of course, she fell out in the Spirit. We prayed for Elizabeth, Carmen, and Maria to be filled, so it was a fruitful evening.

We started Saturday morning with breakfast at Raquel's home. Lipido went with us, and we had such lovely fellowship. I could not understand how her husband could leave her. She is so beautiful, intelligent, educated, well-bred, gracious, obviously a wonderful mother, loving and forgiving. I was a big fan of her! She told us that her husband had come back twice since he left nine months previously, but the last time he left, he said he would not return. She had forgiven him and held no bitterness. Different members of the team had words of wisdom, and she was very receptive. We prayed, and the Lord gave her a fresh infilling of the Holy Spirit. I knew she would come through this like shining gold, but I ached because I knew it would be a painful journey.

We went to the market for gifts to take home. A friend had given me fifty dollars to use if and when I saw a need. Pastor Adamina told us that the children in the jail needed pillows and towels. There was the need, and I had the money! We stopped and used that fifty dollars to bless a lot of children!

We had a late lunch at the home of Esther, wife of one of the seven brothers we had ministered earlier. After eating and sharing, Esther requested prayer for brother Walberto. We told her we had prayed personally for him that morning, but would be glad to pray again. Her beautiful daughter Marcia was concerned about her factory job, plus she was twenty-three and not married. They were both Christians, so we prayed over their concerns and for a refilling of the Holy Spirit. It was important that they knew we cared, that their concerns were our concerns.

We returned to the parsonage to make candy bags for the children to be distributed at the New Year's Eve party after the service the following night. There were always lots of children, and they had such fun. They also were very sensitive to the things of God. They were like empty pots with the lids off, just eager to be filled. The Bible instructs us not to hinder them, "for of such is the kingdom of heaven" (Matt. 19:14, NKJV). Jesus said:

> *Except ye be converted, and become as little children, ye shall not enter into the kingdom of heaven. Whosoever therefore shall humble himself as this little child, the same is greatest in the kingdom of heaven. And whoso shall receive one such little child*

in my name receiveth me. But whoso shall offend one of these little ones which believe in me, it were better for him that a millstone were hanged about his neck, and that he were drowned in the depth of the sea.
—*Matthew 18:3–6*

Jesus had a lot to say about children. These little ones had much to teach us through their simple faith, and it was critical that they be nourished, protected, and encouraged. If only little Eric, Michelle, and Jaziel, those dear little children of Fortunato and Susana, could be with us!

Manuel told us that the last night when he had prayed at the altar, he saw a light with a form in it, but he could not tell who it was. Manuelito, his son, said that when the Americans entered the home of Maria Luisa after the service, "There were lights around their heads, and you could not see their faces." Wow!

At the evening service, Maria Luisa testified that she had been healed. Mickey shared her testimony, and Whit preached. Many came forward for prayer, and the Lord moved mightily. He was eager to meet the needs of His children.

The service continued as we left the church and went to Paulo and Sedalia's home for supper. There were two rooms full of people. Juan Carlos, the youth leader, requested prayer for healing, and Ramiro, the worship leader, had cut his hand and burned his face. We had special prayer for these two dynamic men of God. The Lord was with us as He promised: "For where two or three come together in my name, there am I with them" (Matt. 18:20, NIV). The location certainly didn't matter to Him—church, home, hospital, street corner. He was not limited.

The next day, Sunday, was New Year's Eve, so a special church service was scheduled for that evening. We helped prepare breakfast, and after cleaning, the team went to visit María and her family. Actually, there were two families living in one house with a dirt floor and no heat. There were two babies, and both were sick, so we prayed for their healing. The power of God was so strong that it seemed like a river of glory was flowing through the house. As we would touch them and pray, they would fall on the floor. The oldest couple, Cleofas and Francisca, were so filled with the Spirit that they were shaking. In all, we prayed for seven children, two babies, and four couples. Three were saved, and ten, already saved, were filled with the Holy Spirit. Maria was beside herself with gratitude for God's grace poured over her family. I was just awestruck in His presence.

We returned to the parsonage to prepare for the evening celebration. Part of the team worked on shoebox gifts, and the rest of us cooked tortillas. There are no small duties in God's kingdom.

Then we went to the children's jail, where there were eighteen boys and two girls, plus one visiting mother. We served tortillas, cookies, and drinks; and distributed the pillows, towels, caps, and books. The kids were so grateful. Our two youths, Daniel and John, gave their testimonies, and George presented a gospel message. At the invitation, all the children, including the mother, raised their hands to accept Christ. George went over the message again, explaining the seriousness of their commitment, and when he extended the invitation the second time, again they all raised their hands. You can't beat a 100 percent response! We gave God the praise.

At the parsonage, Mickey and I were delighted to receive crocheted doilies from Francisca, the grandmother for whom we prayed that morning during the glory time in her house. This was a very poor family, so these gifts came as a real sacrifice. We were so honored!

We had a late lunch at the home of Lipido's parents. Her father, Juan, and his family had been with us Thursday evening and said they had no prayer needs, so we simply had a quiet, peaceful time, enjoying the fellowship of good friends. Relationship-building is such an important part of missions. The Holy Spirit is like a dove, and I know He enjoyed the serenity and peace in this home. I surely did!

Members of the congregation that evening presented a skit depicting the devil trying to extinguish their lights. It was very clever and to the point. Leslie and Lalí, two of our special little girls, sang. They were so cute that you just wanted to squeeze them! David preached, and again the altar was full. I prayed for one lady who needed healing in her arm, and as I prayed, she was slain in the Spirit. Later, at dinner, she told me her arm was fine! Another lady wanted the baptism of the Holy Spirit, and she fell out also. Another little boy wanted prayer, and he was touched as well.

When ministry ended at the altar, we adjourned to the parsonage to welcome in the New Year. Long tables were set so everyone could eat together, and there were piñatas for the children. It was wonderful to celebrate with friends with whom we spent time all week, and especially those whose lives had been impacted. They were dressed in their best and filled with joy!

At midnight, Pastor Adamina led us in prayer. There were hugs and kisses, and we all ate grapes. At home we eat black-eyed peas for a prosperous New Year; apparently grapes in Mexico are for a fruitful New Year. What a fine tradition!

After the party ended and all the people went home, we helped clean the parsonage, getting to bed around 2:30 a.m. It was difficult to sleep because of the loud music and banging noises in the neighborhood. We were up at 6:45

a.m. Adamina drove us into McAllen for breakfast and then to the airport.

There was a delay in departure, so we used that time to debrief and share our most meaningful moments. The consensus of opinion was this had been an incredible mission! Because our first plane was late in leaving McAllen, we had to make a mad dash to connect in Houston. Frankly, I didn't know I had it in me to run that fast, but we made it!

There had not been an opportunity to witness on the first leg from McAllen to Houston, and on this second leg, I sat next to a young Navy man. He asked where I had been, so I shared about our mission. He said he believed in God but was not settled about religion. I replied that it was simple. Jesus is standing at the door of your heart, knocking; you just invite Him in. He did not reply, but simply moved out into the aisle and was gone. I prayed that the Lord would send another Christian into his life who could better answer his questions, and next time his heart would be soft to receive. Sometimes we merely plant; other times we reap the harvest from seeds others have planted.

In no time I was home again. As I reflected over the mission, I sensed the Lord's approval because the team had given their all. Accordingly, He had advanced His kingdom. In the parable of the talents in Matthew 25:14–28, the Master was pleased with the servants who used what He had given them, but displeased with the one who buried his talent. I could hear in my spirit that His word to us was, "Well done, good and faithful servants." I had been honored to minister along side some exceptionally good and faithful servants, and I wanted to do it again!

CHAPTER 13
CHINA

MAY 2001

This mission was birthed in the heart of my dear friend, Tricia, who is as close to being Chinese as she can be without being born in China. She was a member at that time of Atlanta City Church, and we were in the same care group. When she shared her dream with us, I immediately wanted to go with her, as did Cheryl and Deena. Another friend in the church, Christiana, caught the vision, and that made five. We bonded way before we left through all our fund raising projects. The ideas we had got to be a joke, but we worked hard and had the support of our church family. Best of all, we had God's favor. Still, at our last church service before departure, we were five hundred dollars short of our goal. As I was leaving, a friend told me the Lord awakened him at 5:30 a.m. and instructed him to give me some money, so he handed me a sealed envelope. I sincerely thanked him, and gave him a big hug. I rushed as discreetly as I could to my car, tore open the envelope, and found the exact amount we needed. Thank God for obedient servants! To say our team was overwhelmed would be an understatement, but then, God's will is God's bill.

Our goal was to minister to the Tu people of China. Tricia previously visited one of their villages to photograph a festival, and she saw the need to pipe water from the river below to the village, which was on top of the mountain. When she came home, she raised money for the project, called The Well of Hope, and contacted the necessary people in China to accomplish the work. The leaders of the village had invited her to return for the official dedication of the irrigation project. This was one of the main focuses of the trip.

It was hard for me to conceive of people who have never heard the gospel, and who do not even have the name of Jesus in their language. We were cautioned not to speak His name openly in a group setting, and when speaking or writing (even in our journals), we were to use code letters and words, such as *B* for the Bible, *company* or *club* to talk about church, and *yarp*, which is the word *pray* spelled backwards. It is forbidden by law in China to evangelize or distribute Bibles. The only churches allowed must be registered and under the control of the government. Consequently, believers have resorted to meeting secretly in "house churches." Our group was told that it was, however, permissible to respond to someone if they directly questioned us about our faith. We were a bit nervous, but excited.

We flew from Atlanta to Los Angeles, and then to Inchon, Korea. On the flight from L.A. to Inchon, I sat next to Tricia. Apparently a young man in front of us was listening to our conversation. He turned and said, "God loves you!" He had been in Colorado and was on his way home to Shanghai. It was an encouraging word.

We had a four-hour layover in Inchon. I regretted this, because it gave me too much time to think about the contraband contents of my suitcases. Each of us had two suitcases, plus a carry-on. One suitcase was completely filled with Bibles, and the other had Bibles and other literature interspersed with our personal items. I am transparent, and when I lie, it is very obvious. I was afraid I would betray my team, we would all be caught, and the Bibles confiscated because of me. My butterflies had turned into buzzards. I went off by myself, pretending to be napping, but I was praying. The Lord in His mercy gave me His peace that passes all understanding. As a sign of His favor, on the flight from Inchon to Beijing, we were put in business class. It was a *Daddy* (the code word I used to refer to my Heavenly Father) thing!

Tricia had instructed us when going through customs to space ourselves, so if one were stopped, the others might be successful. Cheryl and I were the last of the team in line, and we had a couple of people between us. Tricia ran up and told us to come quickly with her. The examiner had his back to us, and people were not stopping, so we didn't either. Breathless, we were outside the terminal with nary a word spoken, but there had been a whole lot of silent *yarping*! Our contact persons met us and took us to our hotel, the Asia Vision. What an appropriate name!

When we returned home, a friend e-mailed Tricia, saying the Lord had awakened her at 11:00 p.m., and told her to pray for us as we were going through customs. She prayed the examiner would turn his back to the wall and we would go through unhindered. That is exactly what happened! We had left our schedules with many praying friends, reflecting when we would be at certain places. The time difference was twelve hours. We went through customs at 11:00 a.m., which was 11:00 p.m. for our intercessors. We serve an on-time God!

This was not just a fluke because teams from Japan and Norway, coming through about the time we did, had everything confiscated. A few days later, a team from Texas was questioned by the police, and they had to change hotels. Their contact person was followed and had to jump from taxi to taxi to lose the police. We met many brave people who were laying their lives on the line for Christ. We saw firsthand that prayer covering is vital for any successful mission.

Our friend, Jan, had a word for the team from the Lord before we left home: "Just as Peter was led out by an angel, you will be in similar situations where angels will be there for you." Another friend, Scott, prophesied: "How beautiful on the mountains are the feet of these bringing the gospel. Don't be discouraged; fear not. He will give His angels charge over you so that you will not dash your feet against a stone. It will be God's agenda." Cheryl was especially encouraged because she was having foot problems, but on the mission, she was fine! We certainly had an excellent crew of angels who watched over us.

Another friend urged us to pray for ourselves. Especially on mission trips, it is common to pray for others but not for ourselves. I certainly prayed for myself there in Inchon, and God answered!

Our guide for Beijing was named Sunni; she was a delightful Christian—and a rather bold one. She wore Christian T-shirts and bracelets, which I thought were a no-no. She took us to the famous Tiananmen Square, the Meeting Gate of the Heavenly Peace, and the Forbidden City, with its beautiful gardens. I had to pinch myself! I couldn't believe I was really there in the places I had read about and seen in documentaries. Our God truly does exceedingly and abundantly above all we ask or think (Ephesians 3:20, NKJV). While resting on some steps in the Forbidden City, we met a mother and her adorable little boy, about two years old. We asked if we could take his picture, and she was so happy to "pose" him for us. He was quite a ham for a little guy. Then she took pictures of us. There were also petitions on tables for China to host the 2008 Olympics, so the whole team was signing, to the approval of the watching crowd. This gave us another opportunity for bridge-building between our cultures. Incidentally, China did get the invitation to host the 2008 Olympics, which will open the door for more missionaries and more Bibles.

After a real, honest-to-goodness Chinese meal at the one-hundred-year-old Palace Restaurant, a treat to the tummy and to the eyes, we retreated to Tricia's room for sharing and praying. We prayed together as a team at least once a day during the entire mission, which attributed to its success and our safety.

The next morning, Sunni took us to the unusual and beautiful plant where items are made out of jade. The Chinese people are gifted artisans, and it was a temptation to buy one of everything, but lack of funds and space held me in check.

Then we went to the Great Wall. I had not realized that much of the Great Wall are actually steps, and uneven ones at that! The first section of the Wall was begun in 204 B.C., and it was extended by the succeeding dynasties. When it was completed in 1644 A.D., it reached a length of fifteen hundred miles. Large watchtowers are spaced just over one hundred yards apart. The section where we began went almost straight up, and our youngest member, Christiana, made it to the first watchtower. I went part of the way, but then felt the calves in my legs start to tighten. Tricia warned us to take it easy because the real mission began the next day, and a lot of walking lay ahead. I did get an official plaque at a nominal price, showing I had climbed the Great Wall. It is priceless to me.

Deena was not feeling well, so we prayed for her. She rested while the rest of the team had supper in the hotel. She was able to go with us afterwards to the house church of Dr. Allen, who was eighty-seven years old. He had served twenty-two years of a life sentence in a labor camp for his faith. He went for a period of ten years without being given a letter or any word from his wife and their six children. One of the songs that sustained him in prison was "The Old Rugged Cross," and he sang it over and over. He did not have a Bible. After the Cultural Revolution, the government decided to release all those over sixty years of age who had been imprisoned for more than twenty years. The reasoning was they were too old to labor much longer, and after twenty years in prison, surely their minds had been reformed so that they would not be a threat to the revolution. Wrong! Dr. Allen told us that the previous Saturday he had baptized over 350 people in the river.

His house church was simply his home, and it was packed at every meeting! The custom was for the new visitors to give their names, their country of origin, and share their testimonies. People were there that evening from Japan, Norway, Germany, England, and America. (The Japanese and Norwegian teams were the ones who had been stopped at the airport). After Cheryl shared, two ladies came to her for encouragement because their stories were similar. Several of the local ladies ministered to Deena, even giving her some medicine to take with her. At the end of the meeting, when we asked Dr. Allen what we Americans could do to help, he replied, "Pray!" He asked us to pray for the lost, for the new believers, for the leaders of their government, and that China be opened to the gospel. I had never before—and still have not to this day—met another such dedicated man of God, who endured such hardship and brutality for the cause of Christ, and yet was so full of joy. Dr. Allen died in 2006, and while the world lost a hero of the faith, heaven had to rejoice at his homecoming.

The next morning Deena was well, and that was a praise. On the way to the airport, Sunni shared her testimony. She had been offered a scholarship to attend college in the States, but refused because China is her home. She was editing Christian books, leading a Bible study group, and planning a mission to Tibet that July. She definitely was not one of those quiet Christians.

We flew China North Airlines into Xining and were accompanied by our local contact leader, Nicole. She took us to the Tibet Research Institute, the small college that would be our base for the next ten days. We were able to rent rooms in the dorms, with some of us on the second floor, and others, including me, on the fifth. Actually, walking the steps helped us stay in shape, but there were times when the second floor looked really good! Missionaries do not complain, especially since meeting Dr. Allen! The city was surrounded by barren mountains of dirt, and the fine dust was continually blowing everywhere. Many people wore masks.

Our main transportation was by taxi, and that was an adventure in faith. The drivers were daredevils, but surprisingly there were few accidents, even though they sometimes drove on the sidewalks. A local joke was, "What do the lines in the center of the road mean? Absolutely nothing!"

Lunch was at a Middle Eastern restaurant, and we were introduced to *baba* tea. Various spices are put into the cup with scalding hot water, and it is delicious! We had a huge platter of vegetables, noodles, and chicken that we were attempting to eat with chopsticks. At one point, a new friend from the school who came with us pulled out a whole chicken head—comb, eyes, and all. It was such a surprise that we exploded into laughter, and Nicole had to explain our conduct to the waitresses. We certainly did not want to offend anyone.

We went to the market. People were very cordial and friendly, and when we asked, they let us take pictures of their children. We were creating quite a stir, and used this time to smile and silently pray—more bridge building. There were vendors along the streets with their carts, but we bought groceries at a big, modern supermarket. We were able to cook at Nicole's apartment, which was a short distance from the school.

After a little rest in our rooms, we walked over to Nicole's place and met her roommate Nicky, who was from Colorado. Nicky had a heart for the Mongols, while Nicole was called to the Tus. It was like Christmas as they opened a suitcase full of goodies we had brought from America. We had some snacks, and Nicole briefed us on the mission itinerary. Tricia had her guitar, so we enjoyed singing, then sharing and praying.

On the way "home," we stopped at a Middle Eastern tent across the street from the school and enjoyed a late supper of mutton and fried bread. We were spectacles here as well, even though there were some white students at the school. It was fun sharing with them. They especially like it when you rave about their food! More bridge-building.

China was pushing English as a second language, and many signs were in both languages. China wants to be a world power, and English is a necessity, not just for doing business with the United States but other countries as well. We saw in the paper that China was becoming a member of the World Trade Organization and that Hong Kong was in APEC, and their sign would be the dragon. There was a lot of construction in the area, but it was done by manual labor, not machines. Crowds of men and women would stand on street corners with their shovels, waiting for rides to work. The air quality was terrible from the dust and the smoke from the factories. Xining was a bustling city with a lot of traffic—like home in Georgia.

I was blessed the following morning to have hot water for a shower. The water is not on all day, and some days, not at all. Cheryl and Deena came in for a visit before we left for the morning. As we shared the trip thus far, we agreed that the most touching parts had been getting the Bibles through and the house church with Dr. Allen.

Nicole urged us the previous night to be spiritually prepared for our visit to Kumbum Monastery. This had once been a powerful demonic place, but a lot of the power had gone out because Christians were going there and praying. The monastery was founded in 1560. There are numerous temples, halls, stupas, and dormitories for the monks. At the height of its glory, there were over five thousand monks in residence, but that time had passed. What once must have been majestic was now dilapidated. There was a heaviness hanging over the area, and I interceded in prayer as I walked until the heaviness lifted. I was filled with a gentle sadness at seeing so many deceived—the older ones, the young children, and the monks—all entrapped. The monks were dressed in wine-colored robes, and they were so gracious and so pleased to be photographed.

In one courtyard, we saw a tree that had been planted by a mother who thought her son was the Llama. Legend says that she placed a lock of his hair in the ground and the tree grew, each leaf having an image of his face. It was not a healthy-looking tree; many limbs were dead. I prayed that the Lord would miraculously turn this tree into a dogwood tree, reflecting the cross of Calvary.

We had lunch at a very nice Middle-Eastern restaurant, and then we prayer-walked through some of the streets of Xining. There were marvelous shops, and we were delighted to find gifts for home (especially tea sets). Guess you call this prayer shopping.

We went to the coffee shop at the school so Tricia could meet with Jun Hoo, a Chinese citizen who had been living in Roswell, Georgia, but was there visiting relatives. He was feeling a strong pull to stay in China and help in the development of his country, but he had a good job back in the States, plus a girlfriend. The team used this time to converse with the students, who liked to practice their English. While we could not openly share our faith, we could answer the questions they posed. I met a very special law student named Jasson from Mongolia who wanted to be an attorney. I had worked for attorneys for forty-five years, so he wanted to hear all my war stories. This developed into a very important God-meeting.

Also that evening, Nicole met Dorothy, a student from Guanting, Minhe County, who was a Tu and therefore fluent in the Tu language. She agreed to be our guide and interpreter for the next leg of our journey. We would learn later this was also a divine appointment. Dorothy was a very petite young lady, with long black hair and beautiful dark eyes. She always dressed immaculately, mostly in white, and I was amazed that her clothes never seemed to wrinkle or get dirty. Actually, she personally never seemed to wrinkle or get out of sorts—just always prim, proper, neat, and in control.

The next morning we (the team, Nicole, and Dorothy) departed by bus for Guanting with a stopover in Minhe, where we met Dorothy's mother for a very brief visit at the bus station. We had lunch there and were the main attraction! We boarded another smaller bus for the rest of the ride. The scenery was spectacular. The mountains were terraced and a lush green. Sheep and donkeys were staked out along the slopes to graze. The ride itself was an adventure. Horns are as important to drivers in China as their motors. The loudest one prevails!

When we arrived in Guanting, the entire town treated us like celebrities, and while it was appreciated on our part, it was also a bit scary. The people were so packed around us that it was difficult to walk. I was glad to leave the main street and go down the little dirt alley to Grandmother's house, which was to be our home for the next week.

Nana was the grandmother of Huggee Fon (also known as "Teacher"), who was a professor at the college where we were based in Xining and a close friend to Nicole. Nana took care of Teacher and her brother during the great famine. Their father, Nana's son, was unable to make a living, and he left the children with her because their mother beat them. Nana's husband had been dead for fourteen years, but her son was still alive. She was eighty years old, very small, and hump-backed (probably from osteoporosis). She wore the traditional Chinese clothes: mandarin jacket, pants, and tiny pointed brocade shoes. Her feet had been bound as a young child, and she walked on her heels. She never removed her shoes, not even to sleep, and it was obvious that her feet caused her pain. She was a very devout Buddhist, constantly turning her small prayer wheel, burning incense, and praying with her prayer beads. We had been cautioned to be reserved in our behavior, but when I first met Nana, I spontaneously grabbed her and gave her a big hug. I knew I had made a friend for life. I could feel my love going into her and her love coming into me.

Nicole, Dorothy, and Christiana went to check on the school situation, as we were scheduled to teach English in some of the classes. While they were gone, Tricia played her guitar and we sang, sitting on the concrete wrap-around porch. Nana brought out her beads and prayer wheel, attempting to touch each of us with the wheel, but we smiled and shook our heads no, pointing up to heaven. Thankfully, this did not seem to offend her. We gave her some candy, and she sat down next to me. I started rubbing her back, and she started melting—holding her arms out with palms up. From then on, every time we sat on the porch, she would

249

back up to me for her back rub. I would pray softly over her as I massaged her back.

As Tricia was playing, neighbors arrived. There were lots of children, and we gave them stickers. A boy and girl sang to us. A very industrious lady brought some embroidery pieces with her, and we bought them all. Nana indicated she wanted us to sing again, and as she hummed the notes, Tricia deduced that she was requesting "Honor, Blessing, and Glory." It's amazing how we can communicate without words. She also wanted another massage, so Deena rubbed her hands, but she was still hurting. I motioned for her to stand, and then I prayed for her healing and also that she would come to know Jesus and be filled with His peace. She didn't understand, but she knew that I loved her. I knew that Jesus loved her too! She was one of the main reasons we had come to China.

There were some hitches in our plans to teach in the school, but at last Dorothy corrected everything. She was related to the principal, and he invited us to come the next morning. Our Lord was always a step ahead of us!

At last it was time for bed. Tricia and Christiana shared a room, and the rest of us slept with Nana. That's why I know she never takes off her shoes! Dorothy stayed with her grandparents a few blocks away. This was an awful night for me. The bed was a huge concrete slab, called a *kong*, which ran across the entire end of the room. We had some blankets, but no mattresses or any kind of padding. Our pillows were little beanbags, literally filled with beans. I was put in the middle, so I lay on my back because I did not want to turn and breathe in my neighbor's face. At long last I fell asleep, but I woke myself snoring. Nana coughed all night long, and poor Nicole was next to her. I hurt the next morning in places I didn't know I had!

We were up around 6:30 a.m. and had granola bars and bananas for breakfast. We packed our supplies for the school and left. The classes were divided, and I was assigned to the second class with thirty-six students. Dorothy came to translate, and she wanted them to tell me their names, how many were in their family, and so on. They seemed a bit bored with all that, so I told her she could go to the other classes, and we would be just fine. I taught them to sing "Head, Shoulders, Knees, and Toes" with all the motions, and then mixed it all. They tried to yell out in English the part of my body where I was pointing. I would go faster and faster, and then I got so tickled because they were so tickled. We had a good time laughing together. I did try to get a little more serious with the ABCs and colors, but it just ended in more laughter. I tied a gospel bracelet on each little wrist, but sadly, I could not explain what the colors represented. (Black stands for sin, red for Jesus' blood, white for purity, yellow for the streets of gold, and green for growth). They just delighted in getting a gift with such pretty-colored beads. I prayed silently that one day they would know the reality of what this little bracelet represented. At the conclusion of our class time, the students and teachers met on the courtyard for pictures, at which time the headmaster extended an open invitation for us to return.

We proceeded to the office of the Minister of Culture, where we were graciously served beer. This is a drinking society, and it would have been impolite to refuse, so I pretended to drink mine and nursed it while we talked. A representative from Zhai Zi, the village where the Well of Hope water project had been completed, came to extend a personal invitation to Tricia. He wanted to put her name on a plaque for the dedication. However, she declined, wanting no credit. She did assure him that we would be present for the ceremony the following day.

We visited the temple in town, and Nana was there. She went with us to visit two other temples located on the outskirts of Guanting. The team was silently praying while Nana was worshiping. This had to be such a treat for her because she probably did not visit these last two temples often because of the distance from her home. Dorothy was bowing at each temple, so we assumed she was Buddhist. Later she said she wasn't really anything because, she told us, "until you come to understand, you cannot commit." I asked if she knew anything about Christianity, and she said she didn't. I told her I believed it was something you had to know for yourself, that one day she would know the truth, and she would pursue it. "Do you really think so?" she asked, and I replied yes. That statement was prophetic.

That evening we went to the home of Dorothy's grandparents for supper. We were entertained by beautiful little children, who sang and danced for us. The grandfather proudly brought out a carved wooden plaque, the size of a door. It had been presented to his grandfather by Emperor Quan Sha for "good character and action in example for others." It was an award for excellence. He said that his family was striving to be worthy of the plaque, and when they achieve this excellence by becoming great and famous, they will openly display the plaque. This explained the pressure under which Dorothy studied to become a lawyer.

On the way back to Nana's, we stopped by the hotel to take showers. We were all exhausted and ready to hit the concrete bed, but Grandmother's friends were assembled to see the foreigners—us—so we had to be neighborly and visit awhile.

It had been a very important day. The school was now open for future mission teams, and Dorothy's heart had been softened. We had prayed over three temples, and ties had been established with the city officials.

Dorothy and our two cab drivers came to collect us the following morning for our journey to Zhai Zi and the Well of Hope dedication service. On our way we stopped at a temple, where we saw magnificent artwork. The seven monks we met were very friendly and were pleased to give us a tour. They ranged in age from a very young boy, approximately twelve years old, to an elderly man with snow-white hair. We drove through a barren, mountainous region, so strikingly different from the green fields we had left around Guanting.

We passed through a valley coming into the village and crossed over a shallow river. The village was perched on top of a mountain, and we could see people waving their hands, beating drums, and shooting off firecrackers. We stopped to view the pump house and saw the pipeline running up the side of the mountain. The mayor and architect excitedly explained the mechanics to us. Many villagers had come down to walk us up, carrying our backpacks, and holding us by the arm so we would not fall. As we approached the entrance of the village, children with banners greeted us, lining each side of the road. Men were beating huge drums, which were held steady by young boys. Scarves were draped around our necks (mine was white). I was overcome by this extravagant display of appreciation and felt so unworthy. This was Tricia's project; yet the whole team was reaping the benefits. It reminded me of Jesus entering Jerusalem on Palm Sunday. He deserved the accolades; I did not.

We ate at the Master's house, and were seated on the *kong*, which was made of wood and had lovely fabric coverings. This was a very special honor because women usually sit in chairs and the men get the kong. A low wooden table was set before us, and we ate and ate and ate. Some of the ladies sang and danced, and then two men sang for us. We learned they both were teachers. The first man who sang, Sol, was a real clown, even doing cartwheels and acting like a monkey. The ladies presented us with embroidered squares. The Mayor and other officials involved in the project went over their receipts with Tricia, making a full accounting of the funds they were given. They are honorable people.

The Mayor gave this speech:

> *Respectable friends and people of the noble country. You traveled thousands of miles from your busy schedules to help with the water project; to look at the well yourselves. Before the well project, the people and livestock in our village had difficulty accessing water. To have your generous assistance has helped our village to step out of poverty. You have contributed to their welfare. This is a feat worth a thousand sunrises for the human welfare. I hereby represent the entire village to thank you sincerely for your spirit of giving and warmly welcome you.*

The engineer of the project wrote the following poem as a "celebration to commemorate this visit," and to welcome "the noble guests from far away:"

> *Make a golden dragon descend to the drought platform;*
> *The dragon head lands in the clear water pool;*

*The electric horse happily gallops and the
    dragon plays.
Lead the dragon to ascend the dry platform;
Clear water flows into Zhai Zi village.
Every family smiles brightly;
They drink water and remember the patrons.*

We were given a tour of the village, and it was a joy to see their fertile wheat fields on top of the mountain. They insisted that we eat again before we left, and, of course, we obliged. I had put away enough food to last me at least a week. We took photographs of the entire village by groups: the men, the women, the children, the mayor, the architect, and the poet. Some of the villagers walked down the mountain with us, while the remainder stood at the top waving to us. It was sad to say good-bye to our new friends. They had made an unforgettable impact on my life.

We stopped by two more temples on the way back to Guanting. Quanchinsu was a new temple still under construction, so we were the first Christians to pray there and claim it for Christ. It was to be a beautiful place nestled in the mountains, and artists were working on massive murals that adorned the entrance.

The next temple was located by the Yellow River. The river actually has a yellow tint. We saw numerous jars of seed wrapped in scarves and tied with cords that the farmers had brought to be blessed. While this was an old temple, there was a solar dish in the courtyard, and a teapot had been put on a stand above it so it could be heated. The contrast of old versus new was very interesting.

Back in Guanting, Cheryl and I stayed with Nana while the rest of the team walked to the hotel for showers. She motioned that she had a headache and wanted a pill, so

Cheryl gave her an aspirin. Then she backed up to me for a massage. Her sixteen-year-old grandson, Hunee, came with some water. When we asked about his future plans, he said he would take care of his grandmother. The others had returned, and Nana began to tell us about her life; she was weeping and said she wanted to die. I pulled up a mat and sat next to her, putting my hand on her shoulder; Tricia played her guitar, and we all were singing. Then Nana took my hand, and I put my other hand on top of hers. I was crying, and then I prayed quietly for her. We all were touched by the love present in this little courtyard. Love has a language of its own.

Neighbors were arriving, so our sweet fellowship took a different turn. They wanted to sing with us, and then they sang for us. The atmosphere turned into joy and laughter. At long last, it was time to end another blessed day.

We had been told that there was a very special temple in the mountains, and all good Buddhists make a pilgrimage there. We loaded our two taxis, including Nana, her friend, two aunts, and two small boys, and embarked on an adventure. The mountains were so steep that the taxis could not ascend, so we would all get out and push. Wild flowers dotted the hillsides, and Nana picked a bouquet. Parts of the mountains were covered in green grass, but as you looked in the distance, you could see various shades of brown—barren yet beautiful.

At the temple we were told the story that a *tonka* (painting) had been drawn in blood to be sent to a certain family, but it was never delivered. It was thought to be too important just for that family, so it was put in the temple. The blood had changed into colors, and dripped from the fingers. We were further advised that the Buddhists feel there will be three periods of history, and that we are currently living in the second part, which is good. The third and final part will be bad, but short, and then the earth will end.

There was a smaller temple adjacent to this one, and it was oppressive. I described it in my journal as "awful." At the entrance sat a huge black Buddha, and next to it were two statues of Chinese males facing each other, dressed in elaborate priest-like robes, one a son and the other his friend. On their arms hung various emblems like the ones Nana's neighbor had tried to sell us the night before. Thankfully, we had declined her offer. Here you can burn incense, ask questions, and get answers from a large book. Our two drivers were doing this—similar to a fortune-teller. Cheryl felt a strong burden of intercession, so she stepped outside to one corner of the porch and I stood at the other, praying silently.

While here, Tricia had difficulty breathing, and she felt extremely tired. Once we prayed for her, she recovered. Christiana touched an odd-looking plant and immediately felt pain and numbness in her hand, which soon broke out in bumps and a rash. On the way down the hill, Dorothy bumped her head and the taxi rolled back on her foot, but amazingly she was not hurt. The team was glad to get out of this area!

Back in Guanting, the team, Nana, her friend, and our two drivers stopped for lunch at our favorite (and only) Muslim restaurant in Guanting. Then we collected our Bibles and notebooks and headed for the Yellow River for a refreshing outing after the heaviness of the day. One of the drivers brought his wife and young son. Tricia played her guitar, we sang, took pictures, and even had a rock-throwing contest. Nana loved to be photographed, and she tried to always pose with her hands folded in prayer or holding her prayer beads. While we were not verbally witnessing about

Jesus, we were being His witnesses by extending our love to these dear people, and relationships were being forged.

That evening the team and Nana were invited back to Grandfather's house for a scrumptious dinner that Dorothy had prepared. This was her twenty-first birthday! Dorothy's aunt displayed some traditional embroidery pieces, and the team bought several. When the aunt left the room, Nana said she should have given them to us; that we paid too much. For us, the cost was approximately sixty-five cents per square, but the goodwill was priceless.

Dorothy said, "Before, I knew about a country called America, but by you I can see your country. Now I know a new America. You are in my heart. I will remember you forever."

I could say the same to them, and did: "Before I knew about a country called China, but by all of you I can see your country. Now I know a new China. You are in my heart. I will remember you forever."

We walked back to Nana's house, and thankfully, only one neighbor and her daughter were there. They did not stay very long. Nana showed us pictures of her family. She was weeping, and I tried to comfort her. Nicole slept in the other room, so I slept next to Nana that last night. She had built a fire in the ovens underneath the kong, and it got extremely hot, like being on a griddle.

The next morning it was time to say our good-byes. Dorothy was forty-five minutes late, so we had time for one last concert. We were all weeping as we blessed the house, and we stood on God's promise that His word would not return void. It had been spoken, sang, and prayed over Nana, and I felt in my spirit that we would see her in heaven, that she had been marked for the kingdom. It was encouraging to see her wearing the gospel bracelet we had given her.

Even though she did not know what it meant at that time, one day she would.

Nana walked with us to the bus stop, and even got on with us, hugging us all over again. She did not want us to leave, and neither did I, but our mission had not been completed. There were more appointments to keep, and time was evaporating. We waved at her as the bus departed. It was many miles before I could quit crying. I had left part of my heart with Nana, Grandfather, his family, the taxi drivers, the children, and all our new friends in Guanting. Heaven will be a place of no goodbyes!

It was a bumpy ride to Minhe, where we had lunch with Dorothy's parents and her younger brother David. He went to college with Dorothy, and he was majoring in computers. Their parents had borrowed $20,000 RBM (renminbi) for their education, so we could again see the pressure to excel. The father was a member of the Communist Party and worked with the disabled. He walked with a pronounced limp and had a very tender heart. He asked Tricia for our assistance with the disabled, and she said she would do what she could. Undoubtedly, he knew of her work on the Well of Hope project. These were compassionate people, and I wanted so much to witness to them about our compassionate Jesus. That would have been very dangerous, though. When we asked what they thought of the possibility of the Olympics coming to China, they were ecstatic. We had highest praise for their Dorothy and her good job of herding us, and they reveled in her glory. They walked us back to the bus station when it was time to leave, and it tickled me when the father handed his wife my backpack to carry. They rode with us for a few stops, trying to prolong the visit. The farewell was tempered with the knowledge that we would be seeing David back at the school. This was another important meeting because relationships were established that would assist Dorothy in the future.

How wonderful to be back at school in my soft bed! We went to our rooms to refresh prior to a team meeting in Tricia's room. Unfortunately, or so it seemed at the time, my keys were locked in my room with me outside. We tried to pick the lock, we prayed over it, and we laughed over it. The office ladies were a bit upset, as they did not have a master key. The maintenance man took the doorknob off, but then I could not lock the door. We went to our meeting, each one sharing her heart about our Guanting experience. I was so honored to be a member of this elite team.

We had a team Bible study the next morning, and as I left my room, I simply shut the door behind me. When I returned, it would not open, so I went out to the park on campus to enjoy the sunshine and read. I was surrounded by lilac trees in full bloom and yellow moss roses; it was delightful. I asked the Lord to give me a divine appointment. Jasson, the law student with whom I had talked the week before in the coffee shop, approached and sat beside me. He spoke English fluently, and we were enjoying our conversation. Then he asked if I were a Christian. Since he asked, I was free to respond. I said, "Yes. Are you?" He didn't reply. I offered to get him a Bible, but he said he had one that a man from Norway had given him. As we were talking, Dorothy, our guide, approached. I told her that Jasson and I were talking about Christianity, and she sat on the other side of me. I drew a diagram, showing a sinful man standing on one side of a chasm, with a holy God on the other side. The dilemma was how the man could get over to God, and the answer was by God's bridge, the cross of Christ. In their culture, they present a gift with both hands extended toward the recipient. I asked if they wanted to receive this gift, explaining that Jesus had His hands extended to them, and I extended mine. They each took one of my hands, and I said I would lead them in prayer. Dorothy wanted to know what prayer was, and I explained that it was talking to her Heavenly Father, just like we had talked to her earthly father earlier. They prayed the Sinner's Prayer and were both so happy! How I praised the Lord for being locked out of my room and that seed previously planted had come to fruition in the fullness of His time.

The team had been waiting at the campus gate for me, and when I explained my delay, they rejoiced. We spent the afternoon in Xining. Dorothy and her friend Showbae came with us. That evening we ate at the campus cafe and then went to the park area. Jasson and Howie, a Tu believer, came with some other guys. We talked about idioms and slang, laughing a lot. The others left, leaving Jasson to talk with Cheryl and me, while Howie talked with Tricia, Deena, and Christiana. Jasson said he had good feelings in his heart about what he had done that day in accepting Christ, but it was very dangerous here; there was much tyranny. We assured him he would be in our prayers, and we knew the Lord would send him Christian brothers. Actually, the Lord had already sent Howie, but Howie had not been free to openly witness to Jasson. Now he could share his faith. Nicole told us that Jasson and Dorothy would be discipled one-on-one at first, and then moved to a group. That was comforting to me, as I did not want to leave these babes in Christ to flounder on their own.

Early the next morning we went via bus to Huzhu, a village known for its crafts and dancing. We were told there was a slight possibility of trouble, as there was news that some believers had been arrested and forced to recant. Also, there had been a problem in Beijing in the transfer of Bibles, so we needed to be cautious. A man sitting behind me on the bus was humming Nana's favorite song, bringing her to my mind, and I had to fight back the tears. We passed through an extremely poor section of town, and as I looked through the window, I saw a little woman watering a scrawny plant in a pot. She saw me, pointed at her plant, and gave me a big smile. Even in the most abhorrent conditions, people still search for beauty and take pride and comfort in it. As we came to a town, there was a huge crowd gathered on a corner waiting for work. We see that in America as well, but not often in crowds that size. What was amazing to me was the number of women there holding shovels, ready to do hard manual labor. China is a country of hard-working people.

At Hudzu, we had to walk a dirt road with fields on each side. When the workers saw us coming, they left their tools and ran into the village to prepare for us. Apparently one of their main sources of income is entertainment, using their native dances, songs, and costumes. After the show, they presented their crafts for sale. We were ushered into a very nice home (brick with tile floors), given hot tea and bread, and then we had to "kiss the cup." They fill a cup with liquor, and you must drink when it is passed to you. Tricia had taught us to bring the cup to our lips, and pretend to drink. You must accept the drink the first time it is offered, but it is permissible to decline any further offers. A group of men and women dressed in ornate costumes sang to us, and we had to sing back to them. A young man explained to us that their outfits meant different things, such as if one was married or single and his or her age. We also saw traditional wedding costumes for the bride and groom.

They took us outside to a large dirt field with an apparatus in the middle. It consisted of a small, round wooden base with a pole coming up from it attached to a larger base at the top. Two ladder swings hung from the top, and beautiful silk scarves were tied all around. The point was to get the makeshift merry-go-round going fast by running around it, then jumping onto the ladders and hanging onto the bars. The faster you went, the farther out the swings went. Christiana and I were the only ones on the team brave (or foolish) enough to attempt it, to the delight of the people. Two of the dancers performed on the swings, doing very difficult acrobatics and ballet. It was so beautiful! The villagers performed special dances for us, explaining what they represented. Cheryl and I participated. One dear lady took me under her wing, and showed me the steps. Later she introduced me to her daughter. Back in the house, there was more dancing and singing. Then they brought out their crafts. After wheeling and dealing and a lot of photographs, it was time to leave. Some of them walked us to the bus stop, and I was with the special lady who taught me to dance. We tried to talk, but she spoke no English.

She did give me a thumbs-up sign of approval, which I did understand. I told her that I loved her and wished I could tell her about Jesus, trusting the Lord would let that message pass the brain and sink into her heart. Then the bus came, so it was hugs and goodbyes.

We had a nice ride back to Xining. On the bus Tricia yelled to me, "They think you're fifty!" I replied, "I'll settle for that. Dorothy's father said I was fifty-five!" My age seemed to cause quite a stir in this country where the elderly are so respected. Actually, I was sixty-seven at that time.

We had a belated luncheon celebration of Dorothy's twenty-first birthday at the Muslim Hot Pot Restaurant in Xining. The tables have a hole in the middle with a pot of hot water over a gas burner. The pot has two sides, one with hot spices, and the other with mild. Even the mild was too hot for me. As the water boils, you put in the vegetables and meat you desire. There was yogurt for desert, which was cooling and refreshing. Of course, we took lots of photographs, and Dorothy was elated.

That evening we returned to the campus coffee house seeking divine appointments. There were not many students there because we were a little early. We did get to talk with Cassie, with whom Deena had spoken previously. There were no openings to witness, and we had to leave for supper at Huggee Fon's apartment (Nana's granddaughter), which was located in the building behind the coffee house. Huggee Fon's husband, Boo Din, was a member of the Communist Party, so we had to be mindful of our conversation. Also, at that time Huggee Fon was not a believer. (Nicole led her to Christ a few weeks later, which meant she could share the good news with Nana). They had an adorable two-year old daughter named Annie. Jun came also. He is the first cousin of Boo, and they grew up together. Jun told us that he had a PhD—one of only five in the province—and he is the only one who was educated in the United States. I was shocked at how Jun blasted the government for all the corruption, saying that communism does not work. He had been offered a job by the government, but said he would not work for them, as he wants to help the people and cannot with this system. He had been back in China for seven months and was trying to decide what to do. Back in America, he had been living with a young lady for the past five years, but he did not want to get married. He came from a family of well-educated, caring people, and was feeling that pressure to excel (like Dorothy). He had the potential to do great things, but the bottom line was that he needed Jesus, the grand Director. The team witnessed with comments as we were gently led. We had to be wise and consider our host and hostess.

The following morning at team meeting, we shared how Jun was on our hearts, and we prayed for him. We met with him for lunch at what he called "the cold noodle place." It was his favorite, and he wanted to treat us. If there ever were a misnomer, this was it. The so-called "cold noodle" was so hot, I could not swallow it, but discreetly hid my first mouthful in my napkin. I took tiny bites and flushed my mouth with huge gulps of water. I was not the only one having trouble, but we certainly did not want to be ungrateful to our host, especially since we wanted to introduce him to Christ. There was no opportunity to witness at this time, but he promised to come to our continuing birthday party for Dorothy that night.

Jun and I talked as we walked down the street about our dreams of changing our world. He said his dream was already shattered because it was huge. I reminded him that big dreams don't always happen at once. One small touch in a pond can start a ripple that spreads throughout the whole body of water as one ripple reaches out and touches another. The only way to eat an elephant is one bite at a time. So many people get disillusioned and then they don't do anything. He said maybe that was why he was here—to learn that. Surely the Holy Spirit was stirring in his heart.

We left Jun and went to a local department store to buy Olympic caps to take home. We saw Dorothy and Showbei, and told Dorothy that Jun was coming to her party that night. She said Jun had been a student of her father. She had been told of his excellence, and she was encouraged to be like Jun. She had never met him and was honored that he was coming to her party. This had to be a God-ordained incident.

We went to Nicole's apartment to prepare our Mexican farewell and birthday dinner. Mexican food is good all over the world! Dorothy, Showbei, David (Dorothy's brother), and Jun joined Nicole, Nicky (her roommate), and the team. There were eleven in all. We played crazy games, sang silly songs, gave Dorothy her gifts, and ate birthday cake. I asked Dorothy if David would like to have a Bible, so she asked him, and he replied he would. She was excited about this, and at the end of the evening, she asked me about it again. I told her I had put it in her bag so she could give it to him at school. She promised when she went back to Guanting, she would explain to Nana the meaning of the gospel bracelet.

I asked Jun if he wanted a Bible, but he declined. He said I could pray for him that God would give him direction. I told him I thought he was looking for *something* instead of *someone*. He said he would persevere, and maybe he would know what to do. I said, "Yes, you will." Tricia had also spoken to him about wisdom and direction, so he knew that we loved him and cared about his future. It was hard to say all the farewells, and there were a lot of tears. This is the part of mission work that is so heart wrenching!

On our last morning in Xining, there was no water, like the devil thumbing his nose at us. Thankfully, this was not a real problem because that evening we would be at the hotel in Beijing. Nicole came to help us check out and get us on the road to the airport. She had become a very special sister to us, not just a guide. She promised to meet with us in the States in a few months (which she did that following November). Our flight into Beijing was uneventful, just a time for contemplating all we had seen and done in Guanting and Xining.

Sunni met us at the Asian Vision Hotel and took us to the places we wanted to go, such as the Friendship Store for shopping, Starbucks to get souvenir coffee mugs, and the Internet cafe so some could send messages home. We had dinner at the Hard Rock Cafe, where we met Chris, who worked with Sunni to safely transfer the Bibles. They had put the Bibles in backpacks, gone into a certain restaurant, and, after dining, left the backpacks to be collected. His heart was to get the Word into the hands of believers, and this was what he was doing at every opportunity. I thought about how many Bibles I had in my home and how I had taken that precious freedom for granted.

Sunni stayed with us that night in the hotel, giving us some quality prayer time together. Because the Lord had so marvelously stretched our funds, we were able to help her financially with her scheduled mission trip to Tibet. She gave us neat China T-shirts as parting gifts. Her passionate love of the Lord and her dedication to serve Him at any cost were inspiring. I knew there were many more like her, and China would one day be a Christian nation. It was just a matter of time.

When we left home to come to China, our team chose to use "We're Off to See the Wizard" from *The Wizard of Oz* as our code song. Dorothy had been our guide/translator to the Tu village where we stayed five days; we went to the Yellow River (instead of the Yellow Brick Road); the abbreviation of the airline we flew was *O.Z.*; and as we were going to the airport to catch the flight home, the taxi driver turned on the radio, and we heard "Somewhere Over the Rainbow." Also, just like the main character in *The Wizard of Oz*, our Dorothy had been searching and found what she had been looking for in Jesus when she accepted Him as her Lord and Savior. We could see His hand in even the smallest of details, confirming to us that He had gathered this little team together. He had showed us time and time again His glory.

Even after the long journey home, He gave us many opportunities to share this dynamic experience with various churches and other groups who had supported us, so the trip did not end with our return to America. And, like putting the cherry on top, Deena, the team member who had been so sick at the beginning and so frustrated with her un-pressed clothes, chose to return to China as a missionary to work with children in orphanages. She was commissioned in May 2005.

The mission goes on, and on, and on!

CHAPTER 14
NEW YORK CITY

OCT 2001

I rejoined New Hope Baptist Church in August 2001, having previously been a member there from 1982 to 1989. New Hope is strong on missions, and I was delighted to be a member of this team of thirteen men and women going to New York City to minister to those impacted by the 9-11 tragedy. We left the church around 5:30 a.m. on Thursday, October 11, 2001, for the Atlanta airport, and the short flight into New York. I sat next to a young Jewish businessman who lived in the city, and when I told him that we were on a mission to help the New Yorkers, he was very pleased. He said that everyone was hurting, and they needed to talk; many were still in a daze.

We arrived at our hotel around two thirty that afternoon, and after receiving our room assignments and stowing our luggage, we had a team meeting. We were divided into two groups: one team of seven (including me) led by Charles, who was assigned to the Billy Graham Association; and the other group of six led by Jack, who would be working with the NYC Metro Baptist Association. Because we arrived so late, we all went to the Baptist Association, where Lisa gave us an orientation. The plan was to set up tables on the streets, disburse literature and Bibles, talk to people who stopped, and deliver letters and teddy bears to fire stations and police stations.

That evening was the one-month anniversary of the tragedy, so we attended a service at St. Patrick's Cathedral. The splendor and pageantry of this magnificent church, plus the music ("Amazing Grace") as we entered, was overwhelming. Sadly, we could not stay since there was another service scheduled at Trinity Baptist Church. A simultaneous live broadcast with Franklin Graham and another church in Brooklyn was augmented by the live worship of Trinity. Policemen, firemen, and emergency personnel were asked to stand and be recognized, and they were given a standing ovation. The atmosphere was one of sadness at the great loss, but also of pride, unity, and hope. We were bound together by the common thread of being brothers and sisters—a family in crisis.

Some of the women on the team went to Times Square, where we asked a lady for directions. We introduced ourselves, and she said her name was Doreen and that she had been unable to leave the house for approximately six days after the bombing. I asked if we could pray for her, and she agreed. When I closed with the Prayer of Jabez, she said, "I know that prayer!" She was touched, and so were we; the Lord sent us to be encouragers and lifters of the head.

The next morning (Friday), the teams went to their respective assignments. The Billy Graham team went to Harbor Christian Fellowship, where two gentlemen named Randy and Rich trained us. We were not to do evangelism, but merely let the people know someone cared, to urge them to talk, and offer them cards so they could call the Billy Graham Association twenty-four hours a day if they needed counseling. We also had some beautifully done pamphlets, entitled "Remembrance—Fallen But Not Forgotten," the cover depicting the ruins of the Towers surrounded by smoke, and a single fireman standing in the debris. Inside were brief stories honoring Father Mike, a chaplain to the firefighters and among the first of the 350 firefighters who died, and Rachel Scott, a student who was killed at Columbine High School, concluding with a message from Billy Graham.

We were then dispatched to Central Park. A table was already there with free literature, and we were to engage people in conversations. Our introduction question was, "Where were you when the Towers fell?" Then we followed up, asking how they were doing. An important part of grief counseling is to allow the counselee to talk, releasing the pent-up emotions. The team fanned out, but we kept our eyes on each other so we would not get lost, because Central Park covers an immense area.

I was standing by the table when Pauline and Chris, a mother and son, approached. I introduced myself and pointed to my badge showing my affiliation with the Graham Association. The son, in his sixties, had taken his eighty-something-year-old mother to the doctor to get a new hearing aid, and they were on their way home. When I asked where they were when the Towers fell, he said they had been in their apartment. They were "doing OK," he told us, but still felt that their world had been shaken. Even though I had not made any religious comments, he turned the conversation in that direction. He said he didn't go to church, but his mother prayed all the time. I kept my arm around her, occasionally giving her a squeeze, and rubbing her back. She said she felt so loved, so special (said that twice, in fact), and I told her she was. Her son had moved from California four years earlier to care for her, and that certainly was a sign of great love. Then suddenly she got excited, exclaiming "I can breathe! The lump is gone; I can breathe!" He said she had shortness of breath. In light of what happened, I asked if I could pray for her, and she nodded her head. Since she was a petite lady, I leaned over so she could hear with her good ear and prayed for both of them. As they were leaving, I encouraged them to be cautious and stay safe.

My next encounter was with Jean, a young lady of Chinese descent who was on her lunch hour. She was born in New York, but her parents were from China. I told her that I had been to China on a mission trip, and she asked how it looked. She wanted to know all I could tell her about it. She had been at work when the Towers fell, and now she was just afraid. She had to get back to her job, so I wished her well and gave her a tract and calling card.

I sat next to a young lady on a bench, who was waiting to meet a friend. She said she was engaged and feeling guilty about being happy. Her friend arrived and she had to leave, so I wished her much happiness in her marriage and said goodbye, covering her in a silent prayer.

Yolanda had been a widow for three years, and she had no children. She moved here about forty years ago from Hungary and was a member of the Reformed Church. She lived in Jackson Heights, Queens, in a neighborhood of Hispanics and Muslims. She said that immediately after the tragedy, U.S. flags were everywhere, but when the bombing of Afghanistan started, the U.S. flags were replaced with signs reading Allah is God. All this was dredging up memories of World War II and the Hungarian Revolt. She was afraid and having trouble sleeping. I gave her a card so she could call the Association for counseling and prayer.

Next I met a tall, blonde young lady, who said she was a native New Yorker. She was dealing relatively well with the tragedy, but the recent anthrax scare was too much to deal with, too soon. I told her why I was there, but we could not continue our conversation because she had to leave. I asked if I could give her a hug and she said sure. I gave her a squeeze and said, "Stay safe." She teared up and rushed off.

Anna, also originally from Hungary, was another widow of many years. She had one grown daughter. I wished I could have connected Anna and Yolanda, as they could have been a comfort to each other. Like Yolanda, she said this reminded her of World War II and the Hungarian Revolt. Things she thought she had handled were coming back. She remembered the Russian tanks, food shortage, and assuming so much responsibility for other children when she was just a child herself. On a trip she took to Austria, she defected from Hungary and later came to the United States, where she was interrogated and investigated. She said our problem in America was letting "all these people" into the country and not investigating them. She resented the foreigners who passed by us as we talked, especially the Muslim ladies with veils. She worked with Alzheimer patients and only made $6.50 per hour. She asked if I could go with her to see the boats, and I agreed because she seemed so lonely. We listened to a Chinese musician play the violin, and she showed me the sailboats, the rowboats, the bridge, the apartment building where John Lennon lived, the famous Angel statue, and the swans. She talked continuously and was very negative. She had a date to meet her daughter the following Friday for her birthday, and they were planning to come to the park, ride in the boats, and have the daughter's portrait drawn by an artist friend for free. However, she did not believe her daughter would really come. She told me earlier she was a member of St. Patrick's, so I asked if I could pray for her. Our Lord had blessed me with her as my new friend and tour guide, and I prayed she would have a happy birthday outing with her daughter and that she would always be safe.

I sat on a bench beside a young man who was reading a newspaper. He moved to the city from Virginia in August, the month before 9-11. He was at work when the Towers fell and said he was all right, but that we must be alert. He had to leave abruptly.

That evening we went to Ground Zero. Only people with credentials could visit, as it was very dangerous and now considered a crime scene. We talked with some policemen and some members of the National Guard, and we gave out tracts. Farther down the street, we talked briefly with a fireman who had just walked out of Ground Zero. He was at the point of tears. Even a month after the attack, it was like an oven among the rubble. They still had to pour water on it because the heat was so strong that when the air hit, it would blaze again. It had gotten up to two thousand degrees. We could see fifteen stories on top of the ground; the other eighty-five were compacted underground. They were only recovering parts of bodies. That day we heard they found a woman's hand, holding a child's hand. It was an eerie sight there in the night, with the floodlights beaming on the vast debris that had been scattered over some sixteen acres, from city block to city block. It was hard to breathe with all the smoke. It was like a fog, making things look out of focus. The stores and their contents were covered in ashes. Little memorials were set up from place to place, with pictures of people who were still missing, letters, flowers, and notes. I sobbed as I wrote on one board. This was a heartbreaking sight to see; it was difficult to absorb this happened in New York City, in my America. The memory is permanently etched in my brain.

The next day, Saturday, our team went to South Street Seaport by the East River, close to Ground Zero. As we walked toward the river, wind was blowing the smoke all around and there was a foul odor. Larry said that we were breathing in the ashes of dead bodies. Some people had on masks. We chatted with police officers along the way as we asked for directions, telling them why we had come, giving tracts, and praying for them as they allowed.

The seaport was crowded because it was a beautiful day. The air was clear and crisp by the river. The team spread out to reach as many as we could in our short space of time.

I saw a young man with red hair who was staring at the water. I asked where he was when the Towers fell, and he told me his story. He was working in the Woolworth Building, and saw it all from the office windows. His company had since moved to Connecticut and would not be returning to New York, so he was commuting. Then his friend Karen arrived. She was a music teacher, and two of her students lost parents in the Towers. They were both grieving. We couldn't talk longer because they had an appointment. I wished them well and urged them to take good care of each other.

I met Sough-Ping (which she said meant "pretty apple") and her husband sitting on some steps. They moved here from China in 1945. They lived in Chinatown and had not left their apartment for many days because of the smoke. They came to the river that day for the sunshine and fresh air. I told them about my trip to China, remarking on the beauty of the country. Glen, another team member, arrived and began talking with the husband, leaving me free to converse in more detail with Sough-Ping. She was waking at three o'clock in the morning every day and having difficulty sleeping. Then it was time to say good-bye. We held hands, I prayed for both of them, husband and wife, and especially for her to have the sweet slumber our Lord promises in His Word (Psalm 127:2).

Irene was a young lady from Palestine, an artist, whose specialty was video/sound. She said she was a Christian, "of course," because her parents were. It was amusing how the Billy Graham badge prompted the people to turn the conversation to religion. She boldly proclaimed, "Christianity started in my country." She had just come there a week ago from Germany, so she was not in the city on 9-11. She was hostile at first, but thawed as we talked. I said I was glad she wasn't here at the time of the tragedy. We talked about Bethlehem, and since I had been there, we had that in common. She let me pray for her, and under my spoken prayer was the silent plea that Christ would reveal Himself to her if she really did not know Him personally.

Wim and Joo had moved here from Holland after World War II; they had no children. Actually, I started talking to him first as he was waiting for his wife to return from the restroom. Then she joined us. They had come into the city for the weekend to celebrate her birthday, which was the next day. They commented on my badge and said they knew about Billy Graham. They were born-again Christians and were doing well. They were pleased to receive a tract.

Liz was sitting alone on a bench by the water. She was from England and was departing the next day for Boston. Because of 9-11, she believed it was important she come to New York first. She and her husband had once planned to take this vacation, but he passed away over twenty years ago. This was the first time she could afford to come. She had two daughters; one was unmarried and living with a man, and the other was about to graduate college. Although she had been baptized in the Church of England as a child, she was an atheist and stated that her daughters did not believe in God either. She said she didn't know what, if anything, she could believe. I told her I was not there to shove Christianity down her throat, but I could tell her what I believed and why, and so I did. I ended with the fact that this was a God-appointment: her being here on this particular day at this time, all the way from England, and me here from Georgia. God promised us in His Word that He works all things together for good for those who love Him (Romans 8:28), and He was using this disaster to bring her here to hear about Him. I gave her two tracts (she did not want a Bible), and I asked if she would be willing to allow me to pray the Lord would reveal to her His truth and that the truth would set her free (John 8:32). She replied, yes, so that is what I prayed. I told her I was confident He would do that for her and for her daughters. I expect to see her in heaven one day because our Lord finishes what He starts!

It was Sunday, our last full day. We went to Eastside Baptist, a charismatic, swinging church, and enjoyed great worship. Pastor Rosario spoke from Exodus 1, giving a sermon entitled "The Destiny for Which I Was Born." He taught how the more afflicted the Hebrews were, the more they multiplied. When oppression moved into murder and taskmasters were set over them, God sent the midwives. God has a plan, and it starts in motion when we're born. Satan also has an evil plan. Each of us has an assignment, a unique calling. The midwives, who assist in bringing forth life, move us forward, and in like manner, God uses us to aid others in their journey. When he asked, "What's your taskmaster's name?" many came forward at the altar call, recognizing that fear, unforgiveness, and bitterness, to name a few, had been oppressing them for too long. I prayed for a young woman and her eight-year-old son. She came back later to say that I had prayed from Isaiah 54, and it ministered to her. The Lord had given her those specific promises, so this was a divine confirmation to her. I marveled again at the sweetness of our Lord. He is God of the details.

Then we went to the renowned Brooklyn Tabernacle. You could feel the presence of the Lord in that place; the music is so anointed. Pastor Cymbala preached on the Holy Spirit. Wow! He said that we are God's temple and asked us to consider where we are taking Him. Everywhere we are, that's where God is! Well, we had taken Him to Central Park, Ground Zero, the East River, police stations, fire stations, the subways, restaurants, churches, and the streets.

We came back to the hotel and ate supper together. Most of the team went to Times Square, but I decided I needed some quiet time, so I stayed in the hotel. When my room-mates returned, they said they had ridden in a limousine. I regretted I didn't go, but it was good to be alone for a little while and recharge. Hindsight is always 20/20.

On several occasions we rode the subway, and I was able to converse with many different people. One was a twenty-year-old student going to New York University studying journalism. He said he was fine, but his parents were very concerned. His stop came, so I urged him to be careful and stay in close touch with his Mom and Dad.

Robert was a young man about to graduate from business school in May and already working another job. He said all this was making him think. He lost a friend in the Trade Center, so he was grieving. I gave him a tract to read later, prayed for him right there on the train for peace and guidance, and he thanked me for my concern.

A young woman from California was sad to admit she was not going to church. She was here with her family to see her daughter play soccer. I gave her one of the special tracts containing a Billy Graham sermon and wished her soccer success!

Darrus was a young woman from Uzbekistan, whose name means "wealth." I laughed and rubbed her arm so her wealth would rub off on me. She was doing fine, she said. Was she really?

All of these contacts were very brief, so we had to rely on the Holy Spirit to lead the conversations. It was important to get tracts into their hands so they would have something to read when they had more quiet time and the words could soak in, but the most important thing was to spread the love.

A dear friend of mine, Brother Grogan, was very active in the Gideons, and he wanted me to see if there were a Gideon Bible in our hotel, which there was. One of our team members, Gail, told me she had been convicted by reading Gideon Bibles in every hotel when she traveled. She finally decided to really read the Bible herself at home, and that's how she met Jesus. Brother Grogan was delighted when I gave him that good report. Our Lord's Word never returns void (Isaiah 55:11).

On Monday, our last day, the entire team went to a fire station that had lost fifteen men. They were putting on brave fronts, but you could see tears in many eyes. One man was there on relief duty. He told us that in his station in the Bronx they got attention and compassion the first day, but nothing after that. This station was loaded with flowers, letters, stuffed animals, and other mementoes. We had a good visit there, and on the street I talked with Dan, a fireman from Indiana. He shared how he fully recovered from a broken neck suffered during a call, and now he was back at work. He came to New York City to help his brothers.

Next we went to a police station where three men had died. We talked with Officer Jeff, whose wife was expecting in three months, and Officer Don. They were all exhausted, but seemed glad to see us. They gave me an official patch and said, "All these Southern people sure do smile a lot." These visits hurt your heart, but it was vital that these warriors knew that others were sharing their suffering. It helped the healing, both ways.

In a local souvenir store we met a cashier from Bangladesh. Gail talked with him while I purchased cards, and then I gave him a tract. You just do what you can with the time you have.

281

We talked in the lobby with a Red Cross volunteer from Michigan. She was on a trauma team and had been there three weeks. She was very concerned that people were not talking, but rather bottling their emotions and saying they were all right. They had set up three centers around the perimeter of Ground Zero. The Oklahoma City Center, set up in 1995 after that bombing, had just now closed after approximately six years. She sadly told us that the suicides start in the second year.

The driver who took us to the airport was a Jew from Uzbekistan. The diversity of nationalities in this city was amazing to me!

On the plane home I sat next to Lindsey and Amy, who are sisters, and gave them my testimony. Lindsey was to be married the following February but was concerned that it might not last. I told her there were no guarantees about anything. You trust in the Lord and try to make the best decision you can, knowing that no matter what, you will be able to survive because He will never leave or forsake you (Deuteronomy 31:8; Matthew 28:20).

We caught an earlier flight than scheduled, but our luggage did not. Larry's wife, Cindy, met us at the airport, and we went to the Dwarf House in Hapeville to eat supper. It was a very good ending, actually a debriefing. We returned to the airport and there was our luggage, right on time. Getting your luggage is such a blessing! Then it was off to New Hope to get my car, and home!

From the time I came to know Jesus, I considered Planet Earth my home, and her people my people. Some of my friends had felt called to specific countries, but I wanted to be a missionary to the whole world, to meet my brothers and sisters of all cultures and races, and introduce them to Jesus. However, this mission to New York City holds a unique place in my heart because it was in my *own* country, ministering to my *own* people; I was experiencing their pain because it was my pain, too. Our nation had been attacked, and this act of violence had bonded us together.

It was so personal!

CHAPTER 15
UGANDA

JUN 2002

New Hope Baptist Church in Fayetteville, Georgia, was a partner in Operation Sunrise Africa (OSA), the objective of which was to expose fifty million people in fifty cities in East and South Africa to the gospel in fifty days. The basic strategy was to send one team of ten to each city every ten days, beginning officially July 1, 2002, and extending through August 19, 2002. Additional personnel would be on Prayer Mountain, where a twenty-four-hour prayer chain would cover the operation beginning June 20, 2002, and concluding August 29, 2002. New Hope's assignment was Uganda, and in particular, the cities of Kampala, Jinja, Masaka, and Hoima.

The vision of OSA began in the heart of Peter, founder of Life Ministry in Kampala, and we were to operate under his covering. Peter met with us at our quarters in Kampala our first morning and explained in detail the assignments of our team. The thrust of OSA for 2002 was to win souls, disciple them, train them to be witnesses for Christ, and then send them into all the cities, continuing the wave. The leaders of New Hope's team were Steve and his wife, Anne, former missionaries to Uganda and close friends of Peter and his wife, Elizabeth. Their daughter Jennifer and son Jonathan were also on the team, along with Judy, Susan (my roommate), Jim, Tom, and four married couples: Holly and Mike, TiAnna and Robert, Celeste and Owen, and Terrie and Keith.

Keith was an optometrist, so we collected eyeglasses to dispense in free eye clinics, which would be held in conjunction with stadium soccer championship games. Keith had trained certain members of the team to give vision tests and provide the proper prescription glasses, while he treated the more complex cases. Other members of the team were greeters, and their job was to make the people feel welcome and present the gospel as opportunities arose. Our team was assigned to the stadium in Kampala, where some local doctors were giving other medical assistance. They did not stay the entire time, but we did. We distributed programs, which featured favorite soccer players and also included the plan of salvation. We were able to share the gospel with those who would take the time to listen. When anyone accepted Christ, we would introduce them to the representatives from Life Ministry so they could be connected to a local church for discipleship.

My assignment was to be a greeter, and to my delight, I was honored to present the gospel to Hadigha, a lovely young lady. She said she had no satisfaction in her life, feeling nothing. I led her to Jesus, the source of all satisfaction. She had that great feeling from just meeting Christ, and I took her to Michael for follow-up. Owen had been working with people in line for eye examinations, and he came to get me because some of them wanted to know about Jesus. I prayed with Moses, and he said he felt warmth in his heart. Then I introduced him to Michael for mentoring. Some of the people already knew Jesus, so I shared scripture that applied to their situations and prayed for their needs.

I had a most interesting conversation with Henry, who was working on a small building close to the ticket booth where Keith was conducting eye exams. I walked over to give him a program/tract. I introduced myself, and he said he was a Muslim. I told him that God loved Muslims. He was very disenchanted with both the Muslims and the Christians, saying that no one was real. I told him that we could not be responsible for the actions of others, only for ourselves, and I assured him that I cared, as did our team; that is why we had come all the way from America. I was at the point of tears, and then he wiped at his eyes and put his head down so I could not see. I asked him to pray with me to the one true God, and ask His Holy Spirit to reveal to him the truth, the reality of Jesus. I could feel my spirit touching his spirit, and I was certain this prayer was answered.

The next morning Steve, Robert, and Mike conducted a very fruitful meeting with local business leaders. At the conclusion, they were asked to plan a one thousand-person seminar. Meanwhile, the rest of the team met, had a devotional, and shared experiences from the night before. Susan and Mike had each led two people to the Lord, so, including the people to whom I talked, we had a total of six conversions.

We returned to the stadium that afternoon. It was more of the same, but better, because more came to the Lord! I prayed with Dan, a teenager; Kizza, also a teenager; Sonie William, in his forties; and Saidi, in his late thirties. Saidi turned out to be a big catch! He said he was a bishop in the Muslim Council, and it was very dangerous for him to be seen. We made an appointment to meet the following Sunday at the stadium so I could pray with his wife and eight children for salvation. I showed him how to do that himself using the plan in the program, but he wanted me to meet his family. Unfortunately, that Sunday he did not come. I received a letter from him after I returned home saying that once he made his decision, he had been chased from his home and had lost his job. His wife and children are "saved," he wrote, so he must have prayed with them himself. He wanted to learn more about Jesus Christ and his new religion, so Peter and Benjamin of Life Ministry have since met with him for mentoring. Benjamin also told me later that Saidi literally had to run for his life. Saidi sent me pictures of his little girl, whom he had re-named "Smith Betty." What an honor!

I awakened very early the following morning and could not sleep, so I prayed and asked the Lord to speak to me. He talked to me about time, and later that morning, Jim did our devotional from Ecclesiastes 3 about how God makes all things beautiful in His time. I shared how the Lord had told me that morning that we were here in Uganda for such a time as this; that it was His appointed time; that we had His favor; and that each team member was important. Our Father is such an encourager!

Steve, Robert, and Michael attended a prayer breakfast with local business leaders and returned in time to share in part of our team meeting. Afterwards, we all went shopping, which is an important part of any mission. It's fun for the team, of course, but it is also a good witness to the people, giving us an opportunity to boast about their handiwork and culture, to have personal interchange, and at the same time boost their economy. I could see that God was doing a mighty work here. The salvations were the greatest miracles, but the gift of sight to those who needed glasses was of utmost importance. Also, marriages were being strengthened between our team couples. It was my prayer that every single team member would be bitten by the "mission bug."

That evening we returned to the stadium, and I was able to pray with Moses, who only had one leg, and with Mayanjo, who said he was a Muslim. Benjamin of Life Ministry talked with each of them and made appointments for follow-up.

I had a most interesting encounter with another Muslim named Abdul. He was a very tall man and had come with his friend, who was a Christian. I started sharing with Abdul, and he kept interrupting me, saying, "Please pray for me; please pray for me!" Several other men approached, wanting programs. They all professed to be Christians. One was belligerent, saying he was a Catholic, and he started arguing about denominations. I told him that it didn't matter. The bottom line is, "Who is this Jesus?" We were talking about a personal relationship with Him, not religion. If your church isn't preaching that He is the only Way to God, the Father— the cross and His blood, His death, burial, and resurrection—then you need to get out of there, no matter what the denomination is called. The main thing right then was that Abdul wanted to know the truth, and he had asked for prayer. They agreed, so the Catholic man stood on one side, laid hands on Abdul, and his Christian friend stood on the other side. I stood in front, put my hand over his heart, and prayed for the Holy Spirit to come with His divine revelation. I told Abdul to open the door of his heart and invite Jesus in. He didn't say the sinner's prayer word for word, but he was grinning ear to ear, and thanking everybody. He left with his program/tract, from which I previously explained the plan of salvation, so he could go over it again.

After the games were over, the clinic closed. We were about to leave when a man named Godfrey and his friend arrived. Godfrey was very upset, wanting prayer for his wife, who was at home very ill. He wanted to talk to the doctor. I told him that the medical doctor was gone, but that we could pray for his wife. I summoned Jackson of Life Ministry and explained the situation. In the Bible, the Lord had Isaac pray for his wife, so Godfrey could do the same, and we would stand in agreement with him. The four of us held hands, and Jackson prayed a powerful prayer. Godfrey and his friend left, and on that following Sunday when we were at the stadium for the launching of OSA, Godfrey was excited to see me. He came running with his hands lifted up, praising the Lord. He said when he arrived home that night after we prayed, his wife was healed! I reported this to Jackson, and he was thrilled.

The next day, we left for Masaka and Prayer Mountain, and on our way we crossed the equator. There was a little village there with a post office, so I mailed myself a card so I could have a postmark from the equator: "Hi to me. Jesus is Lord! Love, Betty." We were traveling along a route used by truckers in Zaire to get to Rwanda and Uganda. Our driver said that some of the truckers engaged in prostitution and spread the AIDS virus. This is consistent with the belief of most researchers that AIDS originated in sub-Saharan Africa.[1]

We stopped in one village that was noted for its drums. It was fascinating to see how they were made, and the team contributed greatly that day to their economy. I completed my transactions, and while waiting for everyone else, I saw some ladies gathered in front of a store. I spoke with a young lady named Stoikie, and as I shared with her about Jesus, she said she knew Him. "He is good; I like Him," she said. She told me she went to church every Sunday, and she wanted this God. I asked if she believed that Jesus is the Son of God, that He died on the cross for her sins, and that He rose again. She affirmed, "Oh, yes!" I replied, "Then you have this God!" There was just time for a brief hug and good-bye, as our bus driver was blowing his horn, ready to leave.

The presence of the Lord was strong on Prayer Mountain; I could feel Him as I stepped off the bus. Life Ministry had offered a fifty-acre mountain at Kako in Masaka to serve as an international prayer retreat center. It was to serve as a school of prayer for all nations, offering a video library containing records of past revivals and books for spiritual renewal. There would be an auditorium, chapel, seminar rooms, and dormitories. The vision was to have twenty-four-hour prayer chains taking place at the center, and they would pray until Jesus returns.

We met Abraham who was a part of a group that prays for Israel. He was married to a woman named Sarah and had ten children. We all came together under a tent, where the local leaders, Benjamin, Steve, and Abraham, shared the vision Peter had in 1995. Another pastor had a similar vision, and his church was assisting in OSA. They were expecting a mighty move of God. We had an outstanding prayer meeting together.

We were then led to a praise gathering and joined in singing and dancing to the glory of God. These people could do more than simply pray—they knew how to worship. It was awesome!

Looking across the valley from Prayer Mountain, we saw a village where witch doctors had called an emergency meeting because the demons were not answering them any more. The day of the meeting it rained hard all day, even though it was the dry season. They adjourned the meeting until October, which is the rainy season. Steve led the group in prayer over that area.

We gathered at another point on the mountain overlooking Lake Victoria, where Steve again led us in prayer. The small huts that people lived in while praying dotted the side of the mountain. What a place for a spiritual retreat!

We said our goodbyes and proceeded to Hotel Liston in Masaka for a buffet supper (which we called our "lupper" because we were combining lunch and dinner). Steve, Robert, and Michael went to speak at a meeting of professional men, and Owen and Jonathan went along to work the video. The remainder of the team went to Masaka Pentecostal Church for an evening service. I met a lady named Betty, which was delightful! They were also worshippers, so we danced and sang with them before our Tom gave his testimony. This was Abraham's church, and he shared that it was exactly fifty-two weeks ago—Sunday, July 1, 2001—when they began praying for revival, not realizing that OSA was in the works. They were excited that in fifty cities in fifty days, fifty million people would hear the gospel. (The number fifty is significant because Pentecost, the day that the Lord sent the Holy Spirit, happened on the fiftieth day after Jesus' ascension to heaven. These dedicated Ugandans were following the Lord's pattern of significance with this number and concentrated prayer as set forth in Acts 1:3–5, 8; 2:1–4.)

That Saturday, which would have been my fiftieth wedding anniversary, the Lord gave me an incredible day. That morning we went to Life Ministry in Kampala, where Keith held an eye clinic for the staff and their families. The rest of us went to All Saints' Cathedral, where 200 to 250 students were being instructed by Compassion International. We divided so we could cover all the classes, and there we shared and gave out goodies. These were healthy, happy, vibrant children, as opposed to those we later visited in Jinja at the children's clinic.

In Jinja, the facilities were bare and stark, with paint peeling off the walls. Beds were almost on top of each other. In one large room, cribs were lined, and parents were sitting on the floor beside them. Some had their children out of the cribs, lying on thin blankets on the floor. I sat next to a group of the mothers and tried to share with them. Language here was a barrier, as they were uneducated and spoke very little English. Many families had gathered outside to enjoy the beautiful, warm day. There were more opportunities to give tracts and little love gifts to the children, including sweets for everyone. I had a good conversation with Albert, a security guard, and with a young man and his wife, all who personally knew Jesus! The administrator said they served approximately 150 children daily, mostly suffering from malaria. About twenty die per day. Even though this disease is treatable, many come too late. Patients are given medicine when they first come to the clinic, but when they start feeling better, they stop taking the medicine, wanting to save it for a later day. It must be taken for at least three days. When the malaria flares, the medicine is no longer effective.

We then went to the source of the Nile for some photographs. There was a lovely park, and it was refreshing to be surrounded by God's beautiful creation after our experience at the clinic.

We had "lupper" again at the Triangle Hotel on a balcony overlooking Lake Victoria. An interesting note: Uganda is the size of Oregon, and Lake Victoria is the size of South Carolina. The team commented on the events of the day, and I shared what a special day it had been for me. I had a fantastic would-have-been fiftieth anniversary! There was no place on earth I would rather have been at that moment in time.

The next day, Sunday, June 30, was the official launch day for OSA. We began the day by attending worship services at All Saints' Cathedral in Kampala. It was a surprise to see that the guest speaker was a friend from home, the pastor of River's Edge, a church in Fayetteville, Georgia. After church we went to Peter and Elizabeth's home for a short visit, and then to a local hotel for lunch. That afternoon various groups from churches all over Uganda were marching to the stadium, and excitement was in the air. A huge stage had been erected, and several choirs and musicians dressed in brilliant colors performed. Prayers were lifted for the success of OSA, for Uganda, for Africa, and I silently added America. Our very own Peter, from whose heart OSA was birthed, was the first speaker and, I thought, the best. At the end of the impressive ceremony, the choir sang a praise song and Pastor Ortiz gave a second trumpet call. He said it was a prophetic choir, and he mentioned the trumpet calls in Revelation 8. I thought of the time when the Israelites were facing a massive attack and King Jehosaphat sent the singers and praisers first into battle, followed by the army. They were victorious (2 Chronicles 20:21–22). Then the pastor started prophesying, saying that a wave was coming like a swell, and Jesus, the Son of Righteousness, was coming with healing in His wings for Uganda and Africa. That evening at supper there was some criticism of the pastor's performance, and it made me sad because he had not come to "perform" but to proclaim the Word of the Lord. Some had concentrated on his trumpet playing and missed the prophecy. Jesus said, "They seeing see not; and hearing they hear not, neither do they understand" (Matt. 13:13–14). We were participants in a monumental occasion. They desired fifty million souls in fifty days. I prayed that the Lord would give us a double portion—100 million!

We left the following morning for Hoima, a four-hour bus drive over bumpy dirt roads. The scenery was magnificent. We rode by rolling hills, mountains, and because of Steve's keen eyes, we even spotted some wild animals. It was neat to see pine trees, and, of course, the red dirt, just like home in Georgia.

We checked into another Kolping House (a chain of hotels) and then proceeded to All Saints Church of God, where approximately two hundred people were waiting for the eye clinic. The leaders there had been very efficient, assigning numbers to the people to prevent a mad rush. We were able to process approximately one hundred people that day. We were told that there had been three salvations before we arrived. The team dispersed to their different tasks, and some went with Ann to visit Harriet, who worked for Ann and Steve while they served as missionaries there. Susan and I gave our testimonies to the people who were waiting, and afterwards we moved to another section to be greeters. As the people were called, just a few at a time, the local team would record the information and we would chat with them as they waited. When asked if they knew Jesus, they would gladly tell you how long they had known Him and give you the date of their new birth. It was a valid part of their testimony. It never failed to delight me.

I prayed for healing with a lady whose eye was very red and swollen. She was to return the next day to see Dr. Keith, but she didn't return. I faithfully assumed she didn't need his services.

The next day the team divided and went to two different schools to share and distribute gifts. One special gift was a gospel bracelet, which allowed them to present the good news to the children. Cahooma, head of the local team, requested that Susan and I remain at the eye clinic. His people had not come, and he needed us to continue to greet and intercede. We were glad we stayed because Ida and Sarah came to Jesus; their new birthdates were July 2, 2002! Our job of greeting, talking, praying with the people, hugging, and taking pictures was very important and very fulfilling. We made "friends."

There was one very special young lady who made an indelible impression on me. Her name was Namugga, and she was twenty-one years old and very pretty. Cahooma kept the front doors locked, so that only those with numbered tickets could enter. Namugga, however, came to a back window and motioned me to come to her. She had a pair of glasses that were badly scratched and chipped. I took them to Terri to get a pair with the same prescription, but she declined, saying it would take away from those already in line. Owen cleaned them as best he could and tightened the screws. I gave them back to her, and explained the situation. She went to another window and used the same approach on Jonathan, but he couldn't help her either. She continued to stay at the window, and then a local pastor arrived with six female students dressed in blue-striped shirts and navy skirts. She called me again from the window and said she was a student. She was wearing a blue-checked shirt and navy skirt, so I told Cahooma she was a student. I asked him to let her in with the other girls and he did! After she received her new glasses, we gave her a case so they wouldn't be scratched. As we talked, she said that she was a Christian, her parents had died, and she had to leave school for a time. Another family accepted her, and she returned to school. Recently she moved in with her grandmother. Her goal was to work in human resources as a social worker. I told her how very proud I was of her and asked her to promise me that she would never give up all the rest of her life. She said others had said the same thing to her, and she would keep that promise and give Jesus the credit.

It was sad to leave Hoima the following day. Approximately 225 people had been treated at the clinic, but so many more needed our services. Yet there had to be a cut-off date, and this was it. Jesus said, "For you have the poor with you always" (Matt. 26:11, NKJV).

As we departed, we went to see the house where Steve, Anne, and their family lived when they served as missionaries here in 1981–1982. We couldn't go inside because the family living there was not home, but we did meet William, a former employee. From there we went to the beautiful mountain home of Peter's mother, Juliette. Her husband died that previous April, and she was delighted to have us visit her. We had a final prayer together, and after everyone left, I knelt at her feet to say a special prayer. It is the custom for younger girls to kneel when they meet an adult; I wanted to show her the honor and respect she so richly deserved.

Our destination was the Paraa Safari Lodge in Queen Elizabeth National Park, and on the way we saw monkeys, baboons, warthogs, hippopotami, and little bucks. The sky was covered with puffy white clouds, like little sheep, reminding me that the Lord was my Shepherd. When we came to the ferry to cross the Nile there was a hippo in the water, and another big hippo the locals called Alvin was grazing on the other side. The Lodge was like something in the movies, and I struggled to believe this was reality. Susan and I shared a room overlooking the Nile, where we could see a crocodile sunning on a sand bank, plus more bucks and hippos. Uganda has over 1,008 species of birds, and I think the majority live in this area, as we could hear many different songs and the cooing of doves. It was a beautiful symphony, and as proof of our Lord's sense of humor, a little guinea hen strutted by as I was writing in my journal.

On July 4, our country's birthday, we celebrated with red, white, and blue M&Ms. We left early that morning for a bus ride around the game park. Ishmael, our guide, pointed to a leopard in a tree. It had killed a waterbuck and was having a feast. We saw another leopard and six lions, including a "great lion" named Abraham who was fourteen years old. There were vultures, eagles, various other beautiful birds, lots of giraffes, bushbucks, water buffalo, warthogs, elephants, jackals, and even a huge monitor lizard. Ishmael said we had a very good day!

That afternoon we went on a river cruise up the Nile to Murchison Falls. The river was teeming with life: hippos, water buffalo, warthogs, monkeys, baboons, elephants, birds, eagles, crocodiles, and even another monitor lizard. Weaver's nests hung from trees like big, brown Christmas balls. Rock walls on the cliffs were pitted with holes where determined birds had made their homes. It tickled me to see the big hippos yawning. How could they be so bored? This was such an exciting place to be! The boat stopped at an outcropping of rocks, and we got out for those Kodak moments, as if we needed a photograph to seal this in our memories.

That evening we had a fun team meeting, where each person had to perform for the group. I did my rendition of "Head, Shoulders, Knees, and Toes," that had come in handy on the China mission. It was good for us to have light time before deeper sharing and debriefing. On so many missions, I had to unwind alone after I returned home. It was good to start the process with my teammates.

The next morning, our last day in Uganda, we stopped at Murchison Falls, this time from the land side. Hollie was a brave trooper, so sick, but not willing that we miss this amazing sight. Several of us prayed for her healing, but it was one of those slow answers. We walked to the top of the falls, and watched the water cascade down into the Nile, making rainbows. The rocks along our path were mica, and with the sun shining on them, it seemed we were walking on diamonds. It was a breathtaking sight; our Creator was everywhere!

It was a rush to get back to Kampala, shower, and pack for home. There was no time for lunch, "lupper," or supper, but Susan and I had stashed away rolls and bananas from breakfast, so we did not perish. Our plane departed from Entebbe. We saw the old airport at a distance. It was still riddled with bullet holes from a confrontation on June 27, 1976, when the Israelites, led by America's own Ross Perot, made their daring raid to rescue hostages held by Palestinians who hijacked an Air France Jet.[2]

There was a long layover in Brussels, so twelve of us rode the train into the city. We saw the Central Market, had Belgian waffles, strawberries and cream, and luscious hot chocolate. We felt obliged to go into the shops to see the famous lace. Of course, we saw the statue of the Manneken Pis, the ornate architecture of the Grand Palace, Town Hall, and the Cathedrale Saints Michel et Gudule. Being the Lord's missionary is not all work, though the work is the most important. The play is outstanding and so like our generous Lord. He really wants us to enjoy the beauty of His Planet Earth.

We departed Brussels and flew over Iceland, where we could see snow, mountains, and glaciers. At last we landed at Dulles International in Washington, DC, for a short layover, and then into Atlanta. Unfortunately, my suitcase did not land with me, but I was determined not to let that rob me of my joy. It did follow in due time.

Through the eye clinics, we had ministered to at least 100 in Kampala and 225 in Hoima, and I personally prayed with ten to receive Christ. Several on the team had led others to Christ, and our businessmen had an open invitation to return and lead Christ-based business seminars. There was no way to put a value on the relational bridges we built with countless Ugandans and the impact on our own lives. It had been a fruitful mission indeed; the kingdom had been increased. As always, I personally received much more than I was able to give. But isn't that God's way? We can never out-give Him.

CHAPTER 16
WALES

The mission to Wales was the second trip to begin on my birthday, but this one was special because it was my seventieth—a good, round number. New Hope Baptist Church, my home church, had been partnering with Holland Road Baptist Church in Hove, England, for the past seven years, though only one trip before had involved ministry specifically in Wales. On top of the excitement, the trip marked the one-hundredth year anniversary of the Wales Great Revival, and our pastor, John, had been asked to speak at services commemorating this event.

New Hope holds a meeting at the beginning of each year, at which time mission trips are planned for the coming year. Rich, our mission leader, encourages us to pray diligently about where we are to serve. A remark made at that meeting broke my heart. It was reported that the previous year a man from Wales had told one of the New Hope team that the Holy Spirit had left their valley. When I heard that, my spirit jumped inside me, and my thought was, "The Holy Spirit is in me, and I can take Him back to the valley!" It seemed so simple. Isn't that God's way, though? We try to make things so complicated, but all I had to do was go. Of course, there would be others on the team who would also be taking the Holy Spirit with them, but it was not about them. It was about my obedience to the Lord's call. As Rich suggested, I prayed carefully about the decision, but the more I prayed, the more I was convinced that Wales was where I was to serve next.

As the deadline approached for turning in our money for the trip, I was two hundred dollars short. I prayed some more, because God always pays for what He orders. When I went to the mailbox one afternoon, I had a note from a precious sister in Christ, enclosing a check for one hundred dollars because she wanted to be a part of the mission. That evening a brother in Christ gave me another note of encouragement, together with a check for fifty dollars. Two days after that, I received a card from another friend enclosing fifty dollars in cash. There was my two hundred dollars! In addition, I was able to earn $105 working the concession stand at two Georgia Tech baseball games, so I had the spending money I needed! I knew this was going to be a fantastic mission.

The team of fifty-one consisted primarily of members of New Hope's choir. They were to perform *Encounter God*, a musical/drama presentation of Christ and the Cross, which they performed at various locales in the evenings. During the day, we were divided into school teams (red, white, and blue). The red and white teams went to the elementary and middle schools, and the blue team visited high schools. Each team consisted of mixers, greeters, and the contacts with the local principals and teachers. The high school team consisted of the Two Bare Feet Band and other individuals who were to give their testimonies, present the gospel, and counsel the students as they responded. (Incidentally, this very talented band got its name from the poem "Footprints in the Sand.") I enlisted on the blue team!

We also had four clowns: two men, Dean-o and Bustyn, and two women, Daisy Diva and Lily. They were a tremendous hit with the children, young and old! They were able to witness most effectively through their skits; humor is a marvelous tool of evangelism. Even in church, don't we remember the jokes more than we do the sermons?

Some served on the community action team. They did projects planned by Holland Road Baptist Church, like rebuilding a wall (where one local got saved) and just beautifying the neighborhoods—cleaning up debris, cutting grass, pulling up weeds, etc. This proved to be a vital part of the mission. They were the hands and feet of Jesus to the community.

Our pastor held leadership seminars, while Donna, his wife, spoke on the role of leaders' wives. John, our music director, and his wife, also named Donna, gave messages on marriage enrichment. Phil, of Youth With a Mission, taught about inductive Bible study.

We had a supper meeting at High Street Church on Monday evening after we had registered at the Castle Hotel at Merthyr Tydfil, which would be our base for the coming week. David, the youth pastor from Holland Road, asked for volunteers to do evangelism. A family fun day had been scheduled for that Saturday at Gellideg, and the band was to do a big concert on Friday night at a local park. We were to promote these two events, especially the Friday concert, because that would be the big evangelistic thrust. Pastor Rhys from Holland Road Baptist would speak on the one-hundredth year of the revival, and an altar call would be made. We were told later that at none of the schools could we share testimonies or present the gospel, and that the high schools wanted only the band to come. This was confusing to me because I was sure I was to give my testimony and share the gospel. The leader of the blue team decided he would do evangelism, and so I was free to do the same. As an added blessing, I was asked to go with the band every night and be a counselor for the young people who made decisions for Christ. This was a blast, and during the course of the entire week I was able to pray with five young ladies to receive Christ. They were precious! Their names were turned in to our local partners so they could be discipled, and in turn, this presented an opening to reach their parents.

My friend Kathleen was also assigned as a counselor with the band. At the Aberdare Sports Centre, we met two local ladies who were to assist us in praying for any young people answering the altar call at the conclusion of the concert. One of these ladies had recently been marvelously saved, and she could hardly contain herself! As we were sharing, she hit Kathleen on the shoulder and said, "Hit for sex!" Kathleen and I shared incredulous glances at each other; we couldn't believe what we just heard. On the way back that evening, she asked our driver what the term meant, and he replied that it was used by cricket players. I said, "Cricket players hit for sex when they're playing a game?" He exploded into laughter! "You don't hit for *sex*! You hit for six—six points!" Something had been lost in the translation. Whenever we would meet after that, we would hit each other on the shoulder and burst into laughter.

I roomed with Sherry and Linda at the hotel. They worked on the school teams and with the choir, so we were not together during the day. We exchanged our war stories each night, and when I shared about "hit for sex," they were laughing so hard that our neighbors in the next room were beating on the wall for us to be quiet.

It was not all work and no play. We did have an opportunity one afternoon to go into Cardiff, the capitol of Wales, and see the magnificent architecture of this old city, including the impressive Cardiff Castle. The famous modern millennium stadium stood out like a sore thumb in the midst of these ancient edifices. I thought about home—America is so young!

During the weekdays I was assigned to Gellideg, the poorest community in Wales, and the site of our Saturday Fun Day. It is a huge apartment complex where unemployment, drinking, drugs, and discouragement abound. I worked with some members of St. Luke's Church who were planting a church in the neighborhood. We had some meaningful prayer times in the mornings before we started, and I was pleased to share my testimony with these dedicated warriors. I was especially honored to team with Phil of Youth With A Mission, and we covered the project, giving out flyers for the Friday night concert and the Saturday Fun Day. We witnessed and prayed for people as the doors opened for us.

As Phil and I went door to door throughout the neighborhood, he would take one house and I would take the one next so that we could cover as many homes as possible. We kept close tabs on each other, and at the times when circumstances brought us together to the same house, one would pray silently as the other shared. We were a good team, and I learned a lot about patience from him. Time was short, and I wanted to jump right in, no beating around the bush, but he was much wiser and very much attuned to the leading of the Holy Spirit. The Lord was blessing me again!

I approached one house, and an elderly lady who was very lonely invited me inside. This was considered a no-no, but I felt led by the Holy Spirit to honor her request, leaving the curtain pulled back on the large front window so Phil would be able to see me. My new friend was a widow, a devoted Catholic who loved Jesus, but no one in the church or the neighborhood came to visit. We shared our testimonies, and I showed her in the Bible that Jesus was her husband (Isaiah 54:5) and suggested that she be friendly to others and reach out to them, regardless of their response.

She prayed for me, and then I prayed for her, both of us blessed by that sweet encounter.

Another woman was at the end of her rope and on the verge of tears. Her sister and brother both were in hospitals with serious illnesses, her daughter had recently graduated from high school and needed direction, and she herself was attending nursing school. Her mother had died several months before, having been a faithful member and Sunday school teacher at St. Luke's, so our friend knew all about Jesus. She was overwhelmed by life's circumstances and said she had to have peace. I happened to have a tract entitled "Steps to Peace With God," and we started going through that together. She then abruptly stopped and said she had to think about all this when she was alone. Just then my partner Phil arrived, and I told her to keep the tract to read later. She agreed that we could pray with her. I especially asked that our Lord give her that "peace that passes understanding" because He is the Prince of Peace (John 14:27; Isaiah 9:6). We exchanged hugs, and I knew that was another divine appointment. When she called out to Him in her quiet time, He would be right there!

Pastor John of St. Luke's, affectionately called "The Legend", sent me on separate assignments: one day to the community luncheon, another day to the Mother's Morning Out, and then to the senior citizens luncheon, where a local lady called me nosey for asking so many questions. I told her that folks at home were going to ask me about the people I met in Wales, and I needed to be able to tell them! Actually, I think she was delighted that I asked questions because the man seated next to her responded that he was single, and she said, "You've been coming here for months and we didn't know you were single!" That was good news for her. He also said he was a Calvinist Zionist; I responded that Calvin was a Presbyterian, and I had accepted Jesus in a Presbyterian Church when I was thirteen years old. Then I gave my testimony and encouraged all of them to come back Sunday to the services held there by St. Luke's.

Pastor John also sent me twice to the local primary school, where I answered questions from the four-year-olds about America, such as: Does it rain? Does it snow? Do you have cars? I read stories to the children and ate fruit kabobs with them. One time Phil, my Gellideg partner, went with me, and the other time Vickie, from our America team, came. They also shared with the students. I returned another afternoon to the school with our four clowns, and they put on a delightful show. It was such joy to see the children laughing so heartily. Some of them would recognize us and wave excitedly! No wonder the Lord says His kingdom consists of the little children (Matthew 19:14). They are so innocent and precious—all the children of the world.

The Friday event, billed as a Centenary Celebration of the 1904 Revival, was held at Cyfarthfa Park, a popular recreation area. It was a wet, cold occasion, so it was a blessing to tour the castle on the grounds to get out of the weather. We had a big tent with lots of food, and the team played games on the grass lawns. Then the rains stopped, thanks to the Lord, and the skies cleared. (Maybe He wanted to see if we were serious about our commitment to serve Him.) The band performed under another tent down by the river, and after Pastor Rhys spoke and gave the altar call, many young people came forward. At one point, I had two young ladies to counsel. One of the local ladies came and took one of them. Then four more came to me, but two of our team got them, so that I could continue to counsel nine-year-old Suzanne, who wanted Jesus to help keep her from sin. She was so sincere and really needed to talk. You know the Lord was pleased at this response!

It seemed to me that the Holy Spirit was centering on the young ones. At one band concert, I prayed with Jade, age twelve, who felt she had fallen away and wanted to be sure of her salvation; also, she wanted her family to be saved. Another time, I prayed with Samantha, age ten, who wanted to know God and His miracles. After a school concert, Demi-Leigh, age eleven, and Emma, age ten, invited Jesus into their hearts. I was seeing the youth come to Christ because that was where I was serving, but there was more to this. In a country that seemed to be dying spiritually, God was birthing babies, young ones with tender hearts. Statistics show that the older we get, the harder it is to enter into a salvation experience. It was crucial that these new babes be nourished and protected—they are the future.

At the Saturday Fun Day at Gellideg, I helped with different events at the community center and then at the school. The day started out with a bang—literally! Holland Road and New Hope were having some fellowship fun prior to the opening, including backwards races across the paved lot. There were too many feet, and I got tangled. My head hit the pavement with a thud that I was sure could be heard for miles, and I found myself sitting on a bench surrounded by concerned team members, holding a frozen popsicle on my goose-egg-sized bump. I was praying for myself, saying every healing scripture I could recall, and then my partner Phil came running. I asked him to pray for me, which he did. The Lord honored His Word, and I did not even have a headache. I did stumble on some gravel later in the day as I was walking down the hill to the school, so I bound Satan from me and from my big feet and from that time I was fine. I especially enjoyed doing the gospel bracelets because it presented opportunities to share the meaning of the different-colored beads. Fun-Day was a huge success for everyone, and for me!

Where did the time go? It was Sunday and time to leave for Holland Road Baptist Church in Brighton and Hove, England. It is a scenic city located on the English Channel, with lots of shops and big hotels. Some of the houses were jammed next to each other and painted pretty pastel colors. It was sad to see a beautiful white church with steeples and ornate windows that had been turned into a Blockbuster video store. While the choir rehearsed, some of us made a short walking tour of the city. The wind was blowing from the north, and it was very cold.

The church had a delicious evening meal prepared for us, and there I met my hostess for the next two days, Mary, and Mrs. Chris, Phil's mother. She said Phil told her to look for me. She was coordinator of the Lydia Fellowship for the U.K. and Ireland and gave me her card. I could see how Phil inherited his servant's heart. The choir gave an outstanding performance of *Encounter God*, but there was no altar response, which, I understand, is quite common in English churches. It was probably a matter of the choir preaching to the choir.

Linda, my roommate from Wales, and I went home with Mary, our new sister in Christ. Mary was single and had just turned eighty. She served as a nurse missionary in the Belgian Congo for thirty years and was now officially retired. However, a missionary never retires. She was teaching a Sunday school class, leading a Monday Bible study, and attending a Tuesday home group. She prayed a sweet prayer over Linda and me before we retired for the night.

The next morning we met the team at the church, and it was off to the Brighton train station for a day trip into London. Rich, our leader, was our tour guide, and I was able to see new things this time! There was the changing of the guard at Buckingham Palace, and as we were waiting, I conversed with a pretty young lady from New York City. She had been with an investment firm for six years, but wanted to get her master's degree and become a school teacher. I gave her my school testimony: I was now seventy and received my master's degree in counseling at age sixty-nine. I had retired from a law firm and was now a missionary/volunteer/counselor. If I could do it, so could she!

The team divided after we left Buckingham Palace, and I went with the group to experience British Airways London Eye. It was under construction the last time I was in London but had been completed for the dawn of the millennium. It is a gigantic Ferris wheel with thirty-two glass capsules, each having a capacity for twenty-five people, that slowly ascend and descend to give you a panoramic view of the city for miles around. Afterward, we passed the Tower of London and stopped in the Hard Rock Cafe for the traditional mugs and shirts. We had a fast supper of fish and chips and rushed to Victoria Station for the return trip to Brighton and the Two Bare Feet concert at the church.

The band had toned down their music considerably for this older crowd, and it was sweet and worshipful. There was no altar call, as usual, but that seemed right, as the congregation seemed to be mellow and words were not necessary.

We adjourned to the fellowship hall for a slide show of the trip. It was fun but also touching. There were hugs all around, as we said our farewells to the locals who had been our partners in Wales and to various team members who were leaving at different times the next day. And then it was off to our host homes.

Linda and I sat up with Mary for a little while sharing the events of the day. Linda departed quite early the next morning, leaving me with Mary for another hour or two. She shared her story with me. She had been engaged during World War II to a merchant marine, and they were to be married after the war. When he came home, he was engaged to another woman, and Mary never met anyone else. After her return from Tonga upon her retirement as a nurse missionary, she moved into this house, which her brothers had insisted their father bequeath to her. She had little money, but friends gave her furniture, so she moved into her completely furnished home, which she considered to be a gift from God. We took a walk in her garden and made some pictures of her lovely roses.

As we talked, she shared with me about a particular family on her heart that was in great need. As she told me their story, my spirit was stirred; they truly deserved a break. My friend Mickey (as in the Peru trip) had given me fifty dollars to give as the Lord led, and I had been waiting for that opportune time. This was it, so I gave the money to Mary to deliver to them. We were both blessed with just the thought of helping them, and I knew Mickey would be pleased. We went back inside and had a precious prayer time. And then my ride came. Good-bye, dear Mary!

When we got home and tallied, we had encountered from 2500 to 3000 people through all the outreach, and a total of one hundred had prayed for salvation, even though we were not officially allowed to present the gospel. We were limited everywhere except at those evening concerts with the band and while we were out with the evangelism teams. Our Lord, however, is not limited, and the clowns witnessed through their skits; the choir through their music; the community action team through their work projects; the band through their concerts, games, brief gospel presentations, and counseling; and the entire team through their loving actions and conversations. We were able to build relational bridges and were invited to go into more churches and more schools the following summer.

Upon reflection, I got to do everything! My plan was just to go into the high schools, give my testimony, and pray with students as I had the opportunity. God's plan was much better, so much broader in scope! Additionally, He proved to me again and again His faithfulness. Every need I had was met and then some!

However, this mission did not end upon touchdown in Atlanta, because after returning home, I was invited to speak at a neighborhood Methodist church and another Baptist church, encouraging them to be part of the Great Commission.

And so the story continues.

I pray, dear reader, that you have been encouraged as you shared in my journeys, and that you, too, will follow your Passion. His name is Jesus, and He will make you a fisher of men.

NOTES

CHAPTER 5
SIBERIA, RUSSIA (MAY 1993)

1. Pamphlet, Operation Impact, Won-by-One, a Partnership Program for Siberian Summer Camps.

2. David Filipov, "Assembly Gathers to Shape a New Russia," *The Moscow Times*, June 5, 1993.

CHAPTER 6
MY FIRST JOURNEY TO ISRAEL (APRIL 1995)

1. *Strong's Exhaustive Concordance of the Bible*, s.v. "seismos (4578)" (Nashville, TN: Abingdon-Cokesbury Press, 1950).

2. "Capital Investments at Ramat Negev Desert AgroResearch Center," *The Negev Foundation*. http://www.negev.org/Projects/rndarc.htm (accessed October 4, 2007).

3. "Jerusalem—Beyond the Old City Walls," *Virtual Israel Experience*. http://www.jewishvirtuallibrary.org/jsource/vie/Jerusalem3.html (accessed October 4, 2007).

4. "Chagall in Israel," *Israel Ministry of Foreign Affairs*. http://www.mfa.gov.il/MFA/MFAArchive/2000_2009/2003/5/Chagall%20in%20Israel (accessed October 4, 2007).

5. Natasha Goldman, "Israeli Holocaust Memorial Strategies at Yad Vashem: From Silence to Recognition," *Art Journal* (Summer 2006). http://findarticles.com/p/articles/mi_m0425/is_2_65/ai_n16726441/pg_1 (accessed September 11, 2007).

6. "The Show," *The Tzabarim Folklore Ensemble*. http://www.jerusalemdance.com/ (accessed October 4, 2007).

7. The Tzabarim Folklore Ensemble—The Show, http://www.google.com/Top/Regional/Middle_East/Israel/Localities/Jerusalem/Arts_and_Entertainment (accessed October 27, 2007).

CHAPTER 7
My Second Journey to Israel (November 1997)

1. *Smith's Bible Dictionary*, revised ed., s.v. "Nazareth."

2. Ibid., s.v. "Garden of Gethsemane."

3. Ibid., s.v. "Engedi."

CHAPTER 8
My Third Journey to Israel (June 1999)

1. *Welcome to Christ Church*, pamphlet, P.O.B. 14037, Jaffa Gate, Jerusalem.

CHAPTER 15
Uganda (June 2002)

1. Mark Schoofs, "AIDS: The Agony of Africa," *The Body*. http://www.thebody.com/content/art2761.html (accessed October 4, 2007).

2. "Twenty-seventh of June," *TheHistoryChannel.com*. http://www.thehistorychannel.co.za/site/this_day_in_history/this_day_June_27.php (accessed October 4, 2007).